Case Studies in Classroom Research

This reader is one part of the Open University, MA in Education: Classroom Studies Module and the selection is therefore related to other material available to students. It is designed to evoke the critical understanding of students. Opinions expressed in it are not necessarily those of the course team or of the University.

Case Studies in Classroom Research

A Reader edited by
Martyn Hammersley
at the Open University

Open University Press

Milton Keynes • Philadelphia

Open University Press
12 Cofferidge Close
Stony Stratford
Milton Keynes MK11 1BY, England

and
1900 Frost Road, Suite 101
Bristol, PA 19007, USA

First Published 1986
Reprinted 1989

British Library Cataloguing in Publication Data
Case studies in classroom research: a reader.
  1. Education——Research 2. Teaching
  I. Hammersley, Martyn
  371.1'02'072   LB1028

  ISBN 0-335-15984-2
  ISBN 0-335-15983-4 Pbk

Library of Congress Cataloging in Publication Data
Case studies in classroom research.
  Includes index.
    1. Teaching——Case studies. 2. Expectation (Psychology)——
Case studies. 3. Teacher–student relationships——Case studies.
I. Hammersley, Martyn.
LB1025.2.C292 1986   371.'1'02   86-12688

  ISBN 0-335-15984-2
  ISBN 0-335-15983-4 (pbk.)

Text design by Carlton Hill
Typeset by Colset Private Limited, Singapore
Printed in Great Britain by St Edmundsbury Press Limited,
Bury St Edmunds, Suffolk

Contents

Part Two: Classroom Tasks   61

Part Three: Teacher Typifications and Expectations   157

Acknowledgements

The articles in this collection come from the following sources, to whose publishers grateful acknowledgement is made:

'Teaching styles and pupil progress', by S.N. Bennett, *Teaching Styles and Pupil Progress*, London, Open Books, 1976.

'Teaching styles and pupil progress: a review of Bennett's study', by D. McIntyre, *British Journal of Teacher Education*, 1976, Vol. 2, No. 3, pp. 291-7.

'Coping strategies and the multiplication of differentiation in infant classrooms', by A. Pollard, *British Educational Research Journal*, 1984, Vol. 10, No. 1, pp. 33-48.

'Cognitive objectives revealed by classroom questions asked by social studies student teachers', by O.L. Davis and D.C. Tinsley, *Peabody Journal of Education*, Vol. 45, pp. 21-6. Originally presented as a paper at the annual meeting of the American Educational Research Association, New York, February 1967.

' "What time is it, Denise?": asking known information questions in classroom discourse', by H. Mehan, *Theory into Practice*, (© 1979, Vol. XVIII, pp. 285-294. College of Education, The Ohio State University.)

'Questioning at home and at school: a comparative study', by S. Brice Heath, in G. Spindler (ed.), *Doing the Ethnography of Schooling: Educational Anthropology in Action*, New York, Holt, Rinehart and Winston, 1982.

'Academic tasks in classrooms', by W. Doyle and K. Carter, *Curriculum Inquiry*, 1984, Vol. 14, No. 2, pp. 129-149.

'Research into teachers' expectations and their effects', by C. Rogers, *The Social Psychology of Schooling*, Chapter 2, pp. 16-40, London, Routledge and Kegan Paul, 1982.

'A theory of typing', by D.H. Hargreaves, S. Hester and F. Mellor, *Deviance in Classrooms*, Chapters 6, 7 and 8, London, Routledge and Kegan Paul, 1975.

'Naturalistic studies of teacher expectation effects', by J. Brophy and T. Good, in J.E. Brophy and T.L. Good (eds), *Teacher–Student Relationships: Causes and Consequences*, New York, Holt, Rinehart and Winston, 1970.

'Student social class and teacher expectations: the self-fulfilling prophecy in ghetto education', by R. Rist, *Harvard Educational Review*, 1970, Vol. 40, pp. 411–451.

Introduction

The study of school classrooms is a major aspect of educational research. It is rooted in the belief that if we are to understand the work of schools, and to improve or change their role, then above all we have to understand what occurs in classrooms. That, after all, is where the real business of education is supposed to take place. There has, however, been much controversy about how this research should be carried out: arguments about whether it should be qualitative or quantitative, whether it must be sociolinguistic in character, whether it should be macro or micro, theoretical or applied. These issues are presented in the companion to this volume *Controversies in Classroom Research* (Hammersley 1986). In this volume, we shift the focus to actual examples of substantive research in three areas: the study of teaching styles and their effects; of classroom tasks, their nature and consequences; and of the effects of teachers' expectations on pupils. Each of these areas has been a focus of research for some considerable time, and a wide range of research strategies has been employed. This gives us a basis for assessing the strengths and weaknesses of different methodological approaches and indeed the promise and achievements of classroom research in general.

Teaching Styles

The history of research on teaching styles can be traced back at least to the work of Anderson and Lewin, Lippitt and White in the 1930s (see Amidon and Hough 1967). In this section we include extracts from two recent, and sharply contrasting, British studies in this area, along with critical commentaries upon them. The best known study of teaching styles in Britain is almost certainly that of Neville Bennett (1976), and Reading 1.1 is an extract from his book. Bennett explicitly began from a concern to provide information which might resolve the debate which had taken place in the late 1960s and early 1970s over the superiority of traditional and progressive teaching in primary schools (Wright 1977). He produced a typology of teaching styles on the basis of a questionnaire study of teachers, validated by observation of a subsample. He then examined the performance of pupils in the classes of this subsample of teachers using a variety of tests of attainment, and samples of written work. He found that pupils in classes with formal teachers tended to do better overall in maths, reading and English, and that there was no evidence that children in informal classrooms made compensating gains in other areas.

While Bennett's research received much publicity and the results were widely accepted, it was also subjected to some severe criticism. We include an example of this criticism here in the form of Donald McIntyre's review of the book (Reading 1.2). He criticises Bennett for drawing conclusions on the basis of his research which are 'too wide-ranging, too simple and too confident' (p. 21). He points out that the research focused on only a subset of the outcomes of teaching, and that there are serious problems involved in identifying teaching styles. Furthermore, he argues, the threats to validity are such in this area that 'it is foolhardy to come to firm conclusions on the basis of any one investigation' (p. 22). He also argues that there is insufficient information provided in the book to evaluate its methodology thoroughly. Bennett's study has also been criticised for the use of a particular statistical technique, a form of cluster analysis, in the development of the typology of teaching styles (See Gray and Satterly 1976 and the reply by Bennett and Entwistle 1976.) And in fact Bennett and others have subsequently reanalysed the data and shown that the original differences found between formal and informal teachers disappear when a different and more appropriate form of cluster analysis is employed (Aitken, Bennett and Hesketh 1981; see also Gray and Satterly 1981).

A very different research strategy, ethnography, is exemplified in the article by Andrew Pollard (Reading 1.3). Unlike Bennett, Pollard is not concerned with the effects of different styles of teaching on pupil achievement but rather with whether differences in the working consensus negotiated between teacher and pupils have consequences for the social differentiation of pupils, for the degree to which friendship groups match the academic ranking of pupils in the class. One of the main criticisms made of Bennett's study was that its documentation of teaching style was based primarily upon questionnaire responses, rather than upon observation of teachers' behaviour. A widely used alternative approach is systematic observation (for example the Oracle study: Galton, Simon and Croll 1980; Galton and Simon 1980).

However, while Pollard relies heavily upon the observation of teachers' classroom behaviour, and uses some rudimentary systematic observation, he adopts a wider and less structured approach than the ORACLE researchers. On the basis of a study in depth of the classrooms of two teachers, he argues, tentatively, that formal classroom regimes generate higher levels of social differentiation than do informal ones.

In the final article in the first section I provide an assessment of one aspect of Pollard's analysis, asking how effectively he has measured the variable 'teaching style/working consensus'. I take Pollard's work as a representative piece of ethnography and argue that it falls well short of satisfactorily showing that the two teachers studied do in fact represent contrasting styles in the relevant respects.

Classroom Tasks

Research on teachers' classroom questions seems to have begun early this century in the United States (Stevens 1912). It has continued since then to the present day generating a considerable literature (Gall 1970). Research on other types of classroom tasks, such as written work, seems to have started more recently and has produced a smaller, but not insubstantial body of work (Barnes and Shemilt 1974; Carter 1980; Doyle and Carter 1984; Barnes and Barnes 1984; Bennett *et al* 1984). Much of the research on both oral questions and written work has been concerned with documenting the nature and frequency of different types of task that teachers set their pupils and with suggesting the consequences for pupil learning of the predominance of particular types of task.

The article by Davis and Tinsley (Reading 2.1) is fairly representative of this tradition of research, looking at the frequency of different types of oral question used by a sample of student social studies teachers and their pupils. Questions are coded according to the cognitive operations involved, the classification system used being based on Bloom's taxonomy of educational objectives (Bloom 1956). It is claimed on the basis of the evidence provided that a high proportion of the questions operate at a relatively low cognitive level, a finding which matches those of many earlier studies.

In Reading 2.2 Scarth and Hammersley raise a number of serious methodological problems about the coding of classroom tasks as open or closed. They note for example that some coding schemes are vague about the distinction between open and closed, and about whether it is the teacher's intentions or the pupils' responses which are being coded. They highlight the difficulties involved in identifying questions and tasks, and in assigning them to different categories. They suggest that these methodological problems have not been given sufficient attention in the literature and require systematic investigation.

Mehan's article (Reading 2.3) draws on recent work in conversational analysis to look at the features of teachers' questions and their implications for the classroom competence which is required of pupils. He points out that most questions asked by teachers are designed to elicit 'known information', rather than being genuine questions. Such questions have a three part structure in which pupils' responses are subsequently evaluated by the teacher. He examines the strategies used by teachers in selecting answerers and in dealing with pupils' failure to produce the 'right' answer. He pays particular attention to the ways in which teachers search for the 'right answer' in pupils' responses. He argues that 'the student does not so much answer the question, as the teacher and student create the student's answer out of a number of tentative displays' (p. 101). Mehan argues that it is essential to pay attention to the interactional demands placed upon pupils by the structure of classroom discourse if we are to understand their success or failure at academic tasks.

Shirley Brice–Heath (Reading 2.4) extends this argument by looking at cultural differences in children's orientations to teachers' questioning, and the effects of these on their classroom performances and achievement levels. In a study of Trackton, a black urban community in the south-eastern United States, she contrasts the way questions were used in the home and local community with the kinds of questions the children faced at school. In the home questions related to 'whole events or objects and their uses, causes and effects' whereas teachers' questions demanded 'labels, attributes and discrete features of objects and events in isolation from the context' (p. 104). Moreover, the children were not familiar with questions where the questioner knew the answer. Heath argues that these cultural differences are a major factor in the poor achievement levels of Trackton children in school. She also reports her attempt to intervene and overcome the culture conflict which she had found operating in the classrooms.

Doyle and Carter (Reading 2.5) focus on written work tasks. They define a task as involving three elements: a product; a set of resources available in the situation; and a set of operations that can be applied to the resources to generate the product. And they portray the curriculum as consisting of a set of tasks which pupils encounter in the classroom. The empirical research reported in their article involved analysis of classroom tasks in two average-ability English classes and one high-ability English class, all taught by the same teacher in a junior high school in the south-west United States. The researchers distinguished between major and minor assignments and routine exercises. The major tasks and some of the minor ones were investigated in detail. Doyle and Carter argue that in the classes observed the major tasks, as initially specified, involved higher-level cognitive operations. However, over time, as pupils worked on them 'there was a clear drift toward greater explicitness and specificity concerning the nature of the final products and a narrowing of the range of judgments students were required to make on their own' (p. 151). And they claim that this transformation of the tasks was in large part a product of the efforts of pupils: 'Students consistently sought . . . to reduce ambiguity and risk by clarifying task demands and obtaining feedback concerning the quality of their provisional writing efforts' (p. 151).

Teacher Typifications and Expectations

Most of the research on the effects of teachers' expectations on pupil learning was stimulated by Rosenthal and Jacobson's pioneering study *Pygmalion in the Classroom* published in 1968. This research arose from Rosenthal's earlier work on the effects of experimenters' expectations on the outcomes of psychological experiments (Rosenthal 1966). Arguing that pupils' academic performances might be affected by teachers' expectations of them, they sought to investigate this hypothesis by means of a quasi-experiment. All the pupils in a school were given an attainment test. The teachers were told that this test enabled the identification of pupils who were likely to bloom or spurt intellectually during the coming academic year. In fact, however, the pupils identified in each class as bloomers had been selected at random. One year after the initial test the children were tested again, and it was found that the bloomers had increased their scores by a greater amount, on average, than the other children.

In Reading 3.1, which is an extract from a book devoted to the study of teachers' expectations (Rogers 1982), Rogers summarises the methods and findings of the Pygmalion research and many of the subsequent studies, both those which sought to replicate Rosenthal and Jacobson's work and those which adopted different research strategies. He concludes that these studies:

> do not produce results that provide an immediately obvious and convincing picture. Some show the expectancy effect, some do not. Some show effects only with younger children, some only with older ones. Some show effects with urban teachers, but not suburban. Some show quantitative but not qualitative effects on teacher–pupil interactions, while others show the exact opposite. Most of the studies can be criticised for problems in their design and on balance they indicate that expectancy effects, certainly the type investigated by Rosenthal and Jacobson, do not seem to happen (p. 177).

One of the major criticisms of Rosenthal and Jacobson's study was that it documented the effects of artificially induced expectations rather than of those expectations which teachers routinely develop about their pupils in normal circumstances. Another was that they focused upon only one dimension of teachers' expectations of their pupils. In particular, what is missing from their analysis is teachers' concern with pupils' classroom behaviour. The article by Hargreaves, Hester and Mellor (Reading 3.2), which is an extract from their book *Deviance in Classrooms* (Hargreaves, Hester and

Mellor 1975) contributes to both these areas. It examines the process by which teachers build up typifications of their pupils as regards their conformity to or deviance from classroom rules. The researchers trace this process from initial encounters to a situation of relative familiarity, using ethnographic interviews with samples of teachers from two secondary schools. They present a model of the stages through which these typifications develop from initial speculations through elaboration to stabilisation, though with the ever-present possibility that the typifications may subsequently be revised.

Another important defect of Rosenthal and Jacobson's research was the failure to investigate the mechanisms by which teachers' expectations might affect pupils' academic performances. The final two studies in this volume are attempts to fill this gap, but using very different approaches. Brophy and Good (Reading 3.3) report the results of two systematic observation studies designed to identify the processes by which teachers' expectations might affect pupils. In the first study they observed the interactions between four first-grade teachers and twelve pupils in each of their classes. Of each set of pupils, the teacher had high expectations of six and low expectations of the other six. The observers recorded the frequency of interaction between each teacher and pupil and various qualitative features of these interactions, for instance who initiated the interaction, and the type of feedback given by the teacher. Brophy and Good argue that some of these features, such as the number of pupil initiated contacts, are likely to be a product of pupil characteristics. However, others, for instance whether a correct answer is followed by praise and a wrong answer is followed by criticism, will reflect teachers' expectations of pupils. This first study found differences between high and low expectation pupils on both these types of measure. However, the second study, which was a replication of the first involving a larger sample of teachers, failed to confirm these results.

Rist (Reading 3.4) using ethnographic techniques followed a small group of pupils through kindergarten and on into the first and second grades. He looked at how the teachers differentiated them in terms of allocation to different groups within the classroom and at how the teachers interacted in different ways with pupils in different groups. He claims to show that there is very little movement between groups over the three-year period and he suggests that this is the product not so much of any inherent differences in ability among the children but rather of the teachers' social class-based typifications and differential treatment of the pupils.

Conclusion

This reader draws together research involving rather different research strategies on three important topics in classroom research. The aim is to allow the methodological strategies employed and findings produced by various approaches to be compared and assessed. There has been a tendency within educational research, and indeed within social research generally, to treat different research strategies as competing methodological paradigms involving contrasting assumptions. This has led to the development of distinct research traditions with their own separate literatures. Such a state of affairs impedes rather than advances the development of classroom research. In my view all social research faces the same basic methodological problems, though researchers differ in their awareness of them, the weight they assign to each and the remedies used. If there is to be any significant progress the work produced by different research traditions must be brought together and the effectiveness of different research strategies examined. This volume is intended to facilitate this process of methodological appraisal.

References

AITKEN, M., BENNETT, S.N. and HESKETH, J. (1981). 'Teaching styles and pupil progress: a re-analysis', *British Journal of Educational Psychology*, 51.

AMIDON, E.J. and HOUGH, J.B. (eds), (1967). *Interaction Analysis: Theory, Research & Application*. Reading Mass. Addison-Wesley.

BARNES, D. and BARNES, D. (1984). *Versions of English*. London, Heinemann.

BARNES, D. and SHEMILT, D. (1974). 'Transmission and interpretation', *Educational Review*, 26, 3.

BENNETT, N. (1976). *Teaching Styles and Pupil Progress*. London, Open Books.

BENNETT, N., DESFORGES, C., COCKBURN, A. and WILKINSON, B. (1984). *The Quality of Pupil Learning Experiences*. London, Erlbaum.

BENNETT, N. and ENTWISTLE, N. (1976). 'Rite and wrong: a reply to "A chapter of errors" ', *Educational Research*, 19, 3.

BLOOM, B. (1956). *Taxonomy of Educational Objectives: The Classification of Educational Goals*. Handbook 1: Cognitive Domain, New York, McKay.

CARTER, K.J. (1980). 'Academic task structures in high ability and average ability classes', Ph. D. Diss. North Texas State University.

DOYLE, W. and CARTER, K. (1984). 'Academic Tasks in Classrooms', *Curriculum Inquiry*, 14, 2. Reprinted in this volume (Reading 2.5).

GALL, M.D. (1970). 'The use of questions in teaching', *Review of Educational Research*, 40, 707–721.

GALTON, M. and SIMON, B. (ed.), (1980). *Progress and Performance in the Primary Classroom*. London, Routledge and Kegan Paul.

GALTON, M., SIMON, B. and CROLL, P. (1980). *Inside the Primary Classroom*. London, Routledge and Kegan Paul.

GRAY, J. and SATTERLY, D. (1976). 'A chapter of errors: teaching styles and pupil progress in retrospect', *Educational Research*, 19, 1.

GRAY, J. and SATTERLY, D. (1981). 'Formal or informal? A re-assessment of the British evidence', *British Journal of Educational Psychology*, 51.

HAMMERSLEY, M. (ed.), (1986). *Controversies in Classroom Research*. Milton Keynes, Open University Press.

HARGREAVES, D.H., HESTER, S. and MELLOR, F. (1975). *Deviance in Classrooms*. London, Routledge and Kegan Paul.

ROGERS, C. (1982). *The Social Psychology of Schooling*. London, Routledge and Kegan Paul.

ROSENTHAL, R. (1966). *Experimenter Effects in Behavioural Research*. New York, Appleton–Century Crofts.

ROSENTHAL, R. and JACOBSON, L. (1968). *Pygmalion in the Classroom*. New York, Holt Rinehart and Winston.

STEVENS, R. (1912). *The Question as a Measure of Efficiency in Instruction*. New York, Teachers College.

WRIGHT, N. (1977). *Progress in Education*. London, Croom Helm.

PART ONE
Teaching Styles and Strategies

Teaching Styles and Pupil Progress

S.N. Bennett

[The following is a chapter from Neville Bennett's book *Teaching Styles and Pupil Progress*, London, Open Books 1976. In earlier chapters Bennett has described how he developed a typology of twelve teaching styles on the basis of questionnaire responses from a large sample of primary school teachers. This typology ranges from informal through mixed to formal teaching. In the chapter reprinted here he outlines the way he set about assessing the effects on pupil achievement of differences in teaching style, and the results of his analysis.]

Too often in the past researchers have adopted a one-shot testing programme when attempting to attribute differential effects on pupils to different teaching styles. This is a weak inferential process since analyses of change or progress are not possible. To answer the question 'Do teaching styles result in differential pupil progress?' requires a research design which allows for a follow up of samples of pupils over an extended period of time during which they experience differing teaching approaches. By testing at the beginning and end of this period, progress can be assessed and differential effects, if any, established.

A quasi-experimental design was adopted which is shown diagramatically in figure 1. The first stage involved the selection of thirty-seven teachers to represent seven of the twelve types isolated in the teacher typology. These seven were chosen since they represented the whole range, and could be collapsed into three general styles: informal, mixed and formal. Types 1 and 2 represented informal styles; 3, 4 and 7 represented mixed styles; and 11 and

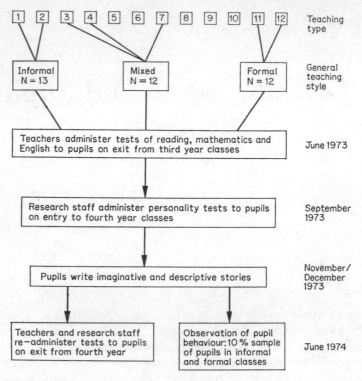

Figure 1   Simplified sampling and research design

12 formal styles. It should not be thought that by choosing styles 3, 4 and 7 to represent mixed teaching approaches a bias towards informal styles was built in. The clear continuum implied by the diagrammatic representation in figure 5.1 is an over-simplification of a highly complex pattern.

Twelve teachers were initially chosen to represent each style, six each from types 1, 2, 11 and 12, and four each from types 3, 4 and 7, but an additional teacher was added to the informal sample because of the small size of one informal classroom. The teachers selected were in each case those whose profiles most closely matched the group profile of their parent type [. . .] This selection procedure gave a pupil sample of approximately 400 per general teaching style.

It was decided that the teachers themselves should administer the attainment tests under normal classroom conditions, to obviate a test atmosphere and, hopefully, to reduce anxiety. The first administration was carried out by third-year teachers who were provided with detailed instructions by the research team. The personality tests were administered by the research team within one month of the pupils' entry into their new fourth-year classes.

These same attainment and personality tests were readministered the following June in the same manner. [. . .]

Analysis of Change

In educational experiments it is rarely if ever possible to allocate pupils to treatments randomly, and as a consequence the average scores of the samples at the pre-test stage could be disparate. In this instance the pupils in the formal sample had higher scores on the three attainment tests. A statistical analysis was therefore required which took differences in initial achievement into account. Analysis of covariance was chosen following the practice adopted in similar types of study, e.g. those of Soar and Barker Lunn. Such an analysis is preferable to the use of raw gain scores, i.e. post-test scores minus pre-test scores, since these suffer from the fact that the unreliability in both pre- and post-test scores are combined. Neither do they take into account differences in initial achievement.

[. . .] In each attainment area the effect of teaching style is highly significant, although the effect of initial level of achievement is most powerful. Residual gain scores were then computed for each type of attainment separately. These scores are interpreted as the difference between observed and predicted scores: i.e. did pupils exposed to the three general teaching styles progress as well as, better than, or worse than would have been expected on the basis of their level of initial achievement?

Reading

It is apposite to consider reading first, in the light of the recent publication of the Bullock Report (1975) *A Language for Life*. [. . .] The Bullock committee were concerned that the reading tests widely used were assessing only a narrow range of reading abilities, and advocated an instrument that combined practicality with a more comprehensive and therefore more realistic sampling of skills. This accorded with our own thinking, and, after a survey of available tests, the Edinburgh Reading Test Stage III (Moray House) was chosen. This covered the required age range, 10 years to 12 years 6 months, without creating a ceiling effect, and at the same time sampled five different reading abilities: reading for facts; comprehension of sequences; retention of main ideas; comprehension of points of view; and vocabulary.

The 'reading for facts' section was designed to sample some of the processes involved in the type of reading used in referring to books and other sources of information, for example in connection with project work. In this the reader has to examine various parts of the material in search of relevant information; he has to disregard what is not relevant and hold some parts in mind as potentially helpful whilst he seeks for further evidence. The reader has to translate statements into other words and to make inferences from the given data in coming to decisions as to the categories into which he will place the statements. To reach the conclusion that a statement is false requires the recognition of statements to the contrary. Success in this section requires a clear understanding of what the passage says and ability to examine the evidence carefully.

'Comprehension of sequences' assesses the pupil's ability to comprehend sequences of events, as in narrative material, or to follow the steps in a piece of reasoning. From a variety of semantic and structural clues within each sentence the pupil has to organise the sentences in such a way as to form a consistent sequence. It is believed that the skills tested in this section are significant for competent reading.

The intention of the 'retention of main ideas' section is to assess the child's ability to learn through reading as he would be called upon to do in individual study. He is asked to decide what the main ideas in the passage are and to reproduce them in a recognition situation within a very short time. In other words this section deals with recall.

'Comprehension of points of view' assesses the extent to which the child is capable of building up clusters of ideas which represent different points of view on topics which could be classified as mildly controversial. In order to match the statements with the characters participating in the discussion outlined in the passage, a thorough assimilation of what is said in the passage is necessary. This process of matching calls for the translation of material into other words, and the making of inferences.

Finally, the 'vocabulary' section assesses the extent of the child's familiarity with the meanings of words and phrases. Deficiencies in vocabulary set limits to competence in all types of reading, and the extension of knowledge of meanings of words is essential if progress in reading is to be maintained.

Differential gain on progress in reading in relation to teaching style is shown in figure 2. The scores represent the average gain or loss over the

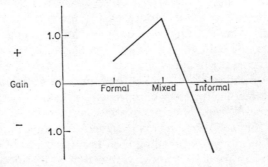

Figure 2   Differential gain in reading by teaching style

school year above or below that predicted from initial achievement. If progress has occurred at the predicted rate the score is zero, if progress is better than predicted the score is positive, and if less than expected, negative. It should be noted that a negative score does not indicate that ground has actually been lost, only that progress has not been made at the level expected.

Children in mixed classes show the greatest overall gain although the difference between mixed and formal is not significant. The differences between mixed and informal, and formal and informal, are both highly significant, however. It is clear that overall progress in informal classrooms is significantly inferior to that in mixed and formal classrooms.

Further analyses were carried out to assess whether this general picture was true across all achievement levels and to examine whether progress for boys and girls exhibited a similar pattern. The results are shown in table 1 and figures 3 and 4.

The table and figures show the post-test achievement of boys at six levels of initial achievement. It would seem that mixed and informal teaching styles are more effective for the lower achieving boys, particularly in the 80 – group. Beyond a reading quotient of 100, however, the mixed and formal boys exhibit superior progress. Among boys of reading quotient 110 + this lead stretches to some six or seven points, equivalent to something in the order of nine months' discrepancy in reading age.

This ineffectiveness of formal teaching among low achieving boys does not appear among low achieving girls. In fact the reverse situation occurs, formal and mixed pupils showing a marked superiority in progress over informal girls (figure 4). Few differences between mixed and formal teaching occur throughout the remainder of the achievement levels, but informally taught girls lag somewhat behind.

There are only minor sex differences, the only significant one being that between boys and girls in the 80 – range in formal classes. The overall trend among formal and mixed pupils is for the girls to perform slightly less well than the boys, whereas among informal pupils the girls tend to progress less well in the lower achievement levels, and slightly better in the higher levels.

Summary

The results provide clear evidence for the better performance of formal and mixed pupils in reading progress. The findings are statistically and educationally significant, showing the equivalent of some three to five months' difference in reading age.

The effect is more apparent among boys, particularly among those with a quotient above 100 where the discrepancies between formal and informal and mixed and informal stretch to some six or seven points. Nevertheless

TABLE 1 Post-test achievement in reading by initial level of achievement, sex and teaching style

Reading Initial achievement	Formal		Mixed		Informal	
	Boys	Girls	Boys	Girls	Boys	Girls
80–	81·3 [12]	91·1 [8]	89·3 [25]	91·3 [24]	87·8 [24]	85·5 [20]
80–89	92·4 [24]	94·5 [17]	92·9 [29]	94·5 [35]	95·7 [29]	94·5 [32]
90–99	101·5 [39]	101·1 [30]	104·1 [33]	100·8 [28]	99·5 [30]	97·1 [39]
100–109	111·9 [41]	110·5 [51]	110·8 [27]	109·9 [27]	108·3 [32]	108·6 [38]
110–119	119·4 [29]	117·8 [29]	120·7 [17]	118·0 [22]	113·2 [20]	118·0 [21]
120+	127·0 [29]	125·4 [26]	127·2 [15]	126·7 [12]	120·7 [17]	123·8 [19]

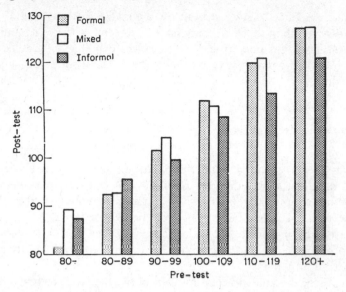

Figure 3   Post-test achievement by initial level of achievement in reading – boys

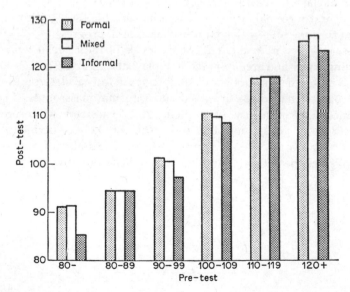

Figure 4   Post-test achievement by initial level of achievement in reading – girls

there is also evidence to suggest that low achieving boys in formal classes perform less well than those of equivalent achievement in mixed and informal classes. This was only true of boys since formal girls showed better progress than their counterparts in other types of classroom. Few sex differences emerged.

Mathematics

[. . .] It has been argued that conventional attainment tests are less valid for the assessment of the new than the old maths. A test was therefore chosen which, in the words of the publisher, is 'broader in content than traditional arithmetic tests'. The Mathematics Attainment Test (DE2, N.F.E.R.) was designed to assess mathematical understanding rather than skill in computation. A proportion of the time taken by a child to complete the test is therefore 'thinking time'.

The results of the analysis relating gain in mathematics to teaching style are presented in graphical form in figure 5.

The pattern here is different from that of reading. Children in formal classes still exhibit substantial progress but this is not so for those in mixed and informal classes. The differences between formal styles on the one hand, and mixed and informal styles on the other are highly significant, being equivalent to some four or five months' differential progress.

Post-test scores were computed for six levels of initial achievement, sex and teaching styles and are presented in table 2 and figures 6 and 7.

Above a mathematics quotient of 90 the boys in formal classrooms exhibit greater progress than those in mixed and informal classrooms. The high performance of informal boys of quotient 120 + is difficult to interpret since this group contains only four boys and is thus unlikely to be reliable. The performance of low achievers is again worthy of note under formal teaching, which replicates the pattern found in reading: boys of a low initial achieve-

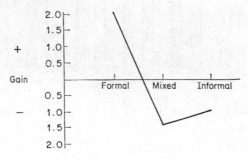

Figure 5   Gain in mathematics by teaching style

TABLE 2   Post-test achievement in mathematics by initial level of achievement, sex and teaching style

Mathematics	Formal		Mixed		Informal	
Initial achievement	Boys	Girls	Boys	Girls	Boys	Girls
80-	81·4 [12]	90·0 [3]	81·4 [13]	82·9 [15]	85·3 [11]	82·0 [10]
80-89	91·0 [26]	90·0 [20]	89·4 [45]	87·7 [31]	92·9 [31]	89·4 [32]
90-99	100·8 [31]	103·0 [44]	98·3 [31]	97·8 [54]	98·9 [38]	96·3 [54]
100-109	110·2 [60]	111·3 [53]	108·2 [34]	107·2 [27]	107·9 [50]	107·3 [45]
110-119	125·8 [26]	120·0 [27]	115·0 [4]	119·6 [16]	115·1 [18]	118·9 [20]
120+	127·4 [19]	130·6 [14]	124·5 [8]	123·8 [5]	131·8 [4]	125·8 [8]

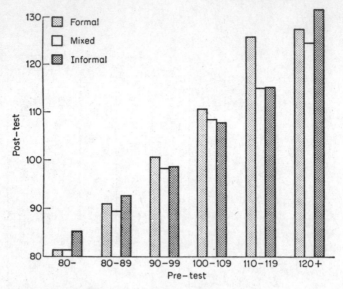

Figure 6   Post-test achievement by level of initial achievement in mathematics – boys

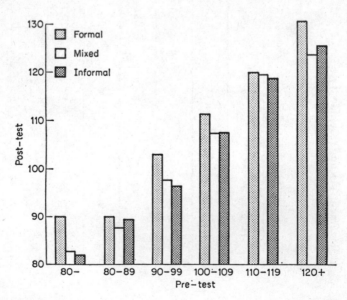

Figure 7   Post-test achievement by initial level of achievement in mathematics – girls

ment level under-achieve, whereas girls of a similar level do not. In fact, girls in formal classrooms show superior progress at every level of achievement, most markedly those with a quotient of 120 + .

Sex differences are again slight, the only significant difference being between boys and girls in formal classes in the range 110–19.

Summary

Better progress in mathematical understanding is evident with formal teaching styles and is apparent at every level of achievement except among the lowest achieving boys. This superiority tends to increase with level of achievement. It could be surmised that class teaching in formal classrooms may be pitched at a level that is beyond the capabilities of the less able boys. On the other hand concern must also be expressed at the apparent inability of mixed and informal teaching to fulfil the potential of the most able pupils.

English

[. . .] Here the analysis of pupil progress is restricted to a conventional English Progress Test (D3, N.F.E.R.), whose major emphasis is on comprehension but includes punctuation and sentence completion sections.

The basic analysis of pupil gain by teaching style is presented in graphical form in figure 8.

The relationship is almost linear, most progress being made under formal teaching, least under informal teaching, with mixed teaching in between. The difference in progress between formal and informal is slightly less than in mathematics and equivalent to approximately three or four months. The differences between formal and mixed, and between formal and informal, are both statistically significant.

Table 3 and figures 9 and 10 show progress at differing levels of achievement and by sex.

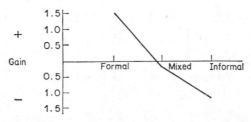

Figure 8   Gains in English by teaching style

TABLE 3   Final achievement by initial achievement level – English

Initial achievement level	Formal		Mixed		Informal	
	Boys	Girls	Boys	Girls	Boys	Girls
80–	82·9 [9]	88·0 [4]	88·8 [18]	88·5 [13]	84·9 [16]	85·3 [12]
80–89	96·3 [23]	91·9 [8]	92·8 [31]	92·6 [27]	92·0 [24]	93·0 [21]
90–99	102·7 [37]	100·9 [24]	100·4 [33]	102·5 [43]	100·1 [43]	101·3 [48]
100–109	111·9 [51]	112·8 [48]	106·6 [31]	111·8 [33]	107·3 [41]	108·4 [43]
110–119	119·9 [28]	119·5 [53]	118·0 [25]	115·5 [21]	114·8 [20]	116·0 [24]
120+	125·3 [26]	126·0 [24]	120·5 [8]	121·3 [11]	121·9 [8]	124·5 [21]

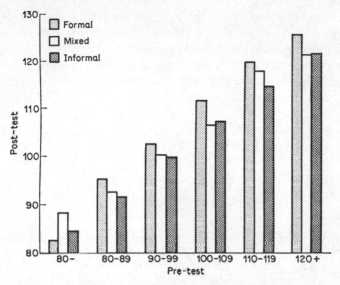

Figure 9   Post-test scores in English by initial achievement level – boys

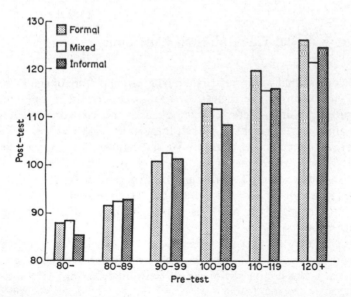

Figure 10   Post-test scores in English by initial achievement level – girls

Formal boys are superior to mixed and informal boys at every achievement level except the lowest, which reveals once again the under-achievement of this group under formal teaching. Also repeated is the finding that the lowest achieving girls do not share this characteristic. Nevertheless girls with an English quotient below 100 in mixed class show superior progress to those in formal and informal classrooms. Thereafter formal girls exhibit most progress.

Sex differences are again slight although the trend is for girls to show slightly better progress than boys in this area.

Summary

Overall, pupils in formal classrooms show significantly better progress in English than those in mixed and informal classrooms. Mixed pupils also show significantly better progress than informal pupils.

The formal boys are superior at every achievement level other than the lowest, whilst mixed girls have higher scores below a quotient of 100, beyond which point formal girls show the greatest progress. Sex differences are slight.

Case Study: A High Gain Informal Classroom

The results presented so far portray a fairly dismal picture of achievement in informal classrooms. Nevertheless there was one such classroom which was categorised high gain in every achievement area; indeed in one area it was the highest gain class. It was therefore felt important that this class and teacher should be examined more closely. All the information on the class was gathered together from the initial questionnaire, the research team and advisors' ratings, children's stories and observation evidence, and was supplemented by an interview with the teacher. From this information an interesting picture emerged, some parts of which differed from the picture of other informal classes.

The teacher was a woman in her middle thirties with ten years' teaching experience. The school was situated in a new town and the class, according to the teacher, was comprised of pupils with the full range of abilities. She felt she was an informal teacher and was in fact categorised as type 2 in the typology, i.e. not the most informal type. Both the research team and advisors also categorised her as informal, and her aims and opinions expressed in the questionnaire were also very informally orientated.

The first factor which differentiated this teacher from other informal teachers was the amount of time spent on mathematics and English, which was equal to, or in excess of, that spent by many formal classes. In other words, the curriculum emphasis was placed on the cognitive rather than the affective/aesthetic. Standards were set by the head. When she was interviewed about the past year in her school, she stated: 'Whilst there was a lot of emphasis on the social aspects in the school the children are encouraged to be work-minded right from the infants. The idea was not to kill learning but that the children should enjoy what they were doing.' Nevertheless, she was free to choose her own syllabus. 'I used "Metric Maths" and "Beta Maths". We followed the method of beta supplemented by hundreds of work sheets and cards. By the third term the children worked mainly from the work sheets. The metric maths involved reading and comprehension. In the third year the children had done some formal classwork in maths.'

She did not use any set books for English. 'We did a lot of creative writing, stories and topic work. All the grammar stemmed from that. Language and vocabulary work was tackled more individually or in groups. I would deal with things like speech marks when they were needed.'

For reading, the Ward–Lock reading workshop was used. The manual recommends that it should be used for short periods: 'so we used it for two six-week periods'.

The teacher had her own system of records, mainly of attainment, including records of group and individual work, and also of social behaviour. She had also built up a large stock of teaching materials over the years. With reference to incentives she stated that she was the main incentive: 'personality has a lot to do with it: they know I will be pleased if they do well.'

When she was told of the progress of her pupils on the attainment tests she indicated that in the main the results were as she had expected. 'I would be disappointed if a class went out without my feeling that all the children achieved something. The poorer ones perhaps did not improve as much as I would have liked. They seemed to improve particularly with regard to maths. At the beginning of the year they groaned when they were to do maths but by the end of the year they liked it.'

An added factor that may or may not be relevant is that her own daughter, whom she was hoping to get accepted by one of the better known girls' public schools, was one of the pupils.

In the context of open-plan primary schools it has been said by practitioners and advisors alike that successful implementation requires good organisation and a clear structure. This would seem to be exemplified in this classroom. Although the classroom was evidently orientated towards informal practices the content of the curriculum was clearly organised and well structured. This would seem to highlight a distinction between how the learning environment is structured, on the one hand, and the emphasis and structure of curriculum content, on the other. At the risk of introducing yet another ill-defined dichotomy, this distinction could be conceptualised as cognitively orientated informality versus affectively or aesthetically orientated informality, the latter laying greater stress on social and moral development, with less emphasis on content and structure [. . .]

General Summary

Reading

1 Pupils taught by formal and mixed styles show significantly superior progress as compared with those taught by informal styles.
2 The effect is more noticeable in average and above average achievers. Low achieving boys in formal classrooms progress less well than expected, but this is not true of low achieving formal girls. Above average boys in informal classrooms markedly under-achieve in comparison to boys of the same ability in mixed and formal classrooms.

Mathematics

1 Pupils taught by formal styles show significantly superior progress to that of those taught by mixed and informal styles.
2 The superiority exists at every level of achievement among boys and girls, with the exception of the least able boys, who again progress less well than expected.

English

1 Pupils taught by formal styles show significantly superior progress as compared with those taught by mixed and informal styles. Mixed pupils also show progress significantly superior to that of informal pupils.
2 Formal boys gain higher scores at every level of achievement, with the exception of the least able. Mixed girls progress most below an English quotient of 100, beyond which formal girls show greatest progress. (. . .)

High Gain Informal Classroom

The most noticeable features of this classroom were the juxtaposition of informal classroom organisation with a clear curriculum structure, and emphasis upon cognitive rather than affective/aesthetic content.

References

BARKER LUNN, J.C. (1970). *Streaming in the Primary School*. National Foundation for Educational Research, Slough.
BULLOCK REPORT (1975). *A Language for Life*. HMSO, London.
SOAR, R.S. (1972). 'Teacher behaviour related to pupil growth', *International Review of Education*, 18, 508–25.

Teaching Styles and Pupil Progress: A Review of Bennett's Study

D. McIntyre

Nearly everyone who is professionally involved in education is responsible, directly or indirectly, for what happens in classrooms and for at least some of the effects upon pupils of what happens in classrooms. This fact is as embarrassing as it is obvious, since we know very little indeed about the ways in which classroom events influence pupils. It is true that, over the last fifteen to twenty years, a considerable volume of relevant and valuable research has been reported; but this research has revealed the immense complexity of classroom processes, has demonstrated the hollowness of much of our 'commonsense' knowledge about classroom teaching and learning, and has raised more questions than it has provided answers. Furthermore, we cannot tell which of the conclusions that can be derived from it are relevant in British contexts, since hardly any of this research has been carried out in Britain.

Research on classroom processes is, then, urgently needed, but it is also frighteningly difficult: every investigation of the effects of 'naturally occurring' events in classrooms which has been reported can justifiably be criticized on several grounds. Such research is also very time-consuming: it is a bad area to choose if one wants an easy Ph.D. or a quick publication. So when a team of competent researchers like Dr Bennett and his colleagues spend several years on such research, our first and dominant reaction must be one of appreciation. It was predictable that they would get few laurels, but they deserve some for attempting to provide information of a kind which all of us badly need, but which very few of us have made the necessary efforts to obtain.

For the reviewer, then, the first task must be warmly to congratulate this research team on having undertaken such demanding and important work. Beyond this, however, the reviewer's task becomes more difficult, because a research investigation and a book about this investigation can be two very different things. Should one be reviewing the book or the research which it is about? In this case, the tension between the two is so acute that the review has been divided into two sections: one concerned with 'the book', the other concerned with 'the research'.

The Book

Dr Bennett has been misguided in writing the book he has written. He has apparently responded to the intense propaganda to which educational researchers have been submitted in recent years to demonstrate the relevance of their research and to communicate their findings more effectively to teachers. This may be inferred both from what is contained in the book and from what is omitted from it, as well as from the highly efficient publicity exercise which accompanied its publication. It is not that there is any distinctive reason why *this* research should not be reported in this way, but rather that this book exemplifies very well the *general* confusion which lies behind the 'relevance' and 'communication' slogans.

The focus and tone of the book are made clear in the preface: 'Teaching methods in primary schools', Dr Bennett writes, 'have been the subject of much controversy among educationalists and parents alike, particularly since the publication of the Plowden Report on primary education in 1967 . . . The only weapon not used appears to be research evidence. There is surprisingly little evidence available and much of this emanates from the United States. The study reported in the following chapters was therefore instigated to provide evidence on such basic pedagogical questions as "Do teaching methods (or styles as they are called in this book) have a differential effect on the academic progress of pupils?" and "Do pupils of differing personality characteristics progress similarly when taught by different approaches?" ' From the beginning, then, the research is presented as a way of resolving popular controversies.

The major conclusion drawn from the research is stated at the end of the book: 'In summary, formal teaching fulfils its aims in the academic area without detriment to the social and emotional development of pupils, whereas informal teaching only partially fulfils its aims in the latter area as well as engendering comparatively poorer outcomes in academic development.' By relating his investigation directly to current debates about policies, Dr Bennett has been drawn into formulating a conclusion which, however perfectly the research had been designed and conducted, could not but be too wide-ranging, too simple and too confident.

The conclusion is too wide-ranging because this investigation, like any other, could only take account of a very limited subset of the outcomes of teaching; it did not, for example, take account of pupils' achievements in art, dance, music or drama, of their skills in discussing or in co-operative working, of their mastery of historical, geographical or scientific concepts, or of the extent to which their lives at home and at school were interrelated.

Within the limits of what was studied, the conclusion is too simple because, even from the internal evidence of this book, it is clear that teaching and its effects are *not* so simple. On page 38, eleven different conceptual criteria are listed on the basis of which teaching can be categorized as progressive (informal) or traditional (formal); are we to conclude that the conclusion is valid irrespective of which of these criteria is used, or is it only valid when teaching with all eleven *informal* characteristics is compared with teaching with all eleven *formal* characteristics? And even if we accept the operational definitions of formal and informal teaching used in this investigation, the data presented appear to show that pupils' attainments are related to complex interactions between their sex, their previous attainments and the teaching style to which they have been exposed.

Finally, however clear the results of this investigation may be seen to be, the conclusion is too confident because, as is made clear in the book, other investigations have led to different results. Nor is this surprising. The internal and external validity of research design which it is possible to attain in this kind of research is severely limited; and furthermore, the lack of precision of most educational concepts is such that it is inevitable, and indeed necessary so long as we use such concepts, that they should be operationalized in different ways. In these circumstances, it is foolhardy to come to firm conclusions on the basis of any one investigation.

Dr Bennett's concern that the book should be widely read is apparent from his emphasis on specific items of data rather than on measures abstracted from sets of items, from his avoidance of precision where there was any danger of being thought pedantic, from his assumption that technical procedures would be of no interest to his readers, and from his omission (with occasional lapses) of inferential statistics. These, the most striking characteristics of the book, merit some exemplification.

We may first look at the treatment given to a crucial part of the research, the collection of evidence about teaching through teachers' completion of a questionnaire. This is important not only because the whole investigation depends upon the validity of these data but also because, if valid data can be collected in this way (contrary to the assumptions of almost every other researcher in this field), then research into teaching can become very much easier, quicker and cheaper than it has been up to now. As Powell (1976) has rightly pointed out, the items of the questionnaire appear to be very crude, and in some cases, ambiguous; but appearances are of little importance if there is clear evidence of the validity of the data collected. The teachers were categorized into twelve types on the basis of their questionnaire responses, and we are told that evidence of the validity of this categorization was sought from three sources: descriptions of classrooms by research staff, descriptions by primary school advisers, and essays written by pupils in nine of the classes on 'What I did at school yesterday'. Although we are led to believe that these various types of evidence showed the categorization to be valid, we are given virtually no information as to how this conclusion was reached. It was clearly considered more important to devote several pages to the description of two classrooms than to report the content analysis procedures which were presumably used, the ways in which measures of validity were calculated, or the results of these validation procedures.

The next chapter of the book is concerned with teachers' aims and opinions as revealed in their responses to 39 attitude statements. The responses to *each* of these items made by three different types of teachers are discussed as if each on its own provided significant evidence. The reliability of the items is not considered, nor is the significance of the differences between the groups of teachers. Neither the conceptual basis for the selection of the items nor the empirical relationships among responses to them are discussed.

A major and potentially interesting part of the study involved the observation of pupils' classroom behaviour. Unfortunately, the rationale underlying the system used for analyzing pupils' behaviour, the way in which, the observation system was prepared and tested, the problems of using it, the reliability with which the various categories were used, and the stability of the pupils' categorized behaviour are all either not mentioned or are passed over in a few sentences. For example, we are told that in the preparation of the system the pupils in three different types of classroom were observed for short periods 'and their behaviours listed'. It's that simple!

Finally, to exemplify the fact that the book 'is refreshingly free from the opaque statistical overkill of dubious data that occupies so many researchers' (Shipman, 1976) – a good example of the irresponsible propaganda which leads to this kind of book – the last two chapters are concerned with interactions between styles of teaching and pupil personality types in their effects on pupils' academic progress and classroom behaviour. Many diagrams and tables are presented, and many claims are made; but we are not told (or given the information from which we could calculate for ourselves) either how much of the variance in criterion measures is accounted for by interaction or other effects, or whether any of the interaction effects are statistically significant.

Because the book is written in this way, it simply does not include many of the results which could be of value; and where the results are given, the information which would enable one to evaluate the methodology on which they are based is not. Thus, despite the many sensible and well-informed things that are said in it, the book is almost completely useless to the serious student of classroom processes. More disturbingly, the book is addressed to those readers who lack the technical knowledge which would enable them to make a rational assessment of the claims which are made in it. It must follow from this, and from the fact that no firm conclusions can be reached on the basis of any single investigation, that the book cannot contribute to the more rational educational decision-making which Dr Bennett claims to seek. On the contrary, it can only bring educational research into disrepute, as pharmacy is brought into disrepute when a drug is put on the market before it has been rigorously evaluated.

Dr Bennett will, however, have done us all a service if, from his mistake, other researchers can learn that they should resist the facile demand that they be concerned about the dissemination of their findings. Researchers need only report their work to people who are technically competent to evaluate it, to use it in developing theories and planning further research, and to relate it to other research findings. There is of course a need for the concepts, perspectives and information which are generated by researchers to be communicated to teachers and others, but that is a different task, and it is a task which should only be undertaken after the results of several investigations have been evaluated and synthesized.

The Research

Very little that has been said up to this point necessarily relates to the quality of the actual research conducted by Dr Bennett and his colleagues. It must be assumed that the conceptual analyses, the explicit methodological procedures and criteria, and the statistical analyses which are lacking in *Teaching Styles and Pupil Progress* will be included in research reports not yet published. In the meantime, although there is much on which one cannot yet comment, there are some issues which are sufficiently clear to merit discussion at this stage.

Teaching Styles

The most striking feature of the research is the unusual way in which teaching is conceptualized. Most recent investigations of teaching have used models which imply that teachers are faced with many different kinds of 'decisions', although they are also subject to many different kinds of constraints. The research to which such models have led has been concerned with *variables* which correspond to the different kinds of decision identified in the models, and has been aimed at exploring the relationships among these variables and between them and other variables reflecting contextual factors, teacher characteristics, pupils' behaviour or pupils' learning. The assumption has been that in this way we can develop a fuller understanding of the constraints limiting teachers' decision-making in particular contexts, and of the effects upon pupils of the different ways in which teachers react to *each kind of decision* with which they are faced.

Dr Bennett and his colleagues have apparently used a different kind of model. They have aimed to discover the effects which different *types of teachers* have upon pupils. Teachers of any one type are recognizable by the distinctive 'style' of their teaching, which means, in this case, that they are relatively similar to each other in terms of nineteen variables which reflect seven independent dimensions upon which teachers' behaviour varies (Bennett and Jordan, 1975). Styles, then, are defined in terms of variables. They cannot, however, be defined at all precisely, as is exemplified very well by the definitions of the twelve types of teacher identified in this investigation. This is because there are, among the teachers within any one type, large or small variations on each of the variables used in defining the type. Furthermore, if one has evidence about, say, the attainments of pupils taught by different types of teacher, one cannot infer from this evidence anything about how any one of the defining variables is related to pupils' attainments.

Categorizing teachers into types according to their styles is therefore not a research strategy which is appropriate for identifying the effects of specific aspects of teachers' behaviour, or for any research based on a model of teaching as an activity involving many different and potentially independent kinds of decisions. The development of a typology of teachers only makes sense if one has quite a different model of teaching. Since neither Dr Bennett nor any other recent writer on teaching has, to this reviewer's knowledge, made explicit any model of teaching in terms of styles, one can only speculate as to what such a model might be.

It does seem, however, that a model of this kind would only be meaningful if the several defining characteristics of any one style of teaching were conceptualized as being linked in some significant way. A typology is only useful where a knowledge of some of an object's characteristics allows one to classify it and therefore to predict with confidence some of its other characteristics, as is the case with biological classifications; and such prediction tends to be possible only where there is some kind of functional relationship among the various characteristics relevant to the classification. A model of teaching in terms of teaching styles would imply that the characteristics of teachers' behaviour are much more closely interconnected than they have yet been discovered to be; and that instead of a teacher having many different choices to make, as has commonly been assumed, his behaviour is very largely determined by a few major choices which define his style. Once we had identified the different styles which teachers could use, we would be able to see that a mixed style was as unusual a phenomenon as is the duck-billed platypus.

This is an intriguing possibility, and the chance that such a model of teaching could be useful should certainly not be dismissed. On the other hand, the use of a research strategy implicitly based on a model of this kind surely requires some justification.

Ideologies as a Basis for Research

A second feature of this research is its concern with the rival claims of different educational ideologies. The disadvantages of reporting the research as if it had immediate implications for educational decision-making have already been discussed. The formulation of research questions in terms of ideological controversies is a characteristic of the research itself, which need not have led to such reporting; it is reflected in the aspects of teaching about which information was collected, in the choice of a sample, including unrepresentatively high proportions of 'formal' and 'informal' teachers, and in the final restriction of the classroom observation part of the study to a simple comparison of 'formal' and 'informal' classrooms.

The issue here is not about whether the research team were biased towards one ideology or another: we can accept their word that the conclusions are, if anything, contrary to their ideological predispositions. Nor is it about the relative value of investigating different aspects of teaching: greater understanding of any aspect of teaching would be of value. The issue is rather one of the relative fruitfulness of different ways of deciding which research questions to ask. If the purpose of educational research is taken to be that of describing and explaining educational phenomena, there are several reasons for believing that research questions derived from ideological disagreements are not likely to be very fruitful. Such disagreements tend to be formulated in terms of simple dichotomies which, as Dr Bennett himself forcibly argues, are not helpful even at a descriptive level. Secondly, ideological disagreements tend primarily to be about what should be considered important, not about which theories can best explain relevant phenomena which are agreed to be important. Thirdly, as Dunkin and Biddle (1974) argue, research questions formulated on the basis of ideological positions have not in practice tended to increase our knowledge about teaching.

The work of educational researchers is most likely to be of value if, instead of attempting to be adjudicators in ideological disputes, we set ourselves tasks which are more demanding but less ambitious. On one hand, rather than relying on educational ideologies for our hypotheses and questions, we are more likely to make progress by developing our questions from sociological and psychological theories, from philosophical analyses, and most of all, through reflecting on the findings of our own and each others' empirical studies. On the other hand, we should do well to recognize that the relevance of 'facts' to most serious educational controversies is marginal; for example, the Lancaster evidence is not relevant to the claim that education should be considered as life itself, not as a preparation for life.

Some Technical Issues

This research has been criticized elsewhere, for example by Rogers and Barron (1976), because of a number of technical weaknesses. Much of this criticism is hardly justified, being concerned with weaknesses which arise from the quasi-experimental nature of the research, such as the possibility of alternative explanations for between-group differences and the unknown nature of the causal relationships underlying the observed statistical correlations. These and other weaknesses are shared by all research of this kind and can only be overcome by using different research designs which have their own inherent disadvantages. The educational researcher has to learn to live with, and to make appropriately cautious use of, imperfect evidence.

One of the interesting issues which is raised by this investigation relates to the choice of measures of pupil attainment. In a context where teachers were not following any common curriculum, there was virtually no option but to use standardized tests; and presumably these were chosen with care, for example to avoid floor and ceiling effects and to ensure that norms were available over the complete range of scores. The use of such tests raises no problems if one is solely concerned to compare the attainments of different groups of pupils on the given criteria. However, if one is attempting to discover the differential effects of different types of teaching, one must also ask about the content validity of the tests: to what extent can the differences between groups be accounted for on the simple grounds that more of the test content was dealt with in some classes than in others, or that more time was spent on this content? These are not easy questions for researchers to examine, but both logical argument and previous empirical findings suggest that they are of critical importance. A useful rule would be that, whatever the particular focus of any investigation relating classroom processes to pupil attainment, *coverage* of the content of each criterion test should be measured, and variance which can be accounted for in terms of differential coverage should be extracted before the possible effects of other classroom variables are examined.

An issue which is raised by Rogers and Barron is that of the relationship between the units used for sampling and the units used in the statistical analysis. Certainly statistical theory demands that these units should be the same, and since classes were sampled, there can be no justification for using the individual pupil as a unit when the general effects of different teaching styles were being compared. However, if one maintained this rigorous position, it would be impossible to ask the important questions about how teaching behaviour interacts with pupils' previous attainments or personality characteristics in influencing pupils' learning. The alternative of sampling individual pupils rather than classes is rarely a practical possibility. Sampling pupils *within* classes, as was done for the pupil observation part of this study, is a possible course of action; but it tends to leave one with a weak basis on which to estimate the residual variance. Probably the least unsatisfactory course of action is to adopt the fiction that, in addition to sampling classes, one has sampled all the individual pupils in each class. The statistical analyses which follow from this must of course take account of the class, as well as the pupil, as a unit; and we must assume that this will be done when the Lancaster data is properly reported.

It was found in this investigation that the initial attainments of pupils in 'formal' classes tended to be higher than those of pupils in 'informal' classes; and to take account of these initial differences, the technique of analysis of covariance was used. This, unfortunately, is wrong. As Evans and Anastasio (1968) conclusively show, one of the necessary assumptions of the analysis of covariance model, homogeneity of between-group and within-group regression, is inevitably violated if, as is claimed in this case, there is a non-zero correlation between the covariate and the treatment effect, i.e. between the initial attainments of pupils and the differential progress which they make as a result of different styles of teaching. When initial differences are found between groups to be compared in research of this kind, the researcher has to settle for statistical techniques, such as multiple regression analysis, which lead to valid but more ambiguous results.

Dr Bennett and his colleagues have collected a great deal of interesting data. It seems likely that, when these data are properly analyzed, they will provide results of which account will have to be taken by anyone attempting to develop an increased understanding of teaching from the complex body of research evidence. It is also possible that this investigation has contributed usefully to our methodological repertoire for the study of teaching, and to our ways of conceptualizing teaching, though both of these seem rather less likely. But on all these points we shall have to suspend judgement until a serious report of the research is available.

References

BENNETT, S.N. and JORDAN, J. (1975). A typology of teaching styles in primary schools. *Brit. J. Educ. Psychol.* 45, 20–8.
DUNKIN, M.J. and BIDDLE, B.J. (1974). *The Study of Teaching* (New York: Holt, Rinehart and Winston).
EVANS, S.H. and ANASTASIO, E.J. (1968). Misuse of analysis of covariance when treatment effect and covariate are confounded. *Psych. Bull.* 69, 225–34.

POWELL, J.L. (1976). After Lancaster: some reflections on the progressive-traditional controversy. *Research in Education* (the newsletter of SCRE). 16.

ROGERS, V.R. and BARRON, J. (1976). Questioning the evidence. *Times Educ. Supp.*, 30 April, 20–1.

SHIPMAN, M.D. (1976). Is it enough? *Times Educ. Supp.*, 30 April, 22.

Coping Strategies and the Multiplication of Differentiation in Infant Classrooms

A. Pollard

This paper is concerned with processes of social differentiation in school classrooms and with the influence of teacher and pupil coping strategies on such processes. It thus relates directly to a core concern of the sociology of education in that it offers an opportunity for analysis at a micro-level to make an unequivocal contribution to the macro-structural debate on schooling and social reproduction.

Of course, the issue of differentiation within classrooms is a well-researched area in which many different approaches have been taken. For instance, the classic study by Rosenthal and Jacobson (1968) claimed to have identified the effects of a 'self-fulfilling prophecy' and argued that pupil performance was dramatically influenced by teacher expectations. Rist (1970) suggested that the kindergarten teacher whom he studied used a 'roughly constructed ideal-type' based on social class criteria with which to classify children into a three table/group 'caste-system' within her classroom. Consequent variation in teacher behaviour resulted in differences in child performance and the caste system began to be institutionalised. From a Marxist perspective, Sharp and Green's (1976) analysis of teacher ideologies and social control in a 'progressive' infant school concerned itself with the formation of child identities through the teacher structured processes of the classroom – in particular as an implication of the teachers' 'busyness' ideology.

The present paper has implications for these arguments, but it retains its primary focus on processes rather than outcomes. More specifically I argue that, in classrooms where a 'working consensus' exists, teachers and children interact to *mutually* reinforce classroom differentiation, as a by-product of the mesh of their coping strategies. The analysis thus particularly utilises the concepts of 'coping strategy' and of 'working consensus' and it is important to clarify my use of them.

The concept of coping strategy has been most formally developed by Andy Hargreaves (1978) who analysed the context of teaching and argued that the constraints and dilemmas impinging on teacher action have macro-structural origins and thus represent 'societal demands' to which teachers have to respond. In my own work (Pollard, 1982), building on Woods' (1977) analysis as well as that of Hargreaves, I sought to develop the concept by emphasising the importance of biography in influencing the particular perception of 'coping' necessities with reference to which teachers *or* children will act. The concept of coping strategy thus has linkages to the macro-concerns of history and social structure *and* to the micro-concerns of biography and the unique social contexts which exist in classrooms.

The concept of 'working consensus' describes a type of negotiated 'truce' between the teacher and the children, by which each recognises the coping necessities of the other. It is a socially constructed set of understandings which reduces threat and enables the participants to mutually accomplish the social situation in their classroom. As David Hargreaves (1975) has put it . . .

> The absolute imposition of the teacher's definition of the situation is really impossible and the side effects of attempts to do so make such a course inadvisable. . . He aims instead at a negotiated settlement whereby teacher and pupil each go half-way with respect to some demands and whereby in other areas the teacher withdraws or moderates his demands on the pupils in return for conformity to other teacher demands. This negotiated settlement may fall short of the teacher's ideal definition of the situation but it is realistic in that it averts discord and ensures that a fair number of his demands are met and that teacher–pupil relationships are generally good. The pupils, realising that their position is not a strong one from which to bargain, are usually content with the concessions made by the teacher (p. 133).

Of course, in the classroom context, the teacher normally has greater power than the children. This gives him or her the advantage of initiation and it is clear that the working consensus will reflect the power differential between the teacher and the children. The children in a sense take up a tactical position, accepting teacher power to a great extent. However, this teacher power *is* circumscribed, because if it is used 'unfairly' or 'unreasonably', from the subjective perspective of the children then they will change from their tactical compliance to more offensive strategies leading to a breakdown of the working consensus. They will defend themselves, often through forms of 'disorder', thus increasing the 'survival threat' experience by that teacher (Pollard, 1980).

When a working consensus is established it thus represents a mutual accommodation for coping. Of course, such a truce cannot be taken for granted. The particular strategies which children develop when faced with their coping problem will vary depending on their biographies and on the particular nature of the cultural, institutional and classroom contexts which exist. Some may try to 'take on' the teacher and to challenge their authority but I would suggest (Pollard, 1979, 1981) that it is far more common, among primary school children at least, to find a type of acceptance of 'how things are' which supports the idea of a working consensus having been negotiated. This may reflect the predominantly class-based organisation of primary schools and the emphasis placed by teachers on 'establishing a good relationship'. Certainly the continuity provided by the class-based primary school system is far more conducive to the establishment of understandings between a class of children and 'their' teacher than is the more time-structured and subject-centred system found in most secondary schools (Bird, 1980).

Even in the primary school there is a range of child response. My own recent research in a middle school (Pollard, 1984) suggests that the nature of this response ranges from a grudging 'doing of time' with a watchful eye out for opportunities for 'messing about', to an active engagement within the teacher's frame of reference and an endorsement of 'pleasing teacher' strategies. One way of placing these alternatives conceptually is to see them as responses to the basic ambiguity of the child's structural position. The 'resistance' strategies generally articulate from peers and child culture whilst the more 'accepting' actions orient more towards adult expectations. Between these alternatives a third type of response represents attempts to be seen favourably in both spheres. In my view the majority of children attempt this third form of adaption and they do so by negotiating the 'working consensus' with the teacher. Since it is normally in the teacher's interests to support this development the working consensus routinely becomes established as 'what-everyone-takes-for-granted' (Ball, 1980). As I clarified above, it is not, in fact, quite what *everyone* takes for granted for 'the children' cannot be regarded as a homogeneous group. However, if it is initially primarily the work of the dominant group of children, I think it can still be argued that in most circumstances in a primary school context it eventually becomes established as the fundamental basis of the 'moral order' of the classroom and hence as a source of legitimation for teacher and child actions which is applied to the class as a whole.

In this paper I wish to attempt to identify what, in terms of sociological consequences, might be called the 'multiplier effect' of some forms of coping and of the 'working consensus'. The working consensus is seen as a product of both teacher and child coping strategies having achieved some sort of balance *vis-à-vis* each other. In each case the particular coping strategies of the other represent a major factor to which their own strategies must have adapted. It follows that over time the strategies of both the teacher and children tend to become 'meshed' together, with those of the children being the more adapted because of the teacher's greater power. Indeed child strategies have sometimes been seen as 'counter-strategies' (Denscombe, 1980) and as primarily reactive. One result of this is that, whatever the sociological significance on the teacher strategies may be the children's reactive coping strategies within the parameters of the working consensus may reinforce and amplify this consequence. Such amplification may reinforce teachers' strategic decisions by leading to their favourable evaluation, their continued usage and their continued 'multiplication' of effect.

In the context of the work on classroom differentiation reviewed earlier, this analysis is suggesting that, in addition to the self-fulfilling prophecy and the consequences of labelling or teacher control ideologies, there are *socially* fulfilling processes at work in classrooms which can powerfully reinforce more individualised factors.

I want now to try to substantiate and illustrate this suggestion that the meshing of teacher and pupil coping strategies produces a multiplication of consequence by drawing on two ethnographic studies of infant-school classrooms. The classrooms were in different schools although the schools were themselves very similar, both being located on the edges of council estates in the inner suburbs of northern towns. They were also of similar age, construction and design. However, the forms of classroom organisation and the teachers themselves were very different. In one Mrs Rothwell maintained what an adviser called a 'good formal regime' whilst the other class, taught by Mr Harman, was run on what might have been called 'progressive' principles[1]. The children in each class were six and seven years old.

In the study of these classrooms I adopted the principle of methodological triangulation (Denzin, 1970) and used a variety of data collection methods. The main one was the classic ethnographic method of observation and field notes but this was supplemented with sociometric analysis of the children's friendship groups, interviews with the teachers, systematic observation of child–teacher contacts, cassette recordings of verbal interaction and the study of non-reactive documents. Contrasts between the two classrooms were clear by whatever type of data was studied. For instance, the very simple classification system which I adopted for collecting data on child–teacher contacts indicated differences particularly with regard to the direction of contact initiation and the number of 'advisory'[2] contacts made (Table 1).

Seventy-three per cent of the child–teacher contacts in Mrs Rothwell's class were teacher initiated and of these over half involved some form of 'advice' which in this classification has a behavioural/disciplinary association. In Mr Harman's class only 13% of the contacts were of this advisory type and over half of child–teacher contacts were child initiated.

Clearly these classrooms were very different. Taking each separately in the body of the paper below I want to present data from interviews which show the perspectives of the teachers and indicate something of their

TABLE 1   Teacher-child contacts %

	Child initiated		Teacher initiated		
	Work related	*Other*	*Work related*	*Other*	*Advisory*
Mrs Rothwell's class	12	15	27	11	35
total		27		73	
Mr Harman's class	20	32	18	17	13
total		52		48	

biographies. This will lead towards an analysis of their classroom coping strategies and pedagogies which will then be augmented with data on the children's social system and classroom actions. Finally the social implications of the teacher strategies will be traced, as processed through the working consensus and the mesh of teacher and child accommodation[3].

We can begin with Mrs Rothwell and her class.

Mrs Rothwell and Her Class

Mrs Rothwell had a teaching certificate and was in her late thirties. She had taught for 12 years. She was married to a civil engineer, had two children and lived in a pleasant rural village outside the town. She had been brought up as, and was, a practising Christian.

A core aspect of Mrs Rothwell's perspective could be decribed as 'familial'. As she explained to me: 'A school should be like a good family, with discipline, love, and room to explore'.

Mrs Rothwell felt a sincere caring duty towards the children in her class whom she believed came from generally poor and unstable home backgrounds. She felt that these homes failed to provide a discipline, standards of behaviour or support for the children and, to compensate for this background, she emphasised 'developing an awareness of right and wrong'.

Mrs Rothwell frequently used personality constructs. Children were often described as 'extrovert' and 'lively' or as 'introverted'. Mrs Rothwell also identified those children who were 'immature' and those who were 'growing up'. From her experience with her own children she believed that she 'knew the stages that children go through'. Mrs Rothwell had a complex array of descriptions to describe the intelligence of the children. These ranged from 'exceptionally bright', 'very bright', 'reasonably bright', 'intelligent', 'capable', 'great ability', 'very able', 'thoughtful' – to 'poor', 'not very clever', 'needs help', 'backward'.

Mrs Rothwell had a clear image of her ideal pupil (Becker, 1952) but felt a type of resigned concern towards many of those who could not match up to this image. As she put it:

> It really is rewarding when you get a child who is bright, one who you can really talk to and rely on, but we don't get many of those . . . most of them here really do need a lot of help. We do what we can for them but some of them are very hard to help even when you want to do your best for them.

Regarding pedagogy Mrs Rothwell felt that learning took place best when she transmitted the knowledge, usually in a discussion → blackboard → book-work sequence, and when the children had had 'enough practice'. Thus there was frequent recitation of maths tables, practice of sums, reading and writing. In Mrs Rothwell's view, the children worked best when they had an 'incentive', and she provided this with a star reward system. Competition was encouraged so that children would 'get on quickly and carefully'. However, some children 'didn't try' and were 'careless' whilst others 'lacked concentration'. These children were regarded as 'unsettled', in contrast to those 'well-adjusted' to school.

Mrs Rothwell's perspective seemed internally consistent. She believed that the skills and the body of knowledge, which it was her duty to teach, were linear by nature and she believed that learning occurs through practice and reinforcement. She therefore introduced work in a careful order and took her planning and preparation very seriously. She provided a fixed time-table in which there was plenty of time for work and practice, and awarded stars to stimulate competition and to provide reinforcement. In Mrs Rothwell's view the structured routines and time-tables which she maintained provided the security which the children needed. In turn she felt that security made it possible for the children to be happy – and: 'They should be happy in school, even if they learn only a little, because they come from broken homes'.

Mrs Rothwell's perspective was thus organised around what she saw as her two main duties: the compensation for poor home backgrounds by providing moral standards and security and the efficient imparting of knowledge and skills.

In Mrs Rothwell's classroom the tables were arranged in two rectangular blocks with the blackboard and the teacher's desk at either ends of the blocks. Seating places were officially allocated by Mrs Rothwell and fixed. The 'brightest' and 'average' children each occupied the majority of a table block (the 'top' and 'middle' groups), with a group of 'less able' children split between the two blocks and clustered at the end of each nearest to the teacher's desk (the 'bottom' group).

Mrs Rothwell used classwork for almost everything – during craft activities everyone made a flower in the way they were shown, in writing practice everyone copied the patterns from the board, in number lessons everyone chanted their 2-times, 3-times, 5-times and 10-times tables; in poetry times children spoke verses chorally, in creative English everyone wrote on the subject suggested using the words written on the blackboard. These examples occurred consistently and regularly.

The consistencies in Mrs Rothwell's image of her ideal pupil, her typifications and dominant constructs, her formal pedagogy, classroom organisation and child-grouping methods, are quite clear. They are all associated with the particular teaching technology (Hammersley, 1980) by which she sought to cope in the classroom. They were the means by which she reconciled her image of herself and her role with her daily practical situation.

From their close similarity to those found by Rist (1970), Mrs Rothwell's teaching strategies appeared likely to produce a social hierarchy within the class and this was investigated by analysing the relationship between the friendship structure of the class and indices of academic achievement.

A sociometric analysis showed that friendship groupings of girls and boys were distinct, and this was confirmed by observations of their play in the playground. The boys tended to be interested in 'Action Man', guns, fighting, chasing, 'Steve Austin', space etc, whilst the girls tended to be more involved with skipping, dolls and home-games. This distinction was often reinforced by Mrs Rothwell: for instance, boys and girls lined up separately, were dismissed from the classroom separately, were given different types of classroom 'jobs' and were spoken to in qualitatively different ways. It was also found that the friendship groupings corresponded closely with the official academic stratification system used by Mrs Rothwell. Two indices of academic achievement were immediately available – official group seat places and reading book level and the relationship between these and informal friendship groupings is shown in Table 2.

There is a pattern of association between informal friendship groups, group seat places and reading book levels revealed here. For instance, in the case of the girls, all of Group 2 sat on the Top table and were on the 14th reading book in the scheme or beyond, whilst the other girls' group was mainly made up of children on the Middle table and of children on or below the 14th reading book. The pattern was very similar for the boys, there being one group basically based on the Top table and one group based on the Middle table. Two children from the Bottom table were shown by sociometric analysis as aspiring to join such groups but their choice was not reciprocated. Two others, Raymond and Catherine, formed the only mixed sex friendship group.

It should be remembered that Mrs Rothwell's criteria for allocation of seat places were not designed to reinforce friendships. The seat places were fixed and maintained by Mrs Rothwell for occasional pedagogic convenience, and the internal stratification which resulted was validated by her perspective concerning the nature of children's abilities and by her view of the competitive spur which the possibility of 'moving to a higher table', or 'being on the

TABLE 2 Seat places and reading book levels in Mrs Rothwell's class by friendship groups

		Seat places by table	Reading book level
Group 1	Sandra	T	14
	Shirley	B	4
	Ann	M	12
	Andrea	M	12
	Denise	M	12
	Valerie	M	8
	Elaine	T	11
	Kathie	M	10
Group 2	Sarah	T	14
	Janet	T	14
	Jane	T	17
	Lee	T	16
Group 3	Clive	B	8
	Duncan	T	17
	Miles	T	17
	Roger	T	13
Group 4	Thomas	M	4
	Denis	M	8
	Charles	M	9
	Terry	M	4
	Peter	M	8
	Geoffrey	M	10
	Alan	T	10
Group 5	Raymond	B	6
	Catherine	B	4
Unplaced	Colin	B	–

highest table' might provide. There are thus good reasons for doubting that the friendships had developed independently of the seat place structuring. My conclusion then is that the children's friendship groups did seem to have been influenced by each child's degree of achievement and by their official identities in the classroom. These are fairly unremarkable conclusions and appear to be a consequence of Mrs Rothwell's perspective, classroom organisation and teaching strategies. One way of putting this is to say that she had created the conditions for 'primary differentiation'. She had a clear image of her 'ideal pupil', and a highly developed set of constructs and typifications. This was combined with forms of classroom organisation and pedagogy which derived from, and reinforced, her perspective.

I want now to focus on what could be termed 'secondary differentiation', which lies in a similar relationship to that between primary and secondary deviance as identified by Lemert (1967). The crucial processual influence which I suggested earlier was that of the children and their coping strategies meshing interaction with the teacher and hers. Indeed I suggested that this could set up a 'multiplier effect' whereby the social consequences of a particular teacher strategy are amplified when children develop their own strategies around those of the teacher. As we have seen, the teacher's use of a particular set of strategies has a primary significance because of the teacher–pupil power differential, but I am suggesting that when a working consensus exists this gains secondary reinforcement from child-coping strategies.

An illustration of child strategies in Mrs Rothwell's class which can briefly be described as 'collaboration to produce' may make this argument clearer. Firstly it should be said that a type of working consensus did appear to exist. The majority of children appeared to accept the dominant definition of the situation, as initiated primarily by Mrs Rothwell, without demur. Indeed, in almost all their work, the majority tried to 'please teacher' by producing correct results; they wanted to 'win a star' and, above all, they did not want to fail. As I have described, the most common setting requiring accomplishment in the class was the 'seat work setting'. In a typical lesson of this type such as 'number', sums were put on the blackboard for everyone to do. Mrs Rothwell's movement pattern was then regular. After setting the lesson-task and checking that the children had begun, she went to her desk to hear readers. The result of Mrs Rothwell sitting at her desk, in combination with her class work and the children's determination to please her, was that the potential for collaboration to find 'the answers' was enormous and such collaboration was widespread. In fact the children appeared to have traded a degree of compliance with Mrs Rothwell's goals in exchange for her unwitting non-intervention with their strategies for attaining them. It was this trade-off that appeared to be the underlying basis of the working consensus.

The collaboration system was very interesting. On those occasions when there was general unease among the children about how to accomplish a set task, such as their sums, observations suggested that a few key children on each table actually did the work and that these 'answers' then flowed through friendship groups in a 'ripple effect' for knowledge comparable to Kounin's (1970) for desists.

In other circumstances when the work set was familiar and most of the children felt confident, then they could work alone. Of course, most commonly situations occurred somewhere between these alternatives and also varied within the class. However, collaboration was far from unusual and was an active process, as the following transcript of a conversation recorded on the Top table shows.

> *Mrs Rothwell*: Today we are going to try to do two sorts of sums at once, we'll try to do the take-away ones and the add-up ones, but I'm going to try and trick you by mixing them up . . . (writes sums on board) . . . this is my day for tricking people.

(The children work. A little later . . .)

Janet: She hasn't caught me out yet.
Sandra: She hasn't caught me out yet.
Nigel: She hasn't caught me out yet – has she . . .?
Janet: She has – you're caught – she's caught him out!
Nigel: Why?
Janet: He's got two 'ten take-aways' . . .
Nigel: I think she has caught me out.
Duncan: Nigel, I think you'd better copy off me, or you'll make a messy job. Ten take away nought makes ten.
Sandra: Ten take away nought makes ten?
Janet: You've done the second one wrong, you've done the second one wrong.
Nigel: I haven't.
Janet: You have – oh, there shouldn't be a four there should there?
Duncan: There should.
Janet: Should there? (Janet alters the answer.)
Nigel: Yes, oh yes, that's right.
Sandra: You've done it wrong, there shouldn't be a four there. (Children change answers.)
Duncan: Mine's right.
Nigel: So's mine.
Janet: Mine is.
Sandra: Mine is.
Janet: Everybody knows ten add ten makes twenty.
Nigel: Ten add ten makes twenty.
Nigel: What's ten add nothing?
Duncan: Nothing.
Sandra: Ten add nothing is nothing – it's nothing.
Nigel: Janet's done it wrong, she's done ten.
Sandra: Mine are right.
Duncan: They are tricky – oh Sandra, you've done that one wrong, no, look. (Shows and Sandra alters.)
Duncan: That's it.

In effect these children were negotiating among themselves for the 'right' answer. As we have seen, academic criteria were important to the children's social system, and observations of 'negotiations for right answers' between children suggested that some children with a reputation for generally 'getting them right' had considerable prestige – for instance, the child who managed to get 'ten add nothing is nothing' accepted was the most chosen child on the sociomatrix.

A related strategy for accomplishing the seat-work lessons which was frequently observed was one of waiting for someone else to have their work marked and then checking and perhaps changing one's own answers. Some children seemed highly dependent on these collaborative strategies, and in these cases, their timing was very important, because if they failed to collect enough answers early in the lesson, they ran a risk that some key children may finish, be marked and put their books away in drawers. In these circumstances the only possible strategy was to attempt to move seats, and some children were repeatedly 'told off' for doing so, as well as subsequently receiving sanctions for 'not having tried'.

Quantitative and non-reactive evidence was available to support observations and cassette recordings of collaboration, in the form of analysis of 'errors-in-common' made by children in their sum books over half a term. This data indicated high percentages of 'errors-in-common' between neighbouring children sitting at the Top and Middle tables. The Top group tended to complete more sums than the Middle group, and also to get more sums correct. The fact that they made relatively few mistakes means that the percentage of 'errors-in-common' was based on fewer items, but this in itself is interesting because observations suggested that they had a more efficient collaboration system than the other tables, in addition to being better able to work alone if necessary. In contrast, the Bottom groups were seated apart. They tended to be shunned by other children and thus to have poor access to correct answers via the collaboration system. To make their difficulties worse, they were often given individual work cards when the class work was considered too hard for them, this meant the comparison of answers was impossible and they tended to do only a small percentage of the work set.

The system of star rewards for 'good work' had a first unintended consequence of reinforcing the collaborative system as well as the work itself. Indeed, on several occasions a complete sequence of negotiation was witnessed, from getting answers from friends to receiving star reinforcement from Mrs Rothwell.

A second consequence of this was that it contributed to the self-fulfilling elements in the internal stratification system of the class: Mrs Rothwell evaluated the work which the children produced and presented, and she consequently assessed that some children were not capable of good work, and should be on the Bottom table, and perhaps do special work cards, whilst others produced good work and therefore should be on the Top or Middle table and could do class work. Those judged not capable thus continued to be sealed off from the hidden means of accomplishing the lessons, whilst those judged capable were enabled to produce overt evidence.

Overall, the collaboration system functioned efficiently as a means of producing the explicit responses required, for it enabled the majority of children to cope with the difficulties of a formal class-based lesson. I do not mean to suggest here that the children learned nothing in the lessons or that they necessarily entirely tricked the teacher, indeed Mrs Rothwell specifically allowed quiet talking so that children could discuss their tasks. A second important point is that from Mrs Rothwell's point of view, she also accomplished these seat-work lessons satisfactorily in terms of her educational perspective and structural position. The children were kept busy on educational tasks which gave them the practice which she felt they needed, during this time there were no discipline problems. Mrs Rothwell was able to hear her readers, and at the end of the lessons their value was tangibly shown in neat rows of sums which in themselves legitimised her work. Thus the collaboration system rewarded the teacher, just as the teacher unwittingly reinforced the collaboration system. It was a stable process, with resources in the perspectives and commonsense knowledge of the participants which provided comprehensive schemes of internal legitimation. The classroom process, with its outcome of social differentiation, was a product of the mesh of the coping strategies of the participants. Although the teacher clearly initiated and continued to structure such process because of her power, the actions of the children significantly reinforced and 'multiplied' the social consequence of differentiation.

We can now look at the second classroom, that of Mr Harman.

Mr Harman and His Class

Mr Harman was an unusual teacher of young children, being male with a degree in Social Sciences as well as a teaching certificate. Aged 25, he had taught for two and a half years at this, his first teaching post. Mr Harman felt somewhat isolated from the school and in particular he disagreed with the general assumption among the staff that their role was to teach the 'basic skills' to children from 'poor home environments'.

Mr Harman derived the most important elements of his perspective from reference groups outside the school. He had been influenced by his degree course in Sociology which he had incorporated into a developed child-centred perspective. In particular, Mr Harman stressed the relativism of his own perspectives and the personal validity of the perspectives of other people. This was particularly so for groups towards which he felt a commitment, and most importantly for the children in his class. For instance, he explained that 'the estate environment, which I find boring, they find endless delight in', and applied this type of argument to a range of situations, including acknowledging the legitimacy of a child to feel 'bored' in class and to find something 'better' to do, because 'if they don't attend to what I'm saying, then it may not have any relevance for them'.

This theme recurs again and again in Mr Harman's attitude to the children, education and practical teaching, and it engendered a wide range of issues on which he disagreed with other staff. For instance, Mr Harman felt that the priority of the school should not be on teaching 'skills' or 'knowledge', but on 'learning how to think and how to learn'.

Because of his isolation Mr Harman valued his classroom autonomy which, being an accepted principle in the school, enabled him to implement his ideas despite general suspicion of them. He was opposed to the Headmaster's insistence on 'discipline' and to his methods of punishment, and linked the issue to that of aims . . . 'It doesn't matter if the children *think* they are in control, as long as the teacher is really controlling the teaching situation so that the results are in line with their broad aims' (Mr Harman).

Mr Harman thus encouraged children to indicate the activities and to follow their interests, and saw his role as: 'asking the right questions – I ask: "what happens if . . .?" ' This approach to learning was based on a belief in the value of intrinsic motivation and Mr Harman was emphatic: 'I try and avoid all sorts of "carrots" – even the unofficial ones like "taking messages" '.

Mr Harman used his ability at generating interest and his charisma as his main control and teaching technique. Frequently this would evolve spontaneously: 'It's my emotive response to situations in the classrooms – it isn't analysable – I just happen to feel its "right" in the relationship between me and the kids'.

This often took the form of humour or deliberately exaggerated acting. These attitudes were the main source of the constructs which Mr Harman used to describe the children, and particularly important to him was the degree of communicative rapport which he was able to develop with them. For instance, children were described as 'aware', 'has a good sense of humour', 'gets a joke' or for some children 'not very inspiring'.

There are several factors in the explanation of the prominence of such constructs. Firstly Mr Harman's control techniques were based on principles which forsook all physical sanctions and extrinsic inducements. This meant that the control techniques were highly verbal and depended upon children reasoning, 'getting the joke' or on having enough awareness to sense teacher expectations. Secondly, because of his sense of isolation, Mr Harman derived a great deal of personal satisfaction from the rapport he was able to develop with the children. Those with quick-witted humour and verbal agility were rewarding to him. Thirdly, Mr Harman interpreted his emphasis on 'thinking ability' in terms of conceptual development. He rejected the school's conventional wisdom that infant children had to learn basic 3R skills before they could learn to 'think', and saw this as a communication problem, the solution to which was the use of:

... verbal language which can be a flexible tool even for young children, rather than trying to communicate on paper and get frustrated with failure – adults find it hard enough to think on paper so why should we expect kids to do it in schools (Mr Harman).

Mr Harman therefore did not emphasise the formal skills of writing very much but used small group work, discussions and 'asking the right questions' as his basic approach in most lesson periods.

At the start of the year the children in Mr Harman's class had not been entirely sure about his approach. Of course, in order to cope within the school Mr Harman could not entirely ignore the institutionalised definitions of standards, behaviour or pedagogy. However, to reconcile his ascribed role with his own beliefs he had to actively adapt and he had generated what might be characterised as a 'subterranean value system' (Matza, 1964) in the classroom. In particular, since he himself rejected many aspects of the institutionalised definition, he had considerable sympathy with the children who shared his views. Thus descriptions of children such as 'a bit devious', 'clever enough to get away with things', and 'a bespectacled Dastardly Dick cartoon freak', contained implicit approval since they indicated 'thinking' and divergence.

In Mr Harman's classroom the tables were arranged for children to work in small groups of five or six. Each child had an official seat at one of the six separate tables and this official seat was for registration and for the first and most 'work'-intensive lesson period of the day. These seat places were broadly based on ability criteria (two Top tables, two Middle, two Bottom) which Mr Harman stated he disliked doing but found it convenient since he could allocate work cards by table. These batches would include literacy and Maths work, and when the quota was finished, 'choosing' and free movement were encouraged.

In other lesson periods work would be 'finished off' and Mr Harman would usually hear readers or take small groups of children for particular instruction on Maths, reading or an interest topic, whilst the rest of the class dispersed to the activities of their choice. These included sand, painting, Wendy House, shop, 'Lego', bricks, plasticine, jigsaws, games, constrcution toys, crayons, 'sticky', interest tables etc.

Thus for the majority of the time, children would be involved individually or in freely chosen groups on their self-chosen activities or on their particular work cards.

Mr Harman's chosen form of classroom organisation and pedagogy represents his form of coping. They represent his resolution at the particular time of this study of the dilemmas and contradictions presented by his beliefs and views of himself with his role and the structural position within the school. The next link in the argument is to see if this particular form of coping was reflected in child strategies or had any social consequences.

In Mr Harman's class sociometric analysis showed six groups, three of girls and three of boys and their table seat positions and official reading book levels are shown in Table 3, thus providing some points of comparison with Mrs Rothwell's class.

Despite the more limited use of fixed seat positions in this class, some relationship between seat position and friendship group is apparent, particularly among the girls. In their case the three groups appeared to have been associated directly with their respective seat positions at the Top, Middle and Bottom tables and the data on reading book level also broadly supports this interpretation that the academic structuring of the classroom was significant for the girls' peer group formation. The same is true of two of the three boys' groups who formed particularly clear friendship groups based on the Top and Middle tables, but it is not the case for the third and largest group of boys who had particularly diverse reading book levels and also relatively diverse seat positions.

It appears from this data that, as in Mrs Rothwell's class, the children's social system was being affected by their official academic status – except, that is, for the large group of boys. Focused observations of this group of boys showed that they were frequently involved in deviant activities but that many of them had a close rapport with Mr Harman. These findings were somewhat unexpected but a possible explanation is provided by considering the early process of establishment of understandings in Mr Harman's class at the start of the year.

In their previous, and their first, school year, the children in Mr Harman's class had been taught by the Deputy Head of the school. She and Mr Harman did not share perspectives and in fact probably provided the greatest contrast of teaching styles existing in the school. In their reception class the children had been used to a daily routine of 'work' in the morning, 'activities' in the afternoon. Mr Harman initially aimed to integrate the two:

> I tried to establish not 'work' and 'play' time but just 'inclass' time – but I totally failed. This distinction between work time and choosing time was forced on me, early on, when I realised they *expected* to do work in the morning. They couldn't cope with the idea of someone 'playing' (in their terms) whilst they were 'working' . . . I had groups in sand, water, painting, Maths, writing etc . . . they kept asking 'what are those children doing?'. They got confused and didn't know what they were meant to do. I found myself policing all the time, checking on what they had and hadn't done. So I've established this system of 'work periods', which they found acceptable and I found productive, and also 'choosing periods' in which I am able to have groups, and gradually I'm getting this idea that some kids can be working when others are choosing.

Thus the children had forced Mr Harman to compromise on his intentions. When he was asked to recall the names of those chilren who had been most confused by his attempt to change their anticipated definition of the

TABLE 3 **Seat places and reading book levels in Mr Harman's class by friendship groups**

		Seat places by table	Reading book level
Group 1	Stuart	M	7
	William	T	24
	Len	M	4
	Marcus	B	1
	Keith	T	16
	Adam	T	19
	Matthew	M	5
	Joe	M	7
	Simon	T	8
	Malcolm	T	7
Group 2	Dick	M	3
	Julian	M	6
	Philip	M	3
	Patrick	B	3
	Peter	M	7
	Sam	M	5
	Edward	M	9
Group 3	Sandra	M	3
	Linda	M	5
	Christine	B	2
	Jill	M	7
Group 4	Paula	T	19
	Maria	M	6
	Susan	T	11
	Janet	T	9
	Carol	T	16
Group 5	Kathleen	B	3
	Barbara	M	6
	Tessa	B	4
Group 6	Gregory	T	27
	Jeremy	T	16
Unplaced	Stephen	B	3
	Gareth	T	15
	Martin	M	3

classroom situation, he mentioned ten names, six were girls, and the four boys were all members of the 'average' group. None of the academically diverse boys were mentioned. From this it appears that a sizeable proportion of Mr Harman's class, including all the girls and the 'academically average' boys, continued to maintain something of the overall definition of the classroom situation which had been established in their first year of schooling and had been maintained by general institutionalised conventions and expectations thereafter.

However, the ambivalence of Mr Harman's structural position and personal perspectives was manifested in the formation of the large group of boys of diverse ability. These children related directly to Mr Harman's 'subterranean value system'. They were regarded as 'good communicators', they could 'get a joke'. Mr Harman thus developed a particularly good rapport with these children, they provided his 'consociates', while the more conformist, 'less inspiring' remainder of the classroom remained 'contemporaneous'. Thus, in a very real sense, this boys' group was 'sponsored' by Mr Harman and his personal value system. This sponsorship included the relabelling of deviant acts. Not only did Mr Harman 'sympathise' with 'bored' children and thus allow peripheral inattention, but some acts, which were deviant within the institutionalised definition, were regarded within the classroom as indicating creative thinking and thus 'learning how to learn'. As Mr Harman said on several occasions: 'Some of them are clever enough to get away with it, and anyway, I don't blame them'.

Thus at the primary stage of differentiation Mr Harman favoured divergent, creative, 'jokers' and at the secondary stage these children took advantage of the scope which he allowed. It is perhaps indicative of external cultural forces that no girls' group took similar advantage and it could well be that Mr Harman's style particularly fitted masculine cultural forms and presented the girls with just another instance of the 'Catch 22' described by Clarricoates (1978).

It appears that there was a close relationship between the coping strategies of Mr Harman and those of his class. Many of the children derived their strategies from the institutionalised child role and definitions which Mr Harman also felt constrained to sustain, but a significant group of boys developed alternative strategies which Mr Harman's values and coping strategies also made possible and this was reflected in the structure of friendship groups within the class.

Conclusion

I have attempted to identify a classroom process in which the coping strategies of the pupils mesh into the coping strategies of the teacher as a mediated product of whatever working consensus is negotiated within the class. This process, by drawing on the partially interdependent nature of teacher and child 'coping', has a social origin and adds another layer of explanation to those studies which have attempted to trace the differentiating influence of labelling and the self-fulfilling prophecy within the classroom. Furthermore, in the classrooms used for illustration, there seemed to be evidence for the suggestion that the mesh of particular coping strategies will be reflected in particular forms of social differentiation within a class and thus provide a type of 'multiplication' and reinforcement of social consequence.

The limited nature of the sample and the interpretive nature of the analysis cause me to be very cautious about claiming to have 'proved' a relationship. However, the analysis does articulate with the commonsense knowledge of practising teachers who 'know' that 'so-and-so's class *is* always like that' and I therefore take the main point of the paper to be in providing one way of analysing such a relationship in more abstract and generalisable terms – to apply, in other words, the 'designatory capacity' which David Hargreaves (1978) claims to be a feature of symbolic interactionism. In addition I hope the analysis has shown that if so-and-so's class is always like that, then the social consequences could be significant and I suspect that such consequences could be documented in class, race and gender terms in the course of further and more detailed research.

It is an established principle of interactionist theory that meanings and identities are constructed and negotiated through social interaction. Similarities in the social contexts of classrooms and in the interests of the participants yield particular patterns of such interaction within schools which ethnographic analysis seeks to describe. This paper represents a contribution to that task.

Notes

1 This contrast does not presage an evaluative argument in this paper, rather it is drawn on simply in attempt to illustrate that that suggested analysis of social amplification processes can be demonstrated in a range of conditions.
2 The 'advisory' classification included managerial and disciplinary contacts.
3 A paper of this sort imposes severe constraints of space and I regret that I have had to edit the data severely.

References

BALL, S. (1980). Initial encounters in the classroom and the process of establishment, in: Woods, P. (Ed.) *Pupil Strategies* (London, Croom Helm).

BECKER, H.S. (1952). Social-class variations in the teacher–pupil relationship, *Journal of Educational Sociology*, 25, pp. 451–465.

BIRD, C. (1980). Deviant labelling in the school and the pupils' reaction, in: Woods, P. (Ed.) *Pupil Strategies* (London, Croom Helm).

CLARRICOATES, K. (1978). Dinosaurs in the classroom. A re-examination of some aspects of the 'hidden' curriculum in primary schools, *Women's Studies International Quarterly*, 1, pp. 353–364.

DENSCOMBE, M. (1980). Pupil strategies and the open classroom in: Woods, P. (Ed.) *Pupil Strategies* (London, Croom Helm).

DENZIN, N.K. (1970). *The Research Act in Sociology* (London, Croom Helm).

HAMMERSLEY, M. (1980). Classroom ethnography, *Educational Analysis*. Vol. 2, No. 2.

HARGREAVES, A. (1978). The significance of classroom coping strategies, in: Barton, L. and Meighan, R. (Eds.) *Sociological Interpretations of Schooling and Classrooms* (Driffield, Nafferton).

HARGREAVES, D. (1975). *Interpersonal Relationships and Education* (London, Routledge and Kegan Paul).

HARGREAVES, D. (1978). Whatever happened to symbolic interactionism?, in: Barton, L. and Meighan, R (Eds.) *Sociological Interpretations of Schooling and Classrooms* (Driffield, Nafferton).

KOUNIN, J.S. (1970). *Discipline and Group Management in Classrooms* (New York, Holt, Rinehart and Winston).

LEMERT, E. (1967). The concept of secondary deviation, in Lemert, E. *Human Deviance, Social Problems and Social Control* (New York).

MATZA, D. (1964). *Delinquency and Drift* (New York, Wiley).

POLLARD, A. (1979). Negotiating deviance and 'getting done' in primary school classrooms, in: Barton, L and Meighan, R. (Eds.) *Schools, Pupils and Deviance* (Driffield, Nafferton).

POLLARD, A. (1980). Teacher interests and changing situations of survival threat in primary school class rooms, in: Woods, P. (Ed.) *Teacher Strategies* (London, Croom Helm).

POLLARD, A. (1981). *Coping with deviance: school processes and their implications for social reproduction*, Unpublished PhD thesis, University of Sheffield.

POLLARD, A. (1982). A model of coping strategies, *British Journal of Sociology of Education*, 3, pp. 19–37.

POLLARD, A. (1984). Goodies, Jokers and Gangs, in: Hammersley, M. and Woods, P. *Life in Schools: the sociology of pupil cultures* (Milton Keynes, Open University Press).

RIST, R.C. (1970). Student social class and teacher expectations: the self-fulfilling prophecy in ghetto education, *Harvard Education Review*, 40, pp. 411–451.

ROSENTHAL, R. and JACOBSON, L. (1968). *Pygmalion in the Classroom* (London, Holt, Rinehart and Winston).

SHARP, R. and GREEN, A.G. (1976). *Education and Social Control* (London, Routledge and Kegan Paul).

WOODS, P. (1977). Teaching for survival, in: Woods, P. and Hammersley, M. (Eds.) *School Experience* (London, Croom Helm).

Measurement in Ethnography: the Case of Pollard on Teaching Style

M. Hammersley

Measurement is not a term generally used by ethnographers. Indeed, many might argue that measurement is central to the experimental and survey research traditions, but not relevant to ethnography. Whether this is so, of course, depends upon what is intended by the term *measurement*.

If what is meant is the development of explicit measurement schemes which produce quantitative indices, such as intelligence tests, attitude inventories or systematic observation schedules, then it is true that ethnographers are not generally concerned with measurement (though there are exceptions, among both anthropologists and sociologists). Such schemes involve the establishment of a set of categories which are exhaustive and mutually exclusive, and ideally these should represent points on an ordinal or interval scale. In addition, the rules for assigning data to the categories should be explicitly stated, should specify concrete indicators, should be unambiguous, and should be applied in the same way to all of the data. For the purposes of this paper, I shall call this conception of measurement the 'standard model'[1]

However, while ethnographers rarely adopt this model, the fundamental issue with which measurement is concerned is the linking of abstract concepts to particular data; and this problem faces ethnographers as much as it does any other social researcher. Given that they are concerned with describing and explaining events in the settings they study, ethnographers are inevitably concerned with the relationship between their accounts and the data they have collected, and between these data and the events described.

Indeed, the issue of the proper relation between concepts and data is an area where ethnographers have often been critical of survey and experimental research. They have argued that the indicators used in such research often have only a highly problematic connection with the concepts presented and that, as a result, the validity of the findings is doubtful. For example, Douglas (1967) has criticized quantitative research on suicide, from Durkheim onwards, on the grounds that the indicators used to measure such concepts as 'social integration' are weak, if not entirely spurious. Similarly, Mehan (1973) has challenged the findings of achievement tests by demonstrating the different ways in which children may interpret test questions.

However, when we turn to ethnographic research itself, there is some vagueness about how concepts and data are linked. Sometimes the model adopted seems to be virtually identical to that of survey and experimental research (see for example McCall and Simmons 1969). On other occasions, an alternative approach seems to be recommended (Blumer 1969, Cicourel 1964). However, the precise nature of such alternatives is elusive (Hammersley 1986). And in my opinion no convincing alternative model has yet been provided. I believe that much the same problems face researchers in relating concepts to data whatever research strategy they adopt. In this paper I want to examine these problems as they arise in ethnographic work.

As an illustration, I shall draw on a recent article on teaching styles and social differentiation by Andrew Pollard (Pollard 1984). I have selected Pollard's article for discussion because, in many respects, it is an exemplary piece of ethnographic research; and it explicitly presents a theory and uses a wide range of data to examine that theory. The author recognizes 'the limited nature of the sample and the interpretative nature of the analysis' (p. 47), and thus by implication the need for further research. What I want to do in this article is to outline the ways in which Pollard's study, and ethnographic work in general, needs to be developed if we are to be reasonably confident that the links between concepts and data are sound.

The theory which Pollard presents is a complex one. While, like many interactionists, he presents his explanation in softened terms – using words like 'influence', 'implication', 'reinforcement' rather than 'causality' or 'determination' – effectively his argument is that the character of the working consensus which a teacher negotiates with his/her class, itself determined by the coping strategies of teacher and pupils, determines the level and nature of social differentiation among the pupils. He compares the 'good formal regime' of Mrs Rothwell's class with the 'progressive' working consensus of Mr Harman's class. He investigates the level of social differentiation among pupils in the two classes, using reading levels, seating position, and patterns of sociometric choice as indicators. And he concludes that the formal regime seems to produce a stronger correlation between academic and social differentiation than does the informal regime.

For the purposes of this discussion, I shall focus upon just one of the variables Pollard discusses: the progressive–traditional dimension along which teaching style varies.[2] He presents descriptions of the perspectives and practices of Mrs Rothwell and Mr Harman, and, in trying to show that these two teachers represent contrasting positions on the dimension, he uses several types of evidence:

(a) *Information about the teachers and classes presumably derived from documents, interviews or observation, but without the source being indicated*: For example:

> Mrs Rothwell felt a sincere caring duty towards the children in her class whom she believed came from generally poor and unstable home backgrounds (p. 36).

> . . . Mr Harman's control techniques were based on principles which forsook all physical sanctions and extrinsic inducements (p. 43).

(b) *Time-generalized observer description*: Here we are provided with a summary of the behaviour of teacher and pupils over time, of their typical behaviour in respects relating to the working consensus. For instance:

> Mrs Rothwell used classwork for almost everything – during craft activities everyone made a flower in the way they were shown, in writing practice everyone copied the patterns from the board, in number lessons everyone chanted their 2-times, 3-times, 5-times and 10-times tables, in poetry times children spoke verses chorally, in creative English everyone wrote on the subject suggested using the words written on the blackboard. These examples occurred consistently and regularly (p. 37).

> In Mr Harman's classroom the tables were arranged for children to work in small groups of five or six. Each child had an official seat at one of the six separate tables and this official seat was for registration and for the first and most 'work'-intensive lesson period of the day (p. 44).

(c) *Frequency-specified, time generalized observer description*: As with (b), but this time the frequencies of the behaviours are provided. Thus Pollard provides a table indicating the percentage of teacher–pupil contacts initiated by each party and the percentages of each type of contact. (See Table 1).

(d) *Time-specific observer description*: Here the researcher provides a description of behaviour on one particular occasion which is taken to be typical, or significant in some other way. For example, Pollard cites the following in support of his claim that 'collaboration was far from unusual and was an active process':

> *Mrs Rothwell*: Today we are going to try to do two sorts of sums at once, we'll try to do the take-away ones and the add-up ones, but I'm going to try and

TABLE 1   Teacher-child contacts %

	Child initiated		Teacher initiated		
	Work related	*Other*	*Work related*	*Other*	*Advisory*
Mrs Rothwell's class	12	15	27	11	35
total		27		73	
Mr Harman's class	20	32	18	17	13
total		52		48	

(Pollard 1984, p. 36)

trick you by mixing them up . . . (writes sums on board) . . . this is my day for tricking people.

(The children work. A little later . . .)

Janet: She hasn't caught me out yet.
Sandra: She hasn't caught me out yet.
Nigel: She hasn't caught me out yet – has she . . .?
Janet: She has – you're caught – she's caught him out!
Nigel: Why?
Janet: He's got two 'ten take-aways' . . .
Nigel: I think she has caught me out.
Duncan: Nigel, I think you'd better copy off me, or you'll make a messy job. Ten take away nought makes ten.
Sandra: Ten take away nought makes ten?
Janet: You've done the second one wrong, you've done the second one wrong.
Nigel: I haven't.
Janet: You have – oh, there shouldn't be a four there should there?
Duncan: There should.
Janet: Should there? (Janet alters the answer.)
Nigel: Yes, oh yes, that's right.
Sandra: You've done it wrong, there shouldn't be a four there. (Children change answers.)
Duncan: Mine's right.
Nigel: So's mine.
Janet: Mine is.
Janet: Everybody knows ten add ten makes twenty.
Nigel: Ten add ten makes twenty.
Nigel: What's ten add nothing?
Duncan: Nothing.
Sandra: Ten add nothing is nothing – it's nothing.
Nigel: Janet's done it wrong, she's done ten.
Sandra: Mine are right.

Duncan: They are tricky – oh Sandra, you've done that one wrong, no, look.
   (Shows and Sandra alters.)
Duncan: That's it.

(pp. 40–41)

(e) *Quotations from participants' accounts:* These can be used in two ways:

(i) To document perspectives: For instance:

Mrs Rothwell had a clear image of her ideal pupil (Becker, 1952) but felt a type
of resigned concern towards many of those who could not match up to this
image. As she put it.

It really is rewarding when you get a child who is bright, one who you can
really talk to and rely on, but we don't get many of those . . . most of them
here really do need a lot of help. We do what we can for them but some of
them are very hard to help even when you want to do your best for them.
(p. 37)

(ii) As a source of description of events: For example:

In their reception class the children had been used to a daily routine of 'work' in
the morning, 'activities' in the afternoon. Mr Harman initially aimed to integrate the two.

I tried to establish not 'work' and 'play' time but just 'inclass' time – but I
totally failed. This distinction between work time and choosing time was
forced on me, early on, when I realised they *expected* to do work in the
morning. They couldn't cope with the idea of someone 'playing' (in their
terms) whilst they were 'working' I had groups in sand, water, painting,
Maths, writing etc . . . they kept asking 'what are those children doing?'
They got confused and didn't know what they were meant to do. I found
myself policing all the time, checking on what they had and hadn't done.
So I've established this system of 'work periods', which they found acceptable and I found productive, and also 'choosing periods' in which I am able
to have groups, and gradually I'm getting this idea that some kids can be
working when others are choosing.

(pp. 45–6)

This range of data used by Pollard is probably a representative sample of the
kinds of information ethnographers usually employ. I want now to look at
some of the problems involved in the use of these different types of evidence.

1 Accuracy of Description

There are two, not clearly distinguishable, aspects of accuracy. At the most
basic level, we need to be sure that the teacher or pupils did actually do, say
or write what Pollard describes. In the case of quotes from audio-recordings

this is a matter of whether the transcription is accurate and whether the verbalization was authored by the person to whom it is attributed. This is a fairly straightforward matter, though if the recordings are of poor quality there can be serious difficulties. Where quotations are recorded by means of field notes, the dangers of inaccuracy are rather greater but still probably minor.

The case of non-verbal elements of action is more difficult. To the extent that these are recorded in detail, what is required is accurate portrayal of patterns of physical movement. Unless still photography, or video or film recording, is used, the problems of mapping physical movement are combined with those intrinsic to the writing of field notes, in particular the immediacy and rapid process of the situation being observed, and the limitations of memory.

However, we are not interested in this etic level of physical sounds and movement for its own sake, but rather to document emic patterns of perspective and action. And here there arises the problem of interpretation given such emphasis by ethnomethodologists (Garfinkel 1967; Heritage 1985). While I do not accept the arguments of ethnomethodologists in toto (Hammersley, 1986), there is no doubt that the attribution of intentions and attitudes on the basis of what people say or do can involve serious problems, and that it is not always handled effectively by ethnographers. For instance let us look again at one of Pollard's descriptions:

> Mrs Rothwell felt a sincere caring duty towards the children in her class whom she believed came from generally poor and unstable home backgrounds (p. 36).

How do we know that the attribution to Mrs Rothwell of a 'sincere caring duty' and of a belief that the children in her class came from 'generally poor and unstable home backgrounds' represents an accurate interpretation? Pollard does not tell us the grounds for these imputations, and as a result we have no basis for judging their accuracy. Moreover, we can imagine that there might be room for considerable disagreement amongst observers over this interpretation.

In other cases Pollard provides at least some evidence. As an instance of time-specific observer description we cited Pollard's use of an account of a conversation among pupils to support his claim that pupils collaborated among themselves over answers (p. 39). Here we are able to assess the relation between the concept of collaboration and the pattern of activity that the pupils are engaging in, as described by Pollard: comparing one another's answers, trying to understand the discrepancies, altering their answers etc. There seems to be little serious doubt that what we have is an instance of collaboration. Pollard does not provide a clear definition of the concept, but those activities would seem likely to fall under most definitions of the term.

The problem of accuracy is perhaps at its most severe when we have to rely upon participants' accounts as a source of descriptions of events. Here the threats to accuracy operate at one remove from the ethnographer as well as in her or his interpretation of the data, and for this reason it may be particularly difficult to get much purchase upon them. The use of multiple accounts, in other words triangulation, is one strategy; but it is no panacea. (Hammersley and Atkinson 1983).

2 The Generalizability of the Descriptions

Pollard, like other ethnographers, makes claims about the stable perspectives and typical behaviour of the people he studied, within some (unspecified) time limits. Clearly, whatever the data used, we need to ask whether they reflect accurately what these people do across different occasions[3]. With accounts, time-specific descriptions and non-frequency time-generalized descriptions, we have to rely upon the researcher's judgment, on the basis of whatever evidence was available, that the opinion or behaviour was typical. This is unsatisfactory because it seems likely that informal estimates of frequency are open to such large errors that all but the most extreme variations are of questionable accuracy. Reliance upon such estimates is perhaps the most serious defect of ethnographic measurement.

However, for one item Pollard does provide a frequency description. This is fairly unusual for an ethnographer, though by no means unique. Pollard's table (see p. 52 above) illustrates both the value and some of the problems involved in providing frequency descriptions. The value is that we can see *how* typical the behaviour is of each teacher's teaching, and the scale of difference between the teachers in this respect. The problems are manifold, and to varying degrees are to be found in 'systematic observation' studies too (Scarth and Hammersley 1986a). In the case of Pollard's table, we need to know:

(a) The period over which the observation of teacher–pupil contacts was carried out; whether it was continuous; and its size relative to the time-span over which generalization is being made?

(b) How rigorously were teacher–child contacts identified? Pollard provides no information about this. Yet variations in identification procedure over the course of observation are a source of error and we need to know how large this error is. This covers both the question of how clear and concrete the identification criteria were and how effectively, practically speaking, these criteria were applied. For example, was the measurement done by live coding or on the basis of video recording?

(c) How rigorously were the child/teacher initiative and work-related/ other/advisory distinctions made? Again, we need to know how closely specified the categories were and how effective the counting of instances was, given practical constraints.

There are serious difficulties involved in devising well-specified category schemes and in applying them rigorously and considerable error can be created by variations in definition, coding procedure and practice (Scarth and Hammersley 1986b). Without information about these matters, even the generalizability of Pollard's frequency description is difficult to judge.

3 Content Validity

By content validity[4] I mean the extent to which the evidence which Pollard uses to document the teachers' perspectives represents all the components of his definition of traditionalism/progressivism (for example didactic versus discovery pedagogy, use of intrinsic versus extrinsic motivation etc.). In order to assess this we need a clear definition of traditionalism/progressivism. Unfortunately, Pollard does not provide one. This failure to provide adequate definitions of key concepts is by no means unusual in ethnographic work.

Of course, in the absence of such a definitions, we could try to explicate the concepts ourselves, or draw on other accounts such as Barth (1971), Berlak and Berlak (1981), Bennett (1976), Hammersley (1977). However, what we are interested in is not what people typically refer to as progressive or traditional teaching, but those aspects of teaching that have the effects (variation in social differentiation) in which Pollard is interested. Alternatively, we could try to retrieve the components of traditionalism/progressivism, as defined by Pollard, from the data he gives. But that undercuts the very possibility of assessing content validity.[5]

Given this lack of clarity about the concepts employed, characteristic of much ethnography, it is impossible to assess the content validity of the indicators Pollard uses for traditionalism/progressivism.

4 Construct Validity

An equally important aspect of measurement is what is often termed 'construct validity': the extent to which an indicator accurately measures the concept or component of a concept it is supposed to measure. In other words, how far do variations in the indicator – for instance frequency of recitation of tables – actually reflect variations in the variable being measured – didactic pedagogy. Once again, we are faced with the problem that there is no clear definition of 'working consensus', nor of the traditional and progressive versions of it. But putting this on one side, there are several reasons why the construct validity of such measures as frequency of the recitation of tables may not be high. For example, a teacher might regard knowledge of tables as an important prerequisite for discovery learning in Mathematics, and this recitation of tables may not be accompanied by other features of didactic pedagogy. Alternatively, there may be other factors which generate recitation of tables besides commitment to traditionalism, for example the imminence of school-wide maths tests, a forthcoming visit by HMI or even the presence of the observer. We are not told how long Pollard spent observing these classrooms, but clearly the longer the time period the less serious the danger from some of these threats to validity.

Another threat to construct validity is idiosyncratic and/or ad hoc use of indicators for traditionalism and progressivism. In order to assess the construct validity of indicators for each component of traditionalism/ progressivism, besides trying to ensure a representative sample of teaching over time, we might use the stability of interpretations of the data across observers: given the identification criteria developed to recognize the indicators, would another observer, or even Pollard himself on another occasion, have interpreted the events in the same way? The aim here is to assess the effects of random variations, as well as systematic error resulting, for example, from bias on the part of the observer. As another check on systematic error we might try to assess the degree to which the various indicators of traditionalism and progressivism which Pollard uses correlate with one another, and do not correlate with aspects of teacher behaviour which the theory would lead us to expect them *not* to correlate with (Evans 1983).

Conclusion

Starting from the assumption that ethnographers have failed to develop any viable alternative to the 'standard measurement model', in this paper I have explored some of the implications of the application of that model to ethnographic work. In doing this I took a recent article by Pollard as an example. I chose this article because he explicitly presents a theory and uses a wide variety of data, including quantitative indices, to support his claims. I have identified four problems of measurement, two (accuracy and generalizability) concern the relationship between descriptions and the events described, and the other two (content and construct validity) involve the relationship between descriptions and theoretical variables or concepts.

In evaluating any study, it is useful to keep three things distinct:

1 Whether the descriptions and explanations provided are correct.

2 Whether the researcher has taken the best precautions and made the best checks so as to maximize the chances of the validity of descriptive and explanatory claims, given available methodology.

3 Whether the researcher provides the reader with the necessary information about the precautions taken and the checks made for an assessment to be made of their effectiveness.

As regards the correctness of the descriptions and explanations, neither the researcher nor, even less, the reader can know this with certainty, one way or the other. Thus, the reader is forced back on assessing whether proper precautions were taken and checks carried out.

The problems I have highlighted are severe and Pollard, like most other ethnographers, gives little indication that he has attended to them. He certainly does not provide the reader with the information necessary to decide whether his treatment of them was effective. Of course, I am not pretending that such problems can be solved easily, or indeed that they can ever be solved perfectly. What I *am* arguing is that they are important, and that they can be dealt with much more effectively than they are at present. My aim in this paper has been to clarify these problems so that ethnographers might address them directly and systematically.

Notes

1 This is represented in sociology by, for example, Blalock (1970).

2 Pollard uses the term 'working consensus' rather than teaching style to indicate that what he is interested in is not just a characteristic of the teacher but a product of the interaction of teacher and pupil strategies. For the purposes of my argument here, these terms can be treated as synonyms.

3 Strictly speaking we need to ensure that both the teachers have been given an equal opportunity to display 'progressive' and 'traditional' behaviours of the various kinds. While in non-experimental research we have to rely upon the natural occurrence of such opportunities, it may be that we could identify such opportunities and sample them. However, at the moment this seems a remote possibility.

4 This is a rather free interpretation of the concept of content validity, but I hope it might prove useful.

5 There are, in any event, areas where we have information on one teacher but not on the other. See the Appendix.

Appendix

Characteristics of the two teachers

Background	*Mrs R.*	*Mr H.*
Sex	F	M
Qualifications	T. Cert.	Soc. Sc. Degree and T. Cert.
Age	Late 30s	25
Experience	12 years	2.5 years
Marital status	M	Unknown
Children	2	Unknown
Residence	Pleasant village outside town	Unknown
Religion	Practising Christian	Unknown
Attitude to school	Unknown	Isolation and disagreement
Origin of perspective	Unknown	Reference groups outside school

Perspective and practice regarding pedagogy

	Mrs R.	*Mr H.*
Aim	Provision of moral standards and efficient transmission of knowledge and skills	Facilitating learning how to think and how to learn
Transmission and practice vs Asking questions and verbal discussion	Transmission	Asking the right questions
Extrinsic vs Intrinsic motivation	Extrinsic	Intrinsic
Physical sanctions	Unknown	No
Careful planning and presentation	Yes	Unknown
More vs Less structured timetable	More	Less
More vs Less differentiated curriculum	Less	More

| More vs Less fixed seating | More | Less |
| More vs Less grouping by ability | More | Less |

Perspective on pupils

	Mrs R.	*Mr H.*
Model	Family	Personal validity of children's perspectives
Criteria	Ability and behaviour	Oral rapport
Cultural deprivation	Yes	No

References

BARTH, R. (1972). *Open Education and the American School*. New York, Agathon Press.

BENNETT, N. (1976). *Teaching Styles and Pupil Progress*. London, Open Books.

BERLAK, A. and BERLAK, H. (1981). *Dilemmas of Schooling*. London, Methuen.

BLALOCK, H.M. (1971). 'The measurement problem', in Blalock H.M. and A. (eds.), *Methodology in Social Research*. New York, McGraw Hill.

BLUMER, H. (1969). *Symbolic Interactionism*. Englewood Cliffs, N.J. Prentice Hall.

CICOUREL, A.V. (1964). *Method and Measurement in Sociology*. New York, The Free Press.

DOUGLAS, J.D. (1967). *The Social Meanings of Suicide*, Princeton, Princeton University Press.

EVANS, J. (1983). 'Criteria of validity in social research', in Hammersley M., (ed.) *The Ethnography of Schooling*, Driffield York, Nafferton.

GARFINKEL, H. (1967). *Studies in Ethnomethodology* Englewood Cliffs, N.J. Prentice Hall.

HAMMERSLEY, M. (1977). 'Teacher perspectives' units 9–10 of Open University course E202, *Schooling and Society*, Milton Keynes, Open University Press.

HAMMERSLEY, M. (1986). 'What's wrong with social theory? Blumer's dilemma reassessed', Unpublished.

HAMMERSLEY, M. and ATKINSON, P. (1983). *Ethnography: Principles in Practice*. London, Tavistock.

HERITAGE, J. (1985). *Garfinkel and Ethnomethodology*. Cambridge, Polity.

MCCALL, G. and SIMMONS, J.L. (1969). *Issues in Participant Observation*. Reading, Mass., Addison Wesley.

MEHAN, H. (1973). 'Assessing children's school peformance' in H.P. Dreitzel (ed.), *Childhood and Socialization*, (Recent Sociology No.5) Collier-Macmillan.

POLLARD, A. (1984). 'Coping strategies and the multiplication of differentiation in infant classrooms', *British Educational Research Journal*, 10, 1.

SCARTH, J. and HAMMERSLEY, M. (1986a). 'Questioning ORACLE', *Educational Research*, 28, 3.

SCARTH, J. and HAMMERSLEY, M. (1986b). 'Some problems in assessing the closeness of classroom tasks', in this volume.

PART TWO
Classroom Tasks

Cognitive Objectives Revealed by Classroom Questions asked by Social Studies Student Teachers

O.L. Davis and D.C. Tinsley

Questions posed in the social studies classroom for over half a century have been recognised as emphasizing memory as the most important cognitive operation (e.g., Adams, 1964; Barr, 1929; Stevens, 1912). Yet, during this period, the attention of the social studies has been focused repeatedly on admonitions to foster pupils' critical thinking and, especially in recent years, discovery procedures. Common also has been the belief that classroom questions of 'fact' and 'thought' productively might be distinguished. Consequently more appropriate social studies objectives have been thought possible by teachers stressing 'thought' questions.

In the past decade considerable progress has been made in the analysis of cognitive operations (Bloom, 1956; Guilford, 1956) and 'memory' and 'knowledge' have come to be seen more adequately as essential and pre-requisite to thinking. Cognitive processes, misunderstood as 'thought' in general, have been identified in hierarchical complexity. Use of these systems as criteria has proved powerful in understanding a variety of educational matters. With respect to instructional objectives, the *Taxonomy of Educational Objectives: Cognitive Domain* (Bloom, 1956) has been particularly influential. For example, objectives revealed in social studies textbook questions have been analyzed (Davis and Hunkins, 1966) as have classroom examinations (Pfeiffer and Davis, 1965), and Jarolimek (1962) has demonstrated the *Taxonomy's* value in planning differentiated instruction.

The *Taxonomy*, however, has not been applied to an analysis of questions in classroom interaction. Previous studies of teaching have considered questions in their analyses (e.g. Bellack and Davitz, 1963). Some of these studies have highlighted thinking processes fostered in the classrooms (e.g., Aschner and Gallagher, 1963; Smith and Meux, 1962; Taba, Levine, and Elzey, 1964), but only recently have rather productive analytic schemes been modified to incorporate attention to cognitive dimensions of teachers' questions (Amidon, 1966; Medley, 1966). Classroom questioning has provided the substance for focused inquiries into teaching (e.g., Dodl, 1966; Sloan and Pate, 1966), but the questions of both teachers and pupils have not been studied against the criteria of the *Taxonomy*.

This study, then, was designed to determine the range of cognitive objectives manifest in secondary school social studies classrooms by questions asked by student teachers and their pupils.

Method

Participating in the study were 44 individuals enrolled in secondary student teaching of the social studies at The University of Texas during the fall semester, 1966. Of these, 32 taught at the senior high school level and 12 taught in junior high schools.

A *Teacher–Pupil Question Inventory (TPQI)* was developed by the investigators and was the source of data analyzed in this study. The *TPQI* schedule requires a classroom observation of 30 minutes divided into alternating five-minute periods. At each instance of a question asked by either the teacher or a pupil, the observer decides which category in which the question may be classified and marks a tally in a provided space. Questions are judged by attention to their form and inferred intent as well as the nature of the response elicited and its reception by the pupil or teacher. The *TPQI* has nine categories, seven of which are based on the Bloom *Taxonomy* and the formulations of Sanders (1966). The remaining two classifications include non-cognitive questions. The nine categories are as follows:

1 *Memory*: The one questioned recalls or recognizes information (facts, generalizations, etc.);
2 *Interpretation*: The one questioned states relationships between various types of data;
3 *Translation*: The one questioned changes information into a different form (linguistic, symbolic, image, etc.);
4 *Application*: The one questioned solves a realistic problem requiring the identification of the crucial issue or points and the selection and use of appropriate knowledge and skills;
5 *Synthesis*: The one questioned suggests answers to a problem that is original, speculative, or creative;
6 *Evaluation*: The one questioned makes a judgment according to explicit criteria (external or internal);

7 *Affectivity*: The one questioned responds with a statement of feeling, emotion, or opinion without a standard of appraisal;

8 *Procedure*: The question relates to classroom organization, student behavior, or instructional management.

Each (teacher) was observed at least twice by his regular university supervisor. Prior to the observations and following a design similar to one used by Flanders (1963), the supervisors underwent a period of training in the use of the *TPQI* and procedures to be followed in the study. By the end of training, the observers reached almost unanimous agreement on classification of questions in the training (audio-taped) materials. Midway during the observation period, observers met again for another training session. Consequently the reliability of observers may be considered adequate.

Results

TPQI item frequencies were determined for the entire group; means of individual teacher's item totals were computed and medians of these means were determined (see Table 1).

Inspection of these data reveals that both teachers and pupils asked more 'memory' questions than all other questions combined. The next largest number of questions fell in the 'interpretation' and 'translation' categories. 'Procedural' questions for both teachers and pupils and 'evaluation' questions for teachers followed as less frequently asked. (The medians of zero (0), as well as the low item frequencies, indicated that questions asking for expressions of 'affectivity' and the higher cognitive processes were seldom

TABLE 1 Total questions and medians and ranges of mean number of questions asked by social studies student teachers and their classes (N = 44)

Question category	Teachers			Pupils		
	Total	*Median*	*Range*	*Total*	*Median*	*Range*
Memory	1313	11.25	0.67–36.33	714	0.25	0–5.00
Translation	187	1.00	0–8.00	123	0	0–4.00
Interpretation	391	3.70	0–10.00	401	0.33	0–4.33
Application	40	0	0–5.00	0	0	0
Analysis	66	0	0–6.00	3	0	0–0.50
Synthesis	10	0	0–4.00	5	0	0–2.00
Evaluation	136	0.70	0–11.00	15	0	0–1.50
Affectivity	78	0	0–8.00	4	0	0–0.50
Procedural	299	2.50	0–11.00	118	0	0–6.00

noted overall and, when observed, were evidenced by only a few of the teachers and their pupils. The types of questions asked by teachers and pupils were highly correlated (r = .90).

Questions of junior high and senior high student teachers were further analyzed by categorizing, for each item, individuals whose item mean fell above and below the group median for that item. On only three items were there obtained significant differences: 'translation' (*chi-square* = 5.47, p < .05); 'evaluation' (*chi-square* = 18.05, p < .001); and 'procedure' (*chi-square* = 4.05, p < .05). These results indicate that a larger proportion of junior high student teachers asked more questions in these categories than did senior high student teachers.

The number and percent of the student teachers and their classes who asked no questions in the question categories are presented in Table 2.

Not one of the student teachers failed to ask a 'memory' question; all but one asked an 'interpretation' question; and less than one-sixth did not ask a 'procedure' question. Over one-half of the student teachers in both groups asked *no* questions categorized as 'application,' 'analysis,' and 'synthesis,' and, for the senior high group alone, 'affectivity.' Pupils in most classes observed failed to ask other than 'memory,' 'procedure,' and 'translation' questions. Pupils in *no* class asked an 'application' question and pupils in most classes did *not* ask questions of the teacher requiring 'translation,' 'analysis,' 'synthesis,' 'evaluation,' 'affectivity,' or even 'procedure.' The types of questions *not* asked by teachers and by pupils were closely related (junior high: R = .93; senior high: R = .76).

Discussion

Memory or the acquisition of knowledge was the major cognitive objective apparent in teachers' and pupils' verbal questions in these social studies classes. Indeed, when the 'translation' and 'interpretation' categories are combined into 'comprehension' (Bloom, 1956), no other cognitive objective seems to have been effectively operational in these 44 social studies classrooms. As a result, the intellectual atmosphere of these social studies classes can only be characterized as meager.

These findings are remarkably similar to those reported by Gallagher (1965). He noted that 'cognitive-memory' was the most dominant thought process for both teachers and pupils in social studies. Also, an overwhelming emphasis upon acquisition of knowledge and a neglect of other cognitive objectives has been reported in an analysis of ninth-grade social studies examinations (Pfeiffer and Davis, 1965).

The accumulating evidence indicates persuasively that the major objectives guiding secondary school social studies classes probably are those

TABLE 2   Number and per cent of social studies student teachers and their classes (N = 44) asking no questions in question categories

Question category	Teacher						Pupil					
	All		Senior High		Junior High		All		Senior High		Junior High	
	No.	%	No.	%	No.	%	No.	%	No.	%	No.	%
Memory	0	0	0	0	0	0	20	45	17	53	3	25
Translation	18	41	14	44	4	33	29	66	24	75	5	42
Interpretation	1	2	0	0	1	8	19	43	17	53	2	17
Application	34	77	24	75	10	83	44	100	32	100	12	100
Analysis	28	64	22	69	6	50	41	93	31	97	10	83
Synthesis	42	95	31	97	11	92	42	95	30	94	12	100
Evaluation	17	39	15	47	2	17	37	84	32	100	5	42
Affectivity	29	66	25	78	4	33	42	95	32	100	10	83
Procedure	7	16	5	16	2	17	28	64	25	78	3	25
	N = 44		N = 32		N = 12		N = 44		N = 32		N = 12	

Percentages rounded to the nearest per cent.

emphasizing 'memory' and 'comprehension.' Since Bloom (1956) described 'comprehension' as the lowest form of intellectual activity, the operational objectives cannot be considered any but having a low cognitive level. This conclusion is particularly depressing in light of the generally held objective for the social studies to foster critical thinking, certainly involving high-level cognitive operations. Too, that student teachers evidenced behaviors typical of the field is surely cause for concern. At least two major observations seem viable:

> 1 More deliberate attention to different cognitive objectives in social studies classrooms is necessary. To be sure, questions requiring memory will be essential, for knowledge is prerequisite to thinking. If other and higher level cognitive objectives *are* considered desirable, the types of questions employed in the classroom must be altered. Not only (but certainly) must social studies teachers change the use of their own language (questions), but also must the type of questions be changed in classroom tests and in instructional materials (Davis and Hunkins, 1966). These suggestions are patently practical for Hunkins (1966) demonstrated that by changing the cognitive emphasis of questions in instructional materials to higher levels, pupil achievement was increased.
>
> 2 Specific understandings and skills of classroom questioning and the purposes of questions need major attention in the pre-service and in-service education of teachers. Apparently, any consideration, if any, of these important learnings by teacher candidates, at least those in this study, was not realistic and specific enough for them to be incorporated as behaviors. If social studies objectives are to emphasize higher thinking processes in practice, such a condition cannot be tolerated. Use of micro-teaching techniques (Allen, 1966), a study program based on classroom-tested materials (e.g., Sanders, 1966), and feedback and discussion of information obtained with the *TPQI* are reasonable possibilities. As a beginning, certainly, courses in social studies methods and student teaching could incorporate a component dealing specifically with questions, their cognitive emphases, and candidates' ability to vary their use of questions in classroom discourse.

References

ADAMS, THOMAS H. *The Development of a Method for Analysis of Questions Asked By Teachers in Classroom Discourse*. Doctor's thesis, New Brunswick, New Jersey: Rutgers, The State University, 1964. 149 pp.

ALLEN, DWIGHT W. 'A New Design for Teacher Education: The Teacher Intern Program at Stanford University.' *The Journal of Teacher Education* 17: 296–300; Fall 1966.

AMIDON, EDMUND. 'Interaction Analysis: Recent Developments.' Unpublished paper read at American Educational Research Association. Chicago, Illinois: February, 1966. 10 pp. (mimeographed).

BARR, ARVIL S. *Characteristic Differences in the Teaching Performance of Good and Poor Teachers of the Social Studies.* Bloomington, Illinois: Public School Publishing Co., 1929. 127 pp.

BELLACK, ARNO A., and JOEL R. DAVITZ. *The Language of the Classroom: Meanings Communicated in High School Teaching, Part I.* USOE Cooperative Research Project, No. 1497. New York: Institute of Psychological Research, Teachers College, Columbia University, 1963. 200 pp.

BLOOM, BENJAMIN S. (editor). *Taxonomy of Educational Objectives: Handbook I: Cognitive Domain.* New York: David McKay, Inc., 1956. 207 pp.

DAVIS, O.L., JR., and FRANCIS P. HUNKINS. 'Textbook Questions: What Thinking Processes Do They Foster?' *Peabody Journal of Education* 43: 285–292; March, 1966.

DODL, NORMAN R. 'Questioning Behavior of Elementary Classroom Groups.' *The California Journal of Instructional Improvement* 9: 167–179; October, 1966.

FLANDERS, NED A. 'Intent, Action, and Feedback: A Preparation for Teaching.' *Journal of Teacher Education* 14: 251–260; September, 1963.

GALLAGHER, JAMES J. 'Expressive Thought by Gifted Children in the Classroom.' *Elementary English* 42: 559–568; May, 1965.

GALLAGHER, JAMES, and MARY JANE ASCHNER. 'A Preliminary Report: Analysis of Classroom Interaction.' *Merrill-Palmer Quarterly of Behavior and Development* 9: 183–194; July, 1963.

GUILFORD, J.P. 'The Structure of Intellect.' *Psychological Bulletin* 53: 267–293; July, 1956.

HUNKINS, FRANCIS P. *The Influence of Analysis and Evaluation Questions on Critical Thinking and Achievement in Sixth Grade Social Studies.* Doctor's thesis, Kent State University, 1966. 301 pp.

JAROLIMEK, JOHN. 'The Taxonomy: Guide to Differentiated Instruction.' *Social Education* 26: 445–447; December, 1962.

MEDLEY, DONALD M. 'OScAR: Still Developing.' Unpublished paper read at American Educational Research Association. Chicago, Illinois: February, 1966. 12 pp. (mimeographed).

PFEIFFER, ISOBEL and DAVIS, O.L., JR. 'Teacher-Made Examinations: What Kind of Thinking do They Demand?' *NASSP Bulletin* 49: 1–10; September, 1965.

SANDERS, NORRIS M. *Classroom Questions: What Kinds?* New York: Harper and Row, 1966. 176 pp.

SLOAN, FRED A., JR., and ROBERT T. PATE. 'Teacher-Pupil Interaction in Two Approaches to Mathematics.' *The Elementary School Journal* 67: 161–167; December, 1966.

SMITH, B.O., and M.O. MEUX. *A Study of the Logic of Teaching.* USOE Cooperative Research Project, No. 258. Urbana: University of Illinois, 1962. 231 pp.

STEVENS, ROMIETT. *The Question as a Measure of Efficiency in Instruction.* Teachers College Contribution to Education No. 48, New York: Teachers College, Columbia University, 1912. 95 pp.

TABA, HILDA, LEVINE, S. and ELZEY, F. *Thinking in Elementary School Children.* USOE Cooperative Research Project, No. 1574. San Francisco, California: San Francisco State College, 1964. 207 pp. (mimeographed).

Some Problems in Assessing the Closedness of Classroom Tasks

J. Scarth and M. Hammersley

There is a considerable body of research analysing the openness/closedness of classroom tasks.[1] Some deals with teachers' oral questions (Stevens 1912; Davis and Tinsley 1967; Barnes 1969; Gall 1970; Mehan 1979; Hargreaves 1984). Some focuses on written tasks (Barnes and Shemilt 1974; Carter 1980; Doyle and Carter 1984; Barnes and Barnes 1984). There is also a related body of work concerned with the analysis of examination questions (Shayer 1972; Fairbrother 1975). In general this literature reports that the bulk of teachers' questions, written work tasks and examination questions are closed, in that they require low-level cognitive operations, notably memory, rather than creative or critical thinking. If we believe that schools should encourage pupils to think for themselves, rather than merely to memorise and reproduce material given to them, this is clearly a disturbing conclusion. But how well-founded is it? While we do not intend to reject this finding or its implications (though see Dillon 1982a), nevertheless we shall raise some serious methodological questions about measuring the 'closedness' of tasks.

The methodological problems involved in this area of research have not been given much attention in the literature.[2] Indeed, frequently statements are made which seem radically to underestimate them. For example Hargreaves (1984:48) talks about having a 'trouble-free coding procedures once he had resolved the problem of 'half-open questions', while Good and Brophy (1984:360) remark that:

> Teacher questioning has been one of the more popular topics in classroom research partly because aspects of it are among the easiest teacher behaviours to observe and code reliably.

The problems we shall discuss can be listed under four headings:

1 The identification of tasks
2 Specification of 'closedness'
3 The reliability and validity of category systems
4 The weighting of tasks

The visibility of these problems, for the reader and perhaps also for the researcher, varies according to the research strategy employed. The problems are most obvious where researchers analyse audio- or audio-visual recordings of classroom activity, identifying each task and then coding it for closedness. This is the approach we shall assume in our exposition. However, the points we make are equally applicable to other research strategies, including those which employ live coding in the classroom.[3]

1 Identification of Tasks

Before we can begin to code tasks, they must be identified. This requires the specification of a set of rules by which to decide when a task has occurred, and to distinguish one task from another. Tasks are not clearly demarcated and labelled in the world, and different sets of rules for identifying them can be developed. There are a number of problems here, and they are particularly severe in the case of oral questions:

(a) Identifying where oral tasks start and finish is problematic because when a teacher asks a question the resulting exchange can take a wide variety of different courses. Figure 1 indicates the possibilities.

The cycle in Figure 1 is a generative mechanism which produces a very large number of possible outcomes, though there is usually great variation in their frequency. With such a complex pattern of routes, the decision as to where one question ends and another begins is not straightforward. For exchanges which have just three parts – teacher elicitation, pupil answer, teacher acceptance of the answer – there may be no problem. However, exchanges which go through more than one phase of the cycle offer alternative cut-off points whose appropriateness is difficult to decide. For instance, one might count every teacher elicitation and answer slot as a separate question, whether or not the slot is filled with a 'right answer', or indeed filled with any answer at all. Alternatively, a question could be defined as a sequence, however long, ending either in acceptance or provision of an answer by the teacher. These are just two of many possibilities.

(b) Another problem is actually *identifying* elicitations, answer slots, and acceptance of answers by the teacher. Though these might be

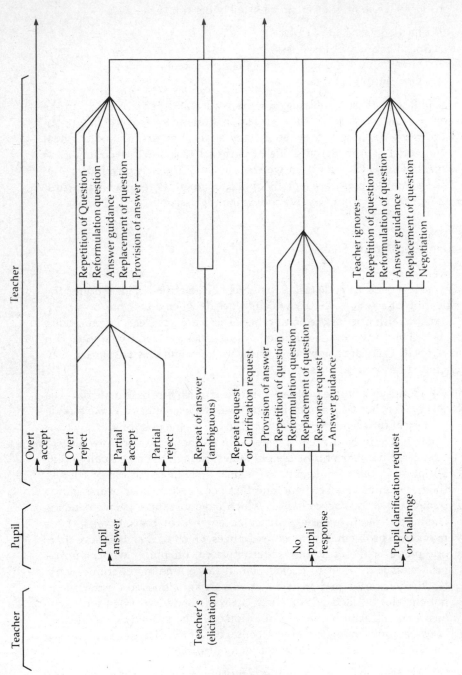

Figure 1   The Teacher Elicitation – Pupil Response Cycle

thought to be easily identifiable, this illusion is soon dispelled once one begins detailed analysis of lesson transcripts. This is because words and syntax are an imperfect guide to pragmatic function. Utterances which have the surface form of questions may not be designed to elicit a response, they may be rhetorical; and statements, or even silence, on the part of the teacher may be designed, or serve, to elicit answers. Similarly, identifying answer slots is complicated both by variations in the nomination system employed by teachers and by the fact that sometimes there is overlap between the talk of teachers and pupils. For instance, where a teacher accepts 'shouted out' answers, it may be particularly difficult to identify answer slots in any rigorous way. Again, acceptance of an answer by the teacher is not always clear. Responses to pupils' answers of the form 'Possibly', 'Oh that's interesting', 'I wasn't thinking of that', 'Okay but' pose problems.

(c) Another source of complexity in the identification of oral tasks is list questions: questions designed to elicit, or which actually elicit, more than one answer. Does one count these as one task or as multiple tasks? Furthermore, does one do this irrespective of whether the list question, and the answers it elicits, are bunched together or are spread over a long period of time, perhaps even over a whole lesson? And does one take any account of whether each answer is specifically elicited and/or accepted by the teacher?

(d) Sometimes one question is embedded within another, notably within a list question. Does one count embedded questions as distinct tasks or count them as part of the question in which they are embedded?

(e) Another source of uncertainty is repetition and clarification requests by both teacher and pupils. Teachers and pupils sometimes do not hear what is said and ask for it to be repeated. One may or may not count these as separate questions and answers. Similarly, teachers and pupils occasionally ask for clarification in response to a question or an answer: 'Do you mean. . .?' 'Do you really think that?' etc. Again, these and the answers they produce can be treated in different ways.

(f) Finally, does one include *all* teachers' questions and pupils' answers, or only those which deal with the lesson topic. In other words, does one exclude procedural and disciplinary exchanges, such as 'Have you got your textbooks with you' or 'Why did you leave the room?'. And if these are excluded how does one deal with ambiguous cases like 'What did we do last week?'

These problems may seem trivial, but the effect of variations in the ways in which they are resolved may not be. We can illustrate this by means of the following extract from a secondary school Humanities lesson in which pupils are looking at the front page of the *Guardian* newspaper. (The square and angle brackets illustrate alternative task definitions and will be explained below.)

T: Now look at the front page and that's – [let's see if somebody can read, like Darren, can you tell me what the main story is on the front page. The rest of you have a look as well, cos I shall be asking you. What do you think the main story is on the front page?

Pl: (No answer)]

T: [Come on Darren, don't be shy.

P2:   There's quite a few here.

P1:   They're all the main ones.]

T: [Yeah, there are a number of stories on the front page, but I will say to you there is only one, there is one main story.

P1:   The one with the picture.]

T: [You reckon that's the one do you?

P1:   The big picture there.]

T: Hang on, hang on, that's the one with the photograph. [Anybody disagree with that? Sean?

P3:   I think the one about Beirut.]

T: Right, I think the main story if you look at the size of the headlines if nothing else, and you'll see this a bit more clearly when we look at the *Daily Mirror*, is the story on the left-hand side of the front page, which is the story about . . .

P4:   (Interruption?) Beirut.

T: . . . the battle for West Beirut in the Middle East 〉. . On the right-hand side we've got another domestic story about closing coal mines and then you've got another story about the Yard, which is sort of home news and foreign news of – the Yard asked Interpol for help.〈 [What's Interpol?

Pn: (No answer)]

T: [What's Interpol?

Pn: (No answer)

T: Don't read it.

Pn: (No answer)]

T: [Interpol?

P5:   I dunno]

T: [Anybody?

Pn: (No answer)

T: No? International Police Organisation, Interpol. Okay, alright, never mind]〉 And then right at the bottom you've got a – you've got another domestic story. 〈[What else have you got on the front page, look very carefully, apart from those stories I've just talked about, look carefully.

P6:   Them little things.]

T: [Pardon?

P6:   Them little things.]

T: [Those little things.
P7:   Yeah.]
T: [Well let's try and be a bit more specific Mark . . .
P7:   The News in Brief.]
T: Okay you've got a very short number of small news items, but what else have these news items got, it's got News in Brief, [but look very carefully at what some of them have got.
P4:   It carries on inside the paper.]
T: Right, they refer you to larger stories inside the newspaper, so if you look at the bottom one about the market information you've got 'few more million' and then there's – it refers you to page seven and so on. [What else have you got on the front page?
P8:   Ed Moses.]
T: Well you've got a little bit – [Why is Ed Moses on the front page?
P8:   He broke the world record.]
T: Right, the world record and he's famous. [Why is he famous at the moment apart from the world record?
P5:   never been – well . . .]
T: [Well, put it this way, why do most people in this room know of Ed Moses or have heard of him?
P1:   On telly.]
T: Yeah, because there's been a lot of athletics recently on the box, the world championships and so on. And this man is in the fore and because he's broken the world record you've got a little photograph of him there. [What else have you got on the front page, look carefully.
P5:   Advertising.]
T: You've got one advertisement in the bottom – well tell a lie – you've got one large advertisement on the bottom right-hand corner and two very small ones at the top, [and what else?
P6:   Contents.]
T: Yes, you've got a contents page haven't you? You've got a list of information which is called 'Inside' which appears underneath that News in Brief.)

Different rules for identifying tasks produce different numbers of questions in this extract. There are many different definitions one could adopt. We have applied just two for the purposes of illustration. If one treats every elicitation and answer slot as a question then there are 20 questions (as marked by square brackets). On the other hand, if tasks are defined as elicitation sequences ending with acceptance or provision of an answer by the teacher, and list questions are treated as single questions and embedded questions are not counted separately, then there are just three questions (angle brackets). Clearly, the choice of identification rules may affect not only the number of tasks but also the balance between open and closed tasks. Using our own coding scheme (Hammersley and Scarth 1986), these two definitions of task produce scores of 40 per cent and 33 per cent respectively for the proportion of open tasks in this extract.[4] How representative of the variations produced by different task definitions this is remains to be seen. And, of course, whether differences of this magnitude are significant depends on the focus of the research. The difference in score does, however, indicate that there is a potential source of error here.

The problem of alternative task identifications also arises with written work. Take the following example of a written work task from a secondary school Geography lesson:

Grid References Exercise: Brecon Beacons Map

A *Give four-figure grid references for*:

1 The square which contains Brecon town centre.
2 A square which contains waterfalls.
3 The square which contains the village of Llanfrynach
4 A square which has marshland in it.
5 The square which has Hollybush Hall in it.

B *What can be found in the following squares?*:

1 0422   2 0829   3 9923   4 0122   5 0521

C *Name the rivers found in squares*:

1 0421   2 0322   3 0024   4 0527   5 0026

D *Name the road in squares*:

1 0730   2 0726   3 9624   4 9929   5 0331

E *What can be found at the following six-figure grid references?* (Name and draw the symbol)

1 073288   2 050236   3 020239   4 995235   5 983204
6 006227   7 066282   8 069258   9 964218   10 014297

F *Give six-figure grid references for the following*:

1 The church at Llanfrynach.
2 The spot height of 555 metres called Pen Milan.
3 The spot height of 561 metres called Bryn.
4 The hospital in Brecon.
5 The triangulation point 293 metres called St. David Without.
6 The village of Battle End.
7 The golf course west of Brecon.

8 The youth hostel at Llwyn-y-celyn.
9 The milestone north of Penwern on the A40(T).
10 The information centre near Mynydd Illtyd.

G Working in pairs:

1 Choose any 20 places on the map; write down the six-figure grid references for those places. See how many your partner can work out!
2 Draw 20 different symbols used on the map. With your partner, find out what they are, and write their names next to your drawing.

Does one count this as a single task, as seven tasks (i.e. A–G), or as 42 tasks (counting each separate numbered question as a task)? The decision is likely to have major consequences for the analysis. Assume for example that all these questions are coded as closed, as on most definitions of closedness they probably would be. The decision as to whether to count them as one or as 42 tasks would almost certainly have a major impact upon the total count of closed tasks.

2 Specification of 'Closedness'

In studies of classroom tasks the aspect of tasks being measured is not always clearly specified. There are two main alternatives here:

(a) The teacher's expectations about the answers pupils will produce.

(b) The cognitive strategies pupils use to tackle a question or written work task.

While sometimes these two things may be the same, they will not always be. Indeed, there is a literature specifically dealing with the match, or lack of match, between teachers' questions and the answers pupils provide (Mills *et al* 1980; Dillon 1982b). However, studies sometimes conflate these two phenomena. For instance, Davis and Tinsley (1967:22) report that in their study:

(Teachers') questions are judged by attention to their form and inferred intent, as well as the nature of the response elicited and its reception by the (. . .) teacher.

Other studies adopt the same catholic approach (Scarth and Hammersley, 1986), probably because of the limited information available about the nature of tasks (see section 3 below).

Moreover, if the focus is the teacher's intentions or expectations, there are a number of different ways in which the concept of closedness can be defined:

(a) Whether or not the teacher assumes that there is a single 'right answer' to the question.

(b) Whether the task is intended to demand 'lower' or 'higher' level cognitive activity: for example, whether it demands reproduction of given material on the one hand or inference or creativity on the other.

(c) Whether or not a clear indication is given to pupils as to what would, or would not, count as an effective performance on the task.

It is obviously important that the particular aspect of the classroom tasks being measured is defined clearly. This is essential if we are to provide a sound assessment of the frequency of different types of task.

3   The Reliability and Validity of Category Systems

In developing a category system for coding tasks, even having specified rules for identifying tasks and defined what is meant by closedness, there remains the question of what set of categories is to be employed. In particular, one must decide how many categories to use. One could distinguish simply between open and closed tasks, but often researchers use a combination of dimensions to produce multiple categories. For example the ORACLE researchers (Galton, Simon and Croll 1980) employed the following categories for coding questions:

Q1 Recalling facts
Q2 Offering ideas, solutions (only one answer acceptable)
Q3 Offering ideas, solutions (multiple answers acceptable)
Q4 Referring to task supervision
Q5 Referring to routine matters
             (Taken from Galton, Simon and Croll 1980, Table 1.2)]

Of course, another reason why researchers use more than two categories for coding tasks is to represent various degrees of closedness. However, it is rare for coding schemes of classroom tasks to be explicitly scaled; most involve only classification.

Even classification requires, ideally, that the categories used are clearly defined and mutually exclusive and exhaustive, so that each and every task is assignable, unambiguously, to one and only one category. This is essential for high reliability. An additional requirement, of course, is that the assignment of tasks to categories is done in a way which reflects accurately the character of each task in terms of the dimension of closedness, as defined in the research. This is of course the issue of construct validity.

Few coding schemes for classroom tasks approximate these ideals. Some specify little more than the names of the categories employed (for example Corey, 1940). However, even where detailed specifications are provided, there remains considerable scope for ambiguous cases, and the question of the construct validity of the indicators used is often not addressed (Scarth and Hammersley, 1986).

There are a number of reasons for the inadequacies of task coding schemes. One is the practical problem of obtaining information about the intentions or expectations of teachers and/or the cognitive operations used by pupils. These cannot be read off unproblematically from what teachers and pupils say in the classroom. For example, even if a teacher asks pupils to 'remember', one cannot be sure whether the question is asking pupils simply to remember information provided previously and to present it, or whether they are required to *use* the remembered information to draw some inference. And one cannot always resolve this problem by means of contextual information. For example, checking what information has been covered previously in a lesson, or in previous lessons, is of limited value since what is critical is the teacher's *memory* of what was covered and/or what pupils *actually* remember. Conversely, if a teacher says 'Can you think . . .', this is no guarantee that the question is not a memory question. 'Think' is sometimes used by teachers as a synonym for 'remember'.

These problems of interpretation are sometimes obscured in coding schemes by a confusion between the psychological operations which pupils must use to produce an answer and the 'logical' status of the information elicited by the question. This confusion occurs, for example, if one classifies as closed those questions which require the recall of facts, and code as open those requiring explanation of facts (see for instance Tisher 1970; Wright and Nuthall 1970) The trouble is that explanations may just as often be subject to recall as descriptions. Whether a particular item of information has the surface form of a fact or an explanation tells one nothing about the psychological processes by which pupils are expected to, or actually do, produce that information as an answer.

Of course, it is possible to ask teachers or pupils to comment on a transcript or recording of a lesson, indicating the intentions behind particular questions and answers. This is a useful source of evidence, but it has rarely been used; and of course doubts may be raised about the relationship between the commentary provided and the original patterns of action.

If we take the teacher's intentions or expectations as the target there is also a problem of indeterminacy. There are two sources of this. First, it seems likely that teachers' expectations are sometimes changed by the responses of pupils. The latter may produce unexpected but acceptable answers or they may not be able to produce the level of answer that the teacher wants. And, indeed, Doyle and Carter (1984) argue that a typical response by pupils to tasks requiring higher cognitive operations is to seek to transform them into tasks involving lower cognitive operations, since the latter generally involve less risk. From this point of view the demands placed upon pupils by tasks should perhaps be seen as the product of negotiation between teacher and pupils (Delamont 1983: ch. 5). To the extent that this is so, the problem of coding tasks becomes more difficult since their character may change over time. As a result one cannot combine evidence from how the task is initially set up with how teachers respond to pupils' answers, since these may reflect different conceptions of the nature of the task. In a situation of lack of information, this is a serious impediment to accurate coding; and indeed raises important questions about what would constitute 'valid coding'.

The second source of indeterminacy relates to teachers' own orientations to the tasks they set. Teachers may not, or may not always, generate or monitor tasks in terms of whether they are open or closed. Or if they do they may not employ the same categories as the analyst. As we have seen, there are a number of different ways in which we may define openness/closedness. Moreover, even if they do employ broadly the same categories as the researcher, it is unlikely, given the circumstances in which they work, that they will use these categories with the same level of clarity and rigour as a researcher can; and they may not use the concepts consistently. As a result of this, the relationship between teachers' categorisations and those of the researcher will be imperfect at best, and it may be very weak indeed.

A problem of indeterminacy of a rather different kind also arises if the target is what pupils do in order to answer teachers' questions. Here indeterminacy results from the fact that different pupils may answer questions or complete tasks in different ways. It may even be that what some treat as an open task others treat as closed. And in fact the same answer from the same pupil at different points in time may suggest quite different cognitive orientations.

Coding schemes for classroom tasks, then, rarely seem to meet the basic requirements for reliable measurement, and indeed very often reliability figures are not provided. Moreover, no studies of which we are aware have addressed the problem of the construct validity of the coding scheme employed: the issue of whether it does indeed measure what it is intended to measure. Dunkin and Biddle (1974:79) suggest that this neglect of validity is typical of classroom research generally.

4 Weighting of Tasks

In most research on classroom tasks, all tasks are assigned the same weight. However, this may be quite misleading. Whether one is concerned with teachers' intentions or pupils' cognitive operations, some tasks may count more than others: they may be regarded as more important by the teacher and/or they may have greater impact on pupils. However, even if one recognises this problem it is difficult to find ways of dealing with it. If one is investigating the propensity of examiners to set closed questions, it may be possible to use the marks assigned to each question as a measure of the weight given to it. Doyle and Carter (1984:135) present one of the few attempts to grapple with this problem in analysing written work tasks. They distinguish between:

(a) Major assignments i.e. those that were specifically designated by the teacher as major (e.g. worth a quarter of the grade for the term or used more than 10 per cent of total class time).

(b) Minor assignments, consisting of one day assignments and quizzes.

(c) Exercises consisting of brief assignments (ten to twelve minutes) for part of a daily grade.

Here teacher intention is the measurement target, and two indicators of the weight attached by the teacher to tasks are employed: proportion of grade marks allocated to a task and the amount of time assigned to the task by the teacher. How closely these two indicators covary and whether the cut-off points used are appropriate is difficult to judge from Doyle and Carter's account. In using the distribution of time across tasks as an indicator problems may also arise with discrepancies between stated and actual time allocations, and where the same time is allocated for finishing off one task and beginning another.

The weighting of teachers' oral questions presents even greater difficulties. The indicators used by Doyle and Carter are not available here: marks are not usually given, except in quizzes, and time spent on a particular question seems more likely to vary with how quickly pupils provide a 'right answer' than with the importance the teacher assigns to it. As far as we are aware there have been no attempts to deal with the weighting problem in the research on oral questions.

How one weights different tasks may make a considerable difference to assessments of the extent to which teachers set, or pupils experience, closed tasks. Of course, while teachers and pupils may see some tasks as more important than others, they may not work on the basis of complete rankings. If they do not, any attempt to apply a weighting scale may force their behaviour into a methodological straitjacket. However, the problem cannot be avoided: to ignore it is to weight all tasks equally and as we have suggested this may also be highly misleading.

Conclusion

In this paper we have discussed a number of problems encountered in measuring the closedness of classroom tasks. These represent important potential sources of error. However, they have been given very little attention in the considerable literature on teachers' questions and written work tasks. Nor are effective solutions to most of them currently available. Yet if we are to be able to make well-founded claims about the types of classroom task pupils experience in school, and to explain this distribution and its consequences, we need such solutions. Systematic investigation of these problems, and of strategies for dealing with them, is overdue.

Notes

1 For the purposes of this article, we include in this category both studies using the open/closed terminology, whatever meaning is given to those terms, and any studies not using this terminology but which refer to distinctions among classroom tasks which this terminology has been used to cover.
2 For general discussions of the methodology of classroom research, see Medley and Mitzel (1963), Rosenshine and Furst (1973), Dunkin and Biddle (1974), McIntyre (1980), Barrow (1984). The issues we discuss in this paper are touched on in some of this literature but not systematically explored.
3 For an outline of the various research strategies used in live coding, see Borich (1977) and Hawkins (1982).
4 There are a number of problems involved in coding the tasks in this extract as open or closed, some of which we will mention in the remainder of the article.

References

BARNES, D. (1969). 'Language in the secondary classroom' in Barnes, D., Britton, J., and Rosen, H., *Language, the Learner and the School*, Harmondsworth, Penguin.
BARNES, D. and SHEMILT, D. (1974). 'Transmission and interpretation',*Educational Review*, 26,3.
BARNES, D. and BARNES, D. (1984). *Versions of English*. London, Heinemann.
BARROW, R. (1984). *Giving Teaching Back to Teachers*. Sussex, Wheatsheaf.
BORICH, G.D. (1977). *The Appraisal of Teaching: Concepts and Process*. Reading, Mass., Addison Wesley.
BROPHY, J. and GOOD, T. (1974). *Teacher-Student Relationships: Causes and Consequences*. New York, Holt, Rinehart and Winston.
CARTER, K.J. (1980). 'Academic task structures in high ability and average ability classes', Ph.D. dissertation, North Texas State University.
COREY, S.M. (1940). 'The teachers out-talk the pupils', *School Review*, 48, 9, 745–52.
DAVIS, O.L. and TINSLEY, D. (1967). 'Cognitive objectives revealed by classroom

questions asked by social studies student teachers', *Peabody Journal of Education*, 45, 1, 21–6.

DELAMONT, S. (1983). *Interaction in the Classroom*. (2nd Edition), London, Methuen.

DILLON, J.T. (1982). 'The effect of questions in education and other enterprises', *Journal of Curriculum Studies*, 14, 127–52.

DILLON, J.T. (1982b). 'Cognitive correspondence between question/statement and response', *American Educational Research Journal*, 19, 540–51.

DOYLE, W. (1983). 'Academic work', *Review of Educational Research*, Summer 1983, 53, 2, pp. 159–99.

DOYLE, W. and CARTER, K. (1984). 'Academic tasks in classrooms', *Curriculum Inquiry*, 14, 2.

DUNKIN, M.J. and BIDDLE, B.J.(1974). *The Study of Teaching*. New York, Holt, Rinehart and Winston.

FAIRBROTHER, R.W. (1975). 'The reliability of teachers' judgement of the abilities being tested by multiple choice items', *Educational Research*, 17, 3, 202–210.

GALL, M. (1970). 'The use of questions in teaching', *Review of Educational Research*, 40, 5, 707–21.

GALTON, M., SIMON, B. and CROLL, P. (1980). *Inside the Primary Classroom*. London, Routledge and Kegan Paul.

GOOD, T. and BROPHY, J. (1984). *Looking in Classrooms*. (3rd edition). New York, Harper and Row.

HAMMERSLEY, M. and SCARTH, J. (1986). 'The impact of public examinations upon teaching in secondary schools', unpublished research report.

HARGREAVES, D.H. (1984). 'Teachers' questions: open, closed and half open', *Educational Research*, 26, 1.

HAWKINS, R.P. (1982). 'Developing a behaviour code', in D.P. Hartmann (ed.), *Using Observers to Study Behavior, New Directions for Methodology of Social and Behavioral Science*, no. 14, San Francisco, Jossey Bass.

MCINTYRE, D.I (1980). 'Systematic observation of classroom activities', *Educational Analysis*, 2, 2.

MEDLEY, D.M. and MITZEL, H.E. (1963). 'Measuring classroom behaviour by systematic observation', in N.L. Gage (ed.), *Handbook of Research on Teaching*, Chicago, Rand McNally.

MEHAN, H. (1979). *Learning Lessons: Social Organization in the Classroom*. Massachusetts, Harvard University Press.

MILLS, S., RICE, C., BERLINER, D. and ROSSEAU, E. (1980). 'The correspondence between teacher questions and student answers in classroom discourse', *Journal of Experimental Education*, 48, 194–204.

ROSENSHINE, B. and FURST, N. (1973). 'The use of direct observation to study teaching', in R.M.W. Travers (ed.), *Second Handbook of Research on Teaching*, Chicago Rand McNally.

SCARTH, J. and HAMMERSLEY, M. (1986). 'Questioning ORACLE', *Educational Research*, 28, 3.

SHAYER, M. (1972). 'Conceptual demands in the Nuffield O-level physics course', *School Science Review*, 54, 26–34.

STEVENS, R. (1912). 'The question as a measure of efficiency in instruction: a critical study of class-room practice', New York, Teachers College, *Columbia University Contributions to Education*, No. 48.

TISHER, R.P. (1970). 'The nature of verbal discourse in classrooms and the association between verbal discourse and pupils' understanding in science', in W.J.

Campbell (ed.), *Scholars in Context: the Effects of Environments on Learning*, Sydney, Wiley.

WRIGHT, C.J. and NUTHALL, G. (1970). 'Relationships between teacher behaviours and pupil achievement in three elementary science lessons', *American Educational Research Journal*, 7, 477–91.

'What Time is it Denise?': Asking Known Information Questions in Classroom Discourse

H. Mehan

There is a significant difference between some of the questions that teachers ask students in classrooms, and the questions that are asked outside classrooms. This difference can be made clear by contrasting the following two question-answer sequences:

1:1 Speaker A: What time is it, Denise?
 2 Speaker B: 2.30
 3 Speaker A: Thank you, Denise

2:1 Speaker A: What time is it, Denise?
 2 Speaker B: 2.30
 3 Speaker A: Very good, Denise[1]

The first sequence is typical of ones that we would expect to encounter in our everyday lives. The first speaker has asked another person for information that the second person presumably has. The second person provides this information, and the first person thanks the second for her trouble.

The second sequence is quite different from the first. And, the difference is found in the first speaker's response to the information provided in response to the question asked. The third component of the second example doesn't seem to do the same conversational 'work' as the third component in the first example. While the 'thank you, Denise' seems to 'acknowledge' the content of the previous reply, the 'very good, Denise' does much more than this. It seems to be more of an 'evaluation' of the previous reply than an 'acknowledgement' of it.

We would be taken aback if, after telling another person the time while waiting for a bus or standing in line, that person said 'very good'. Nevertheless, that kind of a response to a previous reply occurs with great regularity in elementary school classrooms. In fact, the presence of an 'evaluation,' which comments on a reply to a question, seems to be one of the features that distinguishes conversations that take place in classrooms and other educational settings from those that occur in everyday situations.

The difference between question-answer sequences that are followed by 'evaluations' rather than 'acknowledgments' has been explained as the difference between 'known information' questions and 'information seeking' questions. (Searle, 1969; Labov and Fanschel, 1977; Shuy and Griffin, 1978 and Levin, 1977) When a known information question is being asked, the questioner already has the answer, or at least has established the parameters in which a reply can properly fall. The questioner is testing the knowledge of the respondent. The respondent to a 'known information question' is placed in the position of trying to match the questioner's predetermined knowledge, or at least fall within the previously established parameters. When, in contrast, information seeking questions are being asked, the questioner does not have the information, assumes that the respondent has the information, and has an immediate need for the information.

The presence of known information questions (also called elicitations in this paper) in the classroom and other educational settings can be accounted for in terms of the social distribution of knowledge associated with the teacher role. Teachers know things that students don't know, and vice versa. But, because teachers in U.S. schools are both educators *and* evaluators, they are placed in the conversational position of asking students questions to which they already know the answer.

The balance of this paper is divided into two parts. In the first part, I will describe the organization of a variety of interactional sequences that occur between teachers and students when the teacher already has the answer. In the second part, I will draw some of the consequences of asking known information questions.

The Sequential Organization of Known Information Questions

Basic Elicitation Sequences

The following excerpt is from a first grade lesson about numbers. The teacher has placed a row of large, cardboard dice on the wall with corresponding ordinal and cardinal numbers. Students were asked to identify various words as the teacher pointed to them (Table 1).[2]

TABLE 1

Initiation	Reply	Evaluation
3:1 T: . . . what does this 　　word say? Beth.	Beth: One.	T: Very good.
3:2 T: What does this word 　　say? Jenny.	Jenny: One.	T: Okay.
3:3 T: Now look up here. 　　What does this word 　　say? Ramona.	Ramona: Umm.	
3:4 T: Kim.	Kim: First.	T: Okay.
3:5 T: Let's say it together.	All: First.	T: All right.
3:6 T: Say it together again.	All: First.	T: Okay.
3:7 T: Lillian, what does this 　　word say?	Lillian: First.	
3:8 T: Richard, what does 　　this word say?	Richard: First.	T: Oh, you said it so nice 　and loud.

This set of exchanges is a classic example of the three part pattern that has been described repeatedly by observers of classroom conversations (Sinclair and Coulthard, 1975; Mishler, 1975a, 1975b, Mehan, 1978, 1979; Shuy and Griffin, 1978). The first part of this sequence has been called an 'initiation', the second part a 'reply', and the third part either an 'evaluation' (Mehan, 1978, 1979; Shuy and Griffin, 1978) or 'feedback' (Sinclair and Coulthard, 1975). In the example above, each time the teacher asks a question, the students produced a reply. And, in all but two instances in this example (3:3 and 3:7), the reply, in turn, received an overt verbal evaluation.

This basic three-part sequential structure of this type of instructional discourse[3] is depicted in Figure 1.

This structure is composed of what has been defined as adjacency pairs

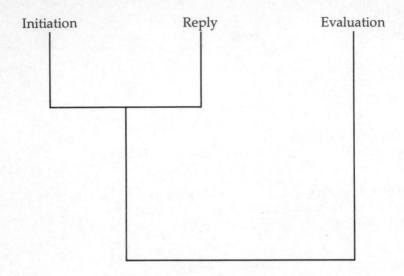

Figure 1   The sequential organization of a typical three part structure

(Sacks *et al*, 1974). Adjacency pairs are 'conditionally relevant'. That is, one item in a pair is conditionally relevant upon the other if, given one item in the pair, the presence of the second is expected. For example, a 'summons' calls forth a 'response' – the ringing of the telephone virtually demands that it be answered; the offering of a greeting seems to compel its return; the asking of a question demands a response.

As illustrated in these examples, conditional relevance means that an obligation to respond (an obligatory co-occurrence relationship) exists between the first and second part of the pair. This relationship accounts for the constraining influence of adjacently related conversational structures. It also accounts for the response that occurs when an expected second half of the pair doesn't occur (e.g. the anger, frustration, and/or questioning, when a friend does not respond to an offered greeting). When a second half of a conditionally relevant pair is absent, its absence is usually made accountable in some way by the participants. In addition, these 'adjacency pairs' are said to be linked together to form chains, which provide a way to understand how stretches of talk longer than the sentence are organized in discourse.

In effect, the three-part Initiation-Reply-Evaluation sequence associated with the classroom contains two coupled adjacency pairs. The Initiation-Reply is the first adjacency pair; the initiation ('What does this word say, Beth?') demands a reply ('one'). When this reply is obtained, a pair is formed. This pair then becomes the first part of a second adjacency pair. The second part of this second pair is the evaluation or the feedback ('very good') of the Initiation-Reply pair (Figure 3).

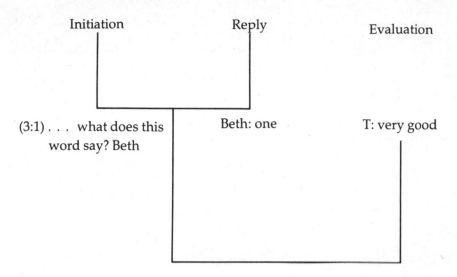

Figure 2

Extended Elicitation Sequences

Once a known information instructional sequence has been initiated, interaction continues until the expected reply is obtained. If the reply appears in
the next turn of talk, then the result is an instructional sequence which has
three adjacently related parts, the initiation, the reply, and the evaluation of
the reply.

However, the reply called for does not always followed immediately after
an initiation. Sometimes students do not answer at all, sometimes they give
partially complete answers, sometimes they reply incorrectly, or out of turn.
If the reply called for by the Initiation act does not appear in the next turn of
talk, the teacher may employ any one of the strategies (e.g. prompting
replies, repeating elicitations, and simplifying elicitations) until the expected
reply does appear. The result is an 'extended sequence' of interaction.

Prompting Replies

The following instance illustrates the teacher's strategy of prompting
incorrect or partially correct replies to obtain the expected reply. The example is from a first grade reading lesson. The lines of a story based on a walk
around the school yard were mounted on a large poster. Students were asked
to read the line of the story that the teacher indicated (Table 2). Here, the
teacher pointed to the line of the story that said: 'See the machine.'

TABLE 2

Initiation	Reply	Evaluation
4:1		
T: See the . . .	E: Tractors.	T: The, yes, tractors, it says mmm.
	E: Tractors.	T: It, it, but it is a tractor, but the word I wrote here, I didn't write tractor. But I wrote a word that, another name for tractor that starts with 'mm.'
	P: Mmmmmmm.	T: It starts with 'mm' Patricia, yes.
4:2		
T: I called the tractor a 'mmm. . .'	R: Machine.	T: Machine, Rafael, good. I called it a machine.

The teacher receiving an incorrect answer ('tractors'), and a partially correct answer ('mmm'), continued questioning the students adding additional information as a prompt, until she obtained a correct reply. Once the correct reply was obtained the teacher positively evaluated it.

Repeating Elicitations
When students answer incorrectly, or do not answer at all, teachers sometimes repeat the elicitation to the same or different students until the expected reply is obtained. In a first grade reading preparedness exercise, the teacher had placed the letters 's' and 'm' on the chalkboard, and asked students to suggest words that started with those letters (Table 3).

Edward declined the teacher's invitation to supply a word that starts with 'm'. The teacher did not evaluate Edward's action; instead she asked another student to supply the answer. When a correct answer was offered, the teacher positively evaluated it.

Simplifying Elicitations
Teachers also reduce the complexity of questions when they do not receive expected replies.

At the outset of the reading lesson about the story described above, the teacher asked the students the questions in Table 4. In this example, the teacher twice attempted to elicit the name of the story from the students.

TABLE 3

Initiation	Reply	Evaluation
5:1 T: What else, what else Edward, what do you think we could put there that starts with an 'm'?	C: (Raises hand).	
5:2 T: Somebody in your family Edward.	E: (Shrugs shoulders 'no').	
5:3 T: All right, Jerome.	A: I know, I know (raises hand)	
5:4 T: What?	A: Man.	T: Man, good for you, Audrey, that's a good one for here. Very good.

Unable to obtain this reply, the teacher changed her questioning strategy. She asked the question in such a way that the students could either agree or disagree with her formulation. Once the students replied to this 'choice' question, the teacher reverted to a questioning form that elicited the specific name of the story. The sequence, like the others presented in this section, ended with a positive evaluation.

A similar example occurred in another reading preparedness lesson. In this sequence, the teacher asks Everett if the phrase 'jumping jacks' starts with the letter 's' or the letter 'j' (Table 5).

When Everett answered incorrectly, the teacher broke the question down into simpler components, then prompted him until he produced the desired reply to the original elicitation. Again, the extended sequences ended with a positive evaluation of the initiation-reply pair.

Summary
Initiation acts compel replies. When a known information question is asked, interaction between teachers and students continues until the expected reply

TABLE 4

Initiation	Reply	Evaluation
6:1 T: Ok, what's the name of this story?	All: (no response)	
6:2 T: Who remembers, what's the name, what's the story about?	All: (no response)	
6:3 T: Is it about taking a bath?	Many: No.	
6:4 T: Is it about the sunshine?	Many: No.	
6:5 T: Edward, what's it about?	E: The map.	T: The map. That's right, this says 'the map.'

is produced. If the reply called for by the question appears in the next immediate turn of talk, the result is an instructional sequence which has three adjacently related parts, an initiation, a reply and an evaluation (see Figure 1). However, if the reply called for by the elicitation does not immediately appear, the teacher 'works' (e.g., prompts, repeats or simplifies elicitations) until that reply is obtained. As soon as the students supply the expected reply (either immediately, or after extended exchanges), the teacher positively evaluates the content of the replies.

The sequential organization of a typical extended sequence is displayed in Figure 3.

Note that the ties that bind three-part sequences together (Figure 1), are apparent in extended sequences (Figure 3). These relationships are simply spread over greater stretches of discourse. Because the reply that completes an elicitation sequence may not appear for many turns, not all instructional sequences are composed of two adjacently related pairs. The existence of extended sequences demonstrates that the reflexive structures that tie inter-actional sequences together are wide ranging, and not limited to adjacently occurring utterances.

TABLE 5

Initiation	Reply	Evaluation
7:1		
T: Everett, you remember, you suggested we do jumping jacks yesterday, remember?	E: Ah ha.	
7:2		
T: Does jumping jacks begin like Sabrina or like Jerome?	E: Sabrina.	
7:3		
T: Say J, J, 'jumping jacks.'	E: Jumping jacks.	T: All right, it's a, it's a beginning of the word jumping jacks.
7:4		
T: Does that begin like Sabrina or like Jerome?	E: (no response)	
7:5		
T: Jumping . . .	E: Jerome.	T: Jerome, that's right.

Thus, the evaluation act plays a significant role in classroom discourse. While it seldom appears in everyday discourse, it is an essential component of instructional interaction. It contributes information to students about the teachers' intentions, and contributes to the negotiation of a mutually acceptable reply.

Some observers of classroom interaction (Bellack *et al*, 1966; Sinclair and Coulthard, 1975) have treated evaluation acts as an optional part of elicitation sequences, while I have found them to be an obligatory component of instructional sequences. This difference seems to be a result of distinguishing between positive and negative evaluation acts. Positive and negative evaluation of student replies do not fulfill equivalent functions in elicitation sequences. Positive evaluations occur as soon as a correct reply appears, while negative evaluations, prompts, or corrections may or may not appear after incorrect or incomplete answers. Thus, the positive evaluation is a terminal

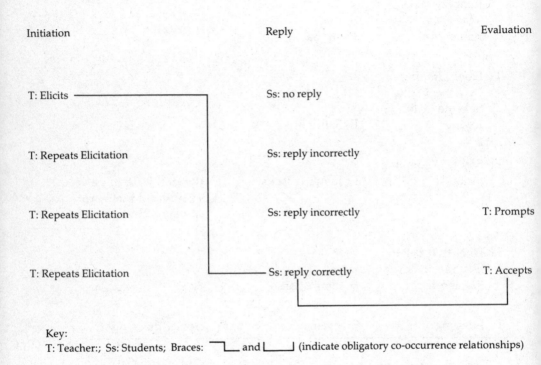

Figure 3   The sequential organization of a typical extended sequence

act; it marks the completion of an instructional sequence. Ending one sequence, it signals that another is to begin.

Negative evaluations, prompts, or corrections are continuation acts. They do not appear at the end of instructional sequences, only in their interior. They function to keep the interaction moving until the answer demanded by the initial interaction is obtained. Thus, positive evaluation acts are an obligatory part of elicitation sequences, while negative evaluations, prompting and the like, are optional parts of these sequences. These relationships are displayed in Figure 4.

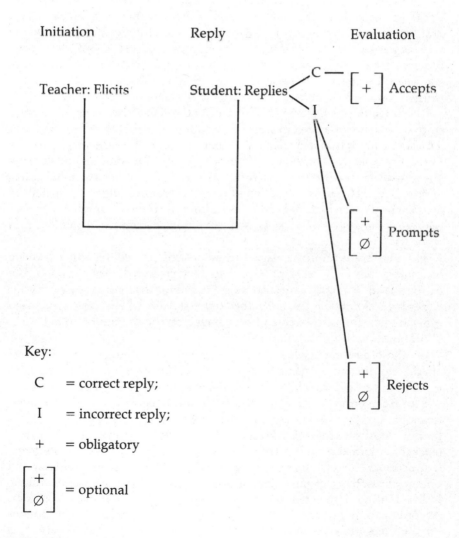

Figure 4

Some Consequences of Asking Known Information
Questions Displaying Knowledge

The use of known information questions has consequences for the knowledge that children display in the classroom. As a way of demonstrating this point, let us return to the first transcript example. The teacher in that sequence asked Beth the question 'what does this word say?' Beth answered 'one,' the teacher complimented her ('Very good'), and asked the same question of a second child, Jenny. Jenny also answered that question correctly. But there was a significant difference in the circumstances available to Jenny and Beth; Jenny had access to the teacher's evaluation of Beth's answer as well as her own knowledge about the numbers on the board. As a consequence, the basis of Jenny's answer was not clear. Did she answer because she 'knew' the answer, or because she attended to the surface features of the preceding discourse, notably, the teacher's response to Beth's answer?

The possibility of students 'imitating' other answers occurs whenever turns-at-talk are allocated to students in such a way that they can reply in a 'chorus' or when the teacher asks the same question of a series of children as in this example. In fact, every way in which turns are allocated to students has consequences for the structural arrangements of instructional interaction. Different turn allocation strategies produce different structural arrangements which are related to the communication of different types of educational material to students, and obtaining academic information from students.

There is a trade off in the use of turn-allocation procedures which provide for individual vs. choral responses, voluntary vs. mandatory responses. On the one hand, if children are encouraged to bid for the floor (e.g., 'raise your hands if you know the answer,'), then only students who want to reply need bid. Competition is fostered and encouraged by this 'invitation to bid' turn-allocation procedure.

On the other hand, when no bid has been requested and an individual child is nominated by name to reply, the teacher then has some access to what that particular child knows. However, this strategy singles the child out from the group. Such a procedure has consequences of particular significance at least for some Native American students. An analysis of a videotape of Odowa students (Erickson and Mohatt, 1977) showed that the native teacher seldom directed instructions or questions at individual students. Instructional conversations were organized such that students could respond voluntarily and in a group, a practice which seemed to be consistent with the Indian's cultural patterns and values which exist outside the classroom. According to Philips (1972, 1976) interaction is structured in Indian community settings on a cooperative, voluntary basis. This cultural pattern is undercut in Anglo-oriented classrooms in which participation is organized to emphasize individual, not group effort, is mandatory, not voluntary, and is competitive, not cooperative.

It is not my intention here to recommend the use of a particular turn-allocation procedure; that is a teacher's and not a researcher's decision. Rather, it is my purpose to point out that various classroom arrangements impose constraints on interaction, and hence, on children who must operate within those constraints. I do this because teachers are sometimes not aware of the organizational consequences of interactional arrangements. What we know about children is constrained by the structure of the task (Cole, Hood, McDermott, 1978), the style of questioning employed, even the way turns are allocated to students. And, knowledge about the organization of inter-action is information that students need to acquire just as much as they learn number facts, times tables, and word attack skills.

'Searching' for Correct Answers

Because there is often only a single correct response to known information questions, and this answer is known in advance of the questioning, teachers often find themselves 'searching' for that answer, while students provide various 'trial' responses which are in search of validation as the correct answer.

An example of this searching practice is found in the following excerpt from a first grade lesson about prepositional phrases. The teacher first asked students to draw a number of objects on their paper. She then asked them to report on their drawing (Table 6).

An interview conducted with the teacher both before and after this lesson (Mehan, 1974) disclosed that she wanted the children to report the result of their drawing in complete sentences with certain prepositional phrases, i.e., 'the red flower is under the tree.' The first time the teacher asked this question, the children responded in unison with an answer which adequately describes the location of the flowers drawn: 'on here.'

However, the teacher wanted *complete* sentences with prepositional phrases, and so she continued questioning the student. Dora provided an answer which employed a prepositional phrase, 'under the tree' (8:2), but since this answer was not in a complete sentence, the teacher continued questioning her:

Teacher: Tell me in a sentence.
Dora: It's under the tree.

Now, Dora has answered the teacher's question. She has provided an answer which, in fact, is a grammatically complete sentence. However, this sentence did not have the proper subject noun, 'The flower,' so the teacher continued to question Dora:

TABLE 6

Initiation	Reply	Evaluation
8:1 T: Make a red flower under the tree. (Pause) OK, let's look at the red flower. Can you tell me where the red flower is?	Ss: Right here, right here.	
8:2 T: Dora?	Dora: Under the tree.	
8:3 T: Tell me in a sentence.	Dora: It's under the tree.	
8:4 T: What's under the tree, Dora?	Ss: The flower.	
8:5 T: Tell me, the flower . . .	Dora: The flower is under the tree.	
8:6 T: Where is the red flower Richard?	Ric: Under the tree.	
8:7 T: Can you tell me in a sentence?	Ric: The flower is under the tree.	
8:8 T: Cindy, where is the red flower?	Cin: The red flower is under the tree.	
8:9 Ric: Hey, that's not red.		

> *Teacher*: What's under the tree *Dora*?
> *Student*: the flower
> *Teacher*: Tell me, the flower . . .

Dora has received information about the desired answer from two sources. First, another child supplies the missing noun phrase. Second, the teacher, employing a 'sentence completion' form of questioning, supplied her with the part of the answer she had been after all along; in effect, the teacher has answered her own question here.

The tempo of the lesson picked up. Richard was asked the same question:

Teacher: Where is the red flower, Richard?
Richard: Under the tree.

One more question-answer exchange was sufficient to get Richard to produce the desired answer form:

Teacher: Can you tell me in a sentence?
Richard: The flower is under the tree.

The teacher then turned to Cindy with the same question, and Cindy, for the first time in the lesson, provided the answer that the teacher had been looking for, all in one turn of talk:

Teacher: Cindy, where is the red flower?
Cindy: The red flower is under the tree.
Richard: hey, that's not red!

There is only one problem. Although Cindy provided exactly the answer that the teacher wanted, it did not accurately reflect the facts of what she had drawn. Richard pointed out, and my examination of her work after the lesson confirmed, Cindy had not, in fact, drawn a red flower; she used a crayon of a different color. Perhaps attending to the cues provided by other children's answers and the structure of the preceding sequences, Cindy was able to provide the desired answer form.

As a result of the teacher's search for the one correct answer to her question, it is difficult to determine whether this child's answer stemmed from a mastery of the conceptual demands of the academic task, or stemmed from a mastery of the conversation demands of the questioning style.

Another example of what happens when a teacher searches for a previously established answer appears in the following excerpt (Table 7) from a social studies lesson about spices from India.

At the outset of this segment, the teacher, looking for 'India' as the place or origin for spices, received a series of replies (9: 2,3,4). All replies were offered hesitantly, with cautious, rising intonation at the end of the utterances (which I have indicated with the (?) mark). The teacher continued to invite replies until the one he wanted was offered. Although that reply (9:4) had the same characteristics of the previous replies, the teacher accepted it. In so doing, he reified the reply. This pattern was repeated as the teacher searched for 'around Africa' as the path to India (9:5–9:9). A number of possible replies were not accepted, until the particular reply appeared. Again, the teacher's acceptance of this reply transformed it from a possible reply into 'the correct answer.' One consequence, then, of the teacher's search for

TABLE 7

Initiation	Reply	Evaluation
9:1 T: OK, why did you think people were so interested in getting over to a place, remember where did they get their spices from?	Pep: from ? Nerea? (Near East)	T: Almost.
9:2	Many: I know, I know.	
9:3	Jose: From California?	T: No.
9:4 T: They didn't know about California. Remember we talked about it	Ss: From Europe? Ss: From India.	T: From India!
9:5 T: And how did they do it? Did they fly over to India?	Many: Nooooo.	T: No.
9:6 T: They had to go around what?	Ss: The long way around?	
9:7 T: They had to go around what?	Ss: On a boat?	T: On a boat.
9:8 T: Around what? Around what?	Ss: Around Africa?	T: Around Africa!
9:9 T: Around here, up through here (tracing trade route on wall map), and India was over here, see?		

answers to known information questions, is that the student does not so much answer the teacher's question, as the teacher and student create the student's answer out of a number of tentative displays.

Conclusions

Children's performance in the classroom involves a wide range of conversational skills which interact with the academic aspects of education. One important communicative skill required to participate in the teaching-learning process includes knowing how to answer questions appropriately, especially given that a unique aspect of the question-asking process in the classroom is that teachers often ask students questions when they already know the answers. On these occasions, the teacher is testing the students' knowledge, not seeking information from them. Thus, an important part of education for children in school is learning that conversations in classrooms have unique features, and that the demands of classroom discourse must be kept separate from the demands of everyday discourse. The students' acquisition of this interactional knowledge seems to be intertwined with the acquisition of the academic knowledge more routinely associated with schooling.

Each of the examples of teacher-student interaction discussed in this paper demonstrates that teachers and students work together to compose the social fact we call an answer to a question. Answers to questions are generated from knowledge about the academic content implied by the question as well as from knowledge about the social conduct of classroom conversations.

The interactional accomplishment of social facts like answers to questions has implications for the way we view students' competence in educational environments. Instead of seeing children's knowledge as private and internal states, as a personal possession, an interactional view of teaching and learning recommends seeing knowledge as *public* property, *social* constructions, assembled jointly by teachers and students that become visible in social contexts. Teachers are sometimes not aware that the child's display of knowledge is constrained by the structure of the task, the organization of discourse, and the physical parameters of the teaching-learning situation. Since each educational arrangement imposes constraints on learning, educators can examine the interactional demands of various educational and evaluation arrangements to determine if any particular arrangement is consistent with their educational goals and the child's previous experience.

Notes

1 This example is based on Sinclair and Coulthard (1975).
2 The materials used for illustrative purpose are excerpts from transcripts of videotape taken in a variety of elementary school classrooms. Information about the
   complete transcripts are available from the author.
3 These three-part sequences are not just the special province of the classroom, as
   example (1) shows. Shuy (1976), Doeblen (1979) and Fisher (1979) are finding that
   doctor-patient interaction is organized into three part sequences, perhaps for the
   same reason that teacher-student interaction is. Goffman (1976) says that riddles
   also have three parts: (1) question, (2) thought and give up, (3) answer. Like the
   elicitation, 'the purpose of the asked person's move is not to inform the asker about
   the answer, but to show whether he is smart enough to uncover what the speaker
   already knows. But here the interaction falls flat if indeed the correct answer is
   uncovered (unlike the asking done by teachers), or if upon being told the answer,
   the asked person does not do an appreciable 'take,' this latter constitutes a fourth
   move' (Goffman, 1976:295).

References

BELLACK, ARNO A. et al. *The Language of the Classroom*. New York: Teachers
   College Press, Columbia University, 1966.
CAZDEN, C.B., VERA, JOHN and HYMES, DELL (eds.) *Functions of Language in
   the Classroom*. Teachers College Press.
COLE, MICHAEL, HOOD, LOIS, and MCDERMOTT, R.P. *Ecological Niche
   Picking: Ecological Invalidity as an Axiom of Experimental Cognitive Psychology*.
   La Jolla, California: Laboratory of Comparative Human Cognition, 1978.
DOEBLEN, RENATE. 'The Social Organization of Doctor-Patient Interaction.'
   Unpublished Ph.D. Dissertation, Konstanz, 1979.
ERICKSON, FREDERICK, and MOHATT, JERRY. 'The Social Organization of
   Participation Structures in Two Classrooms of Indian Students.' Paper presented
   at annual meeting of AERA, New York, 1977.
FISHER, SUE. 'The Negotiation of Treatment Decisions in Doctor-Patient Inter-
   action.' Unpublished Ph.D. Dissertation, University of California, San Diego, La
   Jolla, 1979.
GOFFMAN, ERVING. 'Replies and Responses.' *Language in Society*, 5:257–313,
   1976.
LABOV, WILLIAM and FANSCHEL, DAVID. *Therapeutic Discourse: Psycho-
   therapy as Conversation*. New York: Academic Press, 1977.
LEVIN, PAULA. 'Students and Teachers: A Cultural Analysis of Polynesian Class-
   room Interaction.' Unpublished Ph.D. Dissertation, University of California, San
   Diego, 1977.
MEHAN, HUGH. 'Accomplishing Classroom Lessons.' In A.V. Cicourel et al. *Lan-
   guage use and school performance*. New York: Academic Press, 1974.
MEHAN, HUGH. *Learning Lessons*. Cambridge, Mass.: Harvard University Press,
   1979.
MISHLER, E.G. 'Studies in Dialogue and Discourse: An Exponential Law of Succes-
   sive Questioning.' *Language in Society*, 4:31–52, 1975a.
MISHLER, E.C. 'Studies in Dialogue and Discourse II: Types of Discourse Initiated

by and Sustained through Questioning.' *Psycholinguistics Research Journal*, 4:99–121, 1975b.

PHILIPS, SUSAN. 'Participant Structures and Communicative Competence. In Cazden *et al.*, 1972.

PHILIPS, SUSAN. 'Some Sources of Cultural Variables in the Regulation of Talk.' *Language in Society*, 5:81–96, 1976.

SACKS, HARVEY, SCHEGLOFF, EMMANUEL, and JEFFERSON, GAIL. 'A Simplest Systematics for the Organization of Turn-Taking in Conversation.' *Language*, (50): 696–735, 1974.

SEARLE, JOHN. *Speech Acts*. Cambridge: Cambridge University Press, 1969.

SHUY, ROGER. 'The Medical Interview.' *Primary Care*, 3(3): 365–386, 1976.

SHUY, ROGER, and GRIFFIN, PEG (eds.) *The Study of Children's Functional Language and Education in the Early Years*. Final Report to the Carnegie Corporation of New York, Arlington, Va.: Center for Applied Linguistics, 1978.

SINCLAIR, J.M., and COULTHARD, R.M. *Toward an Analysis of Discourse*. New York: Oxford University Press, 1975.

Note: The author wishes to thank Jürgen Streeck who helped clarify important points in the development of this paper.

Questioning at Home and at School: A Comparative Study

S. Brice Heath

Introduction

'Ain't nobody can talk about things being about theirselves.'

A third-grade boy in a community in the Southeastern part of the United States directed this statement to his teacher when she persisted in asking questions about the story just completed in reading circle.

> TEACHER What is the story about?
> CHILDREN (*silence*)
> TEACHER Uh . . . Let's see . . . Who is it the story talks about?
> CHILDREN (*silence*)
> TEACHER Who is the main character? Um . . . What kind of story is it?
> CHILD Ain't nobody can talk about things being about theirselves!

The boy was saying: 'There's no way anybody can talk (and ask) about things being about themselves.' As an ethnographer who had worked in the boy's community and school for more than five years, I was able to place his summative statement about the kinds of questions asked in school into the context of knowledge about those asked of him in his own community.

The boy was reacting to the fact that teachers' questions were so often about things being about themselves; that is, they asked for labels, attributes, and discrete features of objects and events in isolation from the context. Someone – most often the teacher and the brightest kids in class – always had answers for school questions. These answers could usually be given in one word. In the boy's community, people asked questions about whole events or objects and their uses, causes, and effects. Often no one had an answer which was the 'right answer.' Community members accepted many answers and ways of answering, and their answers almost always involved telling a story, describing a situation, or making comparisons between the event or object being described and another known to the audience.

This paper presents some data on uses of questions in three different situations in a moderate-sized city of the south-eastern United States: a working-class community of black residents, the classrooms attended by children of this community in 1970 – 1975, and the homes of teachers from these classrooms. We will attempt to show how questions varied in proportion to other types of utterances across the three situations, and we shall look at different uses of questions and the assumptions made by the questioners about the functions of questions. Our aim is to indicate how ethnographic data on verbal strategies in community and home settings can be useful for comparison with data collected in studies of the functions of language in the classroom.

Ethnography in the Community and Classroom

The goal of ethnography is to describe the ways of living of a social group, usually one in which there is in-group recognition by the members that they indeed must live and work together to retain group identity. Traditionally, ethnographers have taken up residence in communities made up of one or more of these social groups to record and describe the behaviors, values, and tangible aspects of their culture. More recently, ethnographers have also become participant-observers in settings which do not necessarily have a cross-generational on-going sense of social identity. Anthropologists have studied institutions, such as schools, hospitals, and factories, or short-lived but repetitive group interactions, such as court sessions, conversations, and service encounters. Some anthropologists have made their data available for decision-making by political leadership and institutional management. Anthropologists studying communities in complex societies have also begun to make their studies available to these communities and have offered to provide data about the operations of political/economic institutions through which community members must move in daily interactions outside their own social group.

The fieldwork reported in this paper was carried out over a period of five years in both community and institutional settings. Results of the work were shared with both community and institutional members. One phase of the fieldwork was done in an all-black residential group whose members identified themselves as a community both spatially and in terms of group membership. To distinguish this group from the public community at large, we will hereafter refer to it as Trackton. Over the period of time in which I worked there, its membership declined from 150 to 40, as families moved from the neighborhood into public housing or purchased new homes. Most Trackton households contained one or more members, ages 21 to 45, who worked in jobs providing salaries equal to or above those of beginning public school teachers in the region; however, jobs were seasonal; and work was not always steady. Trackton was located in a south-eastern city with a population of approximately 40,000; in the period from 1970 to 1975, children from the community attended either of two public elementary-level schools. As a volunteer neighborhood service aide, I worked in these schools and with city personnel in a variety of agencies, collecting data on inter-actions of Trackton residents in institutions with which they came in frequent, if not daily, contact. As a professor at a state teacher-training institution for which the region's citizens had a longstanding respect, I had many of the teachers, their spouses, or other family members in classes, and I worked informally with others on local civic or church-related projects. Over the years, I became colleague, co-author, aide, and associate to many of the classroom teachers, and I had access to not only their classrooms, but also their homes and their activities in the public domain.

I began working in Trackton at the request of some of the older residents who had known me for several years. My initial task, in their view, was to read and talk with the children and explain to adults why their children were not doing better in school. Gradually, I was called on to be a source of information about available services and opportunities for them and their children in public institutions, and I was asked to explain the systems of entry and maintenance which made for success in these institutions. In the late 1960s, numerous policy changes in schools and public systems regula-ting housing, employment, and pre-school educational and medical experiences brought the children of all-black communities into many new situations. Desegregation rulings put black students into formerly all-white classrooms, usually with white teachers. There were many com-plaints in the first years, but particularly disturbing to older residents was the hatred of their young for school:

The teachers won't listen.

My kid, he too scared to talk, 'cause nobody play by the rules he know. At home, I can't shut 'im up.

Miss Davis, she complain 'bout Ned not answerin' back. He says she asks dumb questions she already know 'bout.

It seemed clear that parents felt there was little meaningful communication going on between teachers and their children in the classroom. When I talked over this view with classroom teachers, they agreed there was relatively little 'real' exchange of information, feeling, or imagination between them and many of the black students, especially those in the primary grades.

During this period, much research on language pointed out differences between the structures of Black English and those of standard English, and the effects of these differences on academic performance (Labov 1968; Baratz and Shuy 1969; Wolfram 1969). Many local teachers knew of this research (especially Labov 1970, 1972), and some suggested that perhaps differences between the structures of their language and those of their black students were major reasons for communication breakdowns. Other teachers did not agree; they reasoned that almost daily for many years they had lived and worked with Black English speakers in nearly all institutions except schools and churches. Therefore, the structures of the languages used by teachers and their Black English-speaking students were probably not so different as to cause the almost-total lack of communication which seemed to exist in some classrooms. Their view was that reasons for the breakdown lay in the nature of interactions called for in school. The interactional tasks between teacher and child called for particular kinds of responses from students. These responses depended primarily on two kinds of knowledge: first, the rituals and routines of classroom life, and second, the information and skills acquired in the classroom. It was difficult, however, for teachers to pin down exactly what was called for in these interactions; thus they felt they could not help their students achieve success in these tasks. To be sure, the entry of black students into the schools had caused negative attitudes and bitter prejudices to surface, but there were many well-intentioned teachers who, having accepted the desegregation decision as final, wanted to get on with teaching. They felt a strong need to know more about ways in which they could effectively communicate with all their students.

Of the students with whom they had communication problems, teachers said:

They don't seem to be able to answer even the simplest questions.

I would almost think some of them have a hearing problem; it is as though they don't hear me ask a question. I get blank stares to my questions. Yet when I am making statements or telling stories which interest them, they always seem to hear me.

The simplest questions are the ones they can't answer in the classroom; yet on the playground, they can explain a rule for a ballgame or describe a particular kind of bait with no problem. Therefore, I know they can't be as dumb as they seem in my class.

I sometimes feel that when I look at them and ask a question, I'm staring at a wall I can't break through. There's something there; yet in spite of all the questions I ask, I'm never sure I've gotten through to what's inside that wall.

Many teachers and administrators felt they were 'not asking the right questions' of either the children or their own teaching strategies, and I was asked to help them find ways of helping themselves. As an aide, tutor, traveling librarian, and 'visiting fireman' occasionally asked to talk about archaeology or show slides of other countries in which I had done field-work, I served numerous functions in classrooms across a wide range of grade levels and subject areas for five years. I participated and observed, shared data, and acted as change agent at the request of the institution's members. During this period, some of the teachers enrolled in graduate courses of study which included some anthropology and linguistics courses I taught. They then used techniques of ethnographic fieldwork and data interpretation in their own classes and schools and incorporated into their teaching some of the observation skills associated with anthro-pology. Some teachers collected data on their own practices in guiding language learning for their pre-school children at home; others agreed to allow me to participate and observe in their homes, recording uses of language and language input for their children. Particularly critical to these teachers' understanding and acceptance of ethnography in familiar educational settings – both their classrooms and their homes – was their view that the ethnographic/linguistic research was in response to their felt needs, and they were themselves involved.

During the period of participating and observing in classrooms and some teachers' homes, I continued work in Trackton. A major focus of field-work there was the acquisition of uses of language, ways in which children learned to use language to satisfy their needs, ask questions, transmit information, and convince those around them they were competent communicators. Participating and observing with the children and their families and friends intensively over a period of five years, I was able to collect data across a wide range of situations and to follow some children longitudinally as they acquired communicative competence in Trackton and then attempted to take this competence into school settings.[1] Likewise, at various periods during these years, I observed Trackton adults in public service encounters and on their jobs, and I was able to compare their communicative competence in these situations with those inside Trackton. The context of language use, including setting, topic, and participants (both those directly involved in the talk and those who only listened), determined in large part how community members, teachers, public ser-vice personnel, and fellow workers judged the communicative competence of Trackton residents. Proper handling of questioning was especially criti-cal, because outsiders often judged the intelligence and general compe-tence of individuals by their responses to questions and by the questions they asked.

In settings outside Trackton, questions had several functions relatively rarely used by residents there. The first situation in which this difference became important for Trackton children came when they entered school. There they had to learn that teachers did not always make the same assumptions as they did about the uses of questions. What follows here provides an indication of the interrogatives teachers used with their own pre-schoolers at home, questions Trackton adults asked their pre-school children, and the conflict and congruence between these differing approaches to questioning as they evolved in classrooms.

Questions and Language Learning

Questions and their uses by children's caretakers have received relatively little attention in studies of language input and acquisition. In general, what emerges from the literature is the view that questions are used for training children to interact verbally with their caretakers and for directing their attention to what it is they should learn (Holzman 1972, 1974; Snow *et al.* 1976; Goody 1977). Several studies point out that a large percentage of utterances middle class mothers direct to their pre-school children is made up of questions (Newport, *et al* 1977; Snow 1977), and some studies indicate that questions become successively more complex in correspondence with the child's increased language skill (Levelt 1975). Most of these studies consider questions only as they may relate to the child's acquisition of grammatical competence or the structures of his speech community's language system (Ervin-Tripp 1970).

Some attention has also been given to the role of questions in children's acquisition of communicative competence, i.e., how they learn conversational skills (Snow 1977; Ervin-Tripp and Miller 1977) and determine appropriate language uses for different listeners, settings, and topics (Hymes 1962; Blount 1977). Cross-cultural research in child language acquisition has pointed out that the linguistic environment and the language socialization of children vary across cultures. Uses of questions vary in numerous respects. For example, in one society, it may not be the mother or even members of the immediate family who direct the highest proportion of questions to young children, because the language socialization network includes a wide range of participants (Harkness 1977). In another society, questions are not considered highly relevant to learning how to accomplish tasks (Goody 1977); in another, children have very little exposure to *why* or *how* questions (Blank 1975). Among other groups, questions may be intimately linked to imperatives, explaining the reasons for commands or the consequences of not obeying orders (Cook-Gumperz 1973; Sachs, *et al.* 1976).

The specific characteristics of questions and their uses in socializing young children are highly dependent on the network of those who ask questions.

A pre-school child who has frequent contacts with individuals of both sexes, different ages, and varying degrees of familiarity with his world will learn very different uses of questions from the child accustomed to a small network of family and close associates. In particular, the assumptions made by questioners about the functions of their questions in the socialization of the child will be very different. The wide variation possible in child language socialization, and especially in the uses of questions, is exemplified in the community of Trackton and the homes of its classroom teachers.

Classroom Teachers and Their Own Children

Within their homes, children of the classroom teachers involved in this study[2] were socialized into a fairly small network of language users: mother, father, siblings, and maids or grandparents. Children below the age of four rarely communicated with anyone on an extended basis except these primary associates. Visits to Sunday School, the grocery store, shopping centers, and so on provided very limited opportunities for questions addressed to the children by non-intimates. Within the homes, talk to pre-school children emphasized questions. In their questioning routines with pre-verbal as well as verbal children, adults supplied the entire context, giving questions and answering them (cf. Gleason 1973)[3] or giving questions and then pausing to hold conversational space for a hypothetical answer before moving on to the next statement, which assumed information from the hypothetical answer (cf. Snow 1977).

> MOTHER (*addressing an 8-week-old infant*) You want your teddy bear?
> MOTHER Yes, you want your bear.

> MOTHER (*addressing her 2-month-old infant*) You don't know what to make of all those lights, do you? *Pause (3 seconds)*
> MOTHER That's right, I know you don't like them. Let's move over here. (*picks up infant and moves away from lights*)

> MOTHER (*addressing her child age 2;9*) Didja forget your coat?
> MOTHER Yes, you did. Let's go back 'n get it.

When parents wanted to teach a politeness formula, such as *thank you* or *please*, they used interrogatives: 'Can you say "thank you"?' 'What do you say?' (cf. Gleason and Weintraub 1976). Questions served a wide variety of functions in adult-child interactions. They allowed adults to hold pseudo-conversations with children, to direct their attention to specific events or objects in the array of stimuli about them, and to link formulaic responses to appropriate occasions. Perhaps most important, adults' uses of questions trained children to act as question-answerers, as experts on knowledge about the world, especially the names and attributes of items in their environment and those introduced to them through books.

> MOTHER (*looking at a family photograph album with Missy, age 2;3*) Who's that, Missy? (*The mother has pointed to the family dog in one of the pictures.*)
> MISSY That's Toby.
> MOTHER What does Toby say?
> MISSY Woof, woof, (*child imitates a whine*) grrrrrr, yip.
> MOTHER Where does Toby live?
> MISSY *My* house.

The children seemed to feel compelled to give answers to adults' questions. When they did not know answers (or were bored with the usual routine of expected answers), they sometimes invented fantastic answers.

Adults addressed questions to their children in great numbers and variety. During a period of 48 hours, Missy (age 2;3) was asked 103 questions; 47.9 percent of all utterances (215) directed to her during this period were questions (cf. Sachs *et al.* 1976).[4] Table 1 contains a description of these questions. Questions designated Q–I are those in which the questioner has the information being requested of the addressee; A–I questions are those in which the addressee has the information being requested. Unanswerable questions (U–I) are those for which neither questioner nor addressee has the information. Of the A–I questions, 25 percent were clarification requests (Corsaro 1977), in which questioners asked the child to clarify, confirm, or repeat a previous utterance. Q–I questions were often used in game-playing, especially games of hide-and-seek or peek-a-boo. These two types, Q–I and A–I, fit the simplicity of syntax expected in utterances directed to children of this age (cf. New-port, et al. 1977), but the U–I questions do not. These were both Why–questions and 'I wonder' questions which asked for information neither the child nor the adult was expected to have. The syntax of these and the answers they called for was far more complex than that of other types addressed to the child. For

TABLE 1   Percentages and types of questions (Missy 2;3)

Types	Examples	Total	Percentage
Q–I	What color is that?	46	44.7
A–I	What do you want?	24	23.3
U–I	Why is it things can't be simpler than they are?	18	17.5
Others	(directives, etc.)	15	14.5

example, a father walking the child outside before putting her to bed would look up at the sky and ask: 'I wonder what's up there?' These questions seemed to be self-talk, an out-loud sort of reverie. For these questions, the child was expected to be a passive listener, but a listener nevertheless, thus giving the adult an 'excuse' for talking to himself.

Interrogative forms predominated in types of utterances directed to pre-schoolers. Over a six-month period, a teacher arranged for her child (age 2;8–3;2) and the child (age 3;2–3;8) of another teacher to play in one or the other of the two homes each afternoon from 3 to 5. Adult-children interactions were taped one afternoon each week for six months. Adults who interacted with the children usually included either or both of the teachers (mothers), one grandparent, and two older siblings. In the first month (four sessions), interrogatives made up 58.6 percent of the total utterances (640) directed to the children, imperatives 28.1 percent, exclamations 6.7 percent, declaratives 6.6 percent. In the sixth month (four sessions), interrogatives made up 52.4 percent of the total utterances (770) directed to the children, imperatives 30.3 percent, exclamations 4.4 percent, and declaratives 12.9 percent. Lumping all interrogative forms together in the data masks the uses of questions in behavior correction and accusations of wrong-doing. Many of the interrogatives were, in fact, directives or condemnations of the children's behavior. For example, tag questions attached directly to statements were counted here as interrogatives because of their form, but the speakers usually meant these as declarative or directive. For example, in the utterance 'That's a top. You've never seen one of those, have you?' the adult was not calling for a response from the child, but making a declarative statement for the child: 'No, I've never seen one of those.' In the statement, 'You wouldn't do that, would you?' the speaker provides a somewhat softened directive which means 'Don't do that.' Questions similar in type to tag questions were directives in intent and followed immediately after imperatives in form, extending their force: 'Stop it, Jamie. Why can't you behave?' The latter part of this utterance extends the scolding power of the imperative and calls upon the child to *think* about a response to the question, but not to respond verbally to the condemnation.

Adults and older siblings seemed compelled to communicate to the pre-schoolers in questions. At the end of the third month, when the strong patterning of questioning was definitive in the data, the teachers agreed to make a conscious effort for one month to reduce their questions and use statements instead. This change evolved out of discussions surrounding analysis of the past three months' tapes. One teacher believed (though she admitted perhaps ideally so) that statements transmitted more information than questions did. Therefore, since she also believed her purpose in holding conversations with her pre-schoolers was to pass on information, she should make statements, not ask questions. The other teacher was skeptical, believing questions necessary to check on information-transmission. However, both agreed to try to reduce their level of questioning (and that of adults around them) directed to the children for one month to see if their feelings about statements and questions could be borne out in the data in any concrete way. During this period, the percentage of questions dropped to 50.6 percent and the percentage of statements increased to 11.9 percent. However, both teachers reported they were not satisfied with what was happening. They felt they gave more orders, the questions they did ask were scolding in nature, and they were not getting the behavior modifications they expected from their children. They reported they felt they did not involve their children when they used statements. They received no sense of interaction and felt they were 'preaching' to a third party; they could not be sure they were being heard. They viewed questions as a way to 'share talk' with children of this age. Just 'talking *to* them' (interpreted now by both teachers as using statements only) seemed to have no impact; questions allowed adults to 'talk *with* children.'

Without being aware of any change in their behavior, in the last month of data collected from these adult-children interactions, adults seemed to focus on teaching the children to ask the right questions in the right places and not to ask questions which seemed to challenge the authority of adults. The children were told:

Don't ask why people are sick.

Don't ask that kind of question.

Don't ask so many questions.

Don't ask why.

These corrections seemed to increase dramatically when someone from outside the family circle entered the home. Adults seemed to use correctives to questions to announce they were training their children in the right way. If a child asked an 'impertinent' question of a visitor, the adult would reprimand the child and offer an explanatory aside to the visitor. 'What do you say?' as a request for politeness formulas such as 'please' and 'thank you' was an especially favorite question when outsiders were present.

In summary, teachers socializing their own pre-schoolers to language depended heavily on questions. They used questions to teach their children what they should attend to when looking at a book ('What's that?' 'Where's the puppy?' 'What does he have in his hand?'). The children were taught to label (Ninio and Bruner 1978), to search out pieces of pictures, to name parts of the whole, and to talk about these out of context. As the children grew older, adults used questions to add power to their directives ('Stop that! Did you hear me?') and to call particular attention to the infraction committed ('Put that back. Don't you know that's not yours?'). Adults saw questions as necessary to train children, to cause them to respond verbally, and to be trained as conversational partners.

Language Learning in Trackton

In the past decade, linguists have described the structure of Black English, its history, and its particular systems of usage in appropriate contexts. Numerous myths about the language of the black child have been exploded by research, which has shown this language to be rule-governed and as capable of providing an adequate basis for thinking as any other language. Speech acts given particular labels in Black English, such as 'signifying,' 'playing the dozens,' and 'jiving,' have been described in their uses by adolescent and adult members of black communities (Labov, *et al.* 1968; Mitchell Kernan 1971; Kochman 1972).

Nevertheless, many stereotypes still exist about language learning in black communities. Studies of black communities provide only bits and pieces of evidence on adults interacting with young children for language socialization. Ward (1971) describes a community in Louisiana in which the children have numerous language difficulties in school, but little systematic attention is given to the acquisition of communicative competence by young children in the community. Adult-child interactions described in Young 1970 and Stack 1976 provide few data directly relevant to language socialization. Teachers who participated in the study reported here initially held a variety of stereotypes about how black children learned language: black parents don't care about how their children talk; black children don't have adequate exposure to language, because their parents are probably as nonverbal as the kids are at school; black parents don't spend enough time with their children to train them to talk right. All of these views show that teachers thought black children's language socialization was somehow different from that of other children. Yet in their interactions with black children in the classroom, teachers invariably assumed they would respond to language routines and uses of language in building knowledge, skills, and dispositions just as other children did. Some teachers were aware of this paradox, but felt that since they did not know how language was taught in black communities and how it was used to make children aware of the world around them, they had no basis on which to rethink their views of the language socialization of black children. The teachers could only assume these children were taught language and cognitive skills in the same ways they used to teach their own children.

That was not the case for children in Trackton, as examination of the role of questions in their language socialization indicates. Questions addressed by adults to children occurred far less frequently in Trackton than in the homes of teachers. In Trackton, adults were not observed playing peek-a-boo games with young children; thus, a major source of Q-I questions was eliminated. Adults and siblings also did not direct questions to pre-verbal infants; instead, they made statements about them to someone else which conveyed the same information as questions directed by teachers to their children. Trackton adults would say of a crying pre-verbal infant: 'Sump'n's the matter with that child.' The equivalent in the teacher's home would be to direct a question or series of questions to the child: 'What's the matter?' 'Does something hurt you?' 'Are you hungry?' Trackton adults did not attempt to engage children as conversational partners until they were seen as realistic sources of information and competent partners in talk.

It has been suggested that the language used by adults, especially mothers, in speaking to young children has numerous special properties; some of these develop because of the limited range of topics which can be discussed with young children (Shatz and Gelman 1977). In addition, most of the research on mother-child interaction has been done in homes where a single child and a single parent were recorded in their interactions (Brown 1973). In this situation, mothers have no one other than their children to talk to or with, and language interactions with their children may thus be intensified over those which would occur if other conversational partners were consistently present. In Trackton, adults almost always had someone else around to talk to; rarely were mothers or other adults left alone in the home with young children (cf. Young 1970; Ward 1971; Stack 1976). The children did not have to be used as conversational partners; others more knowledgeable and more competent as conversants were available. Children were not excluded from activities of adults or from listening to their conversations on any topic. Trackton parents, unlike teachers with their pre-schoolers, never mentioned the fact that something should not be talked about in the presence of children or that particular words were inappropriate. However, if children used taboo words, they were scolded (cf. Mitchell Kernan's comments in Slobin 1968:15). Young children would often sit on the laps of conversants, at their feet or between them on the sofa, listening. They were rarely addressed directly, however, in an effort to bring them into the conversation. Sometimes they were fondled, their faces and mouths touched, and food offered by community members as well as older siblings. In these cases, the person offering the food would address a comment such as 'Hey, he really goes for these!' to someone else in the room. Questions directed by a teacher to her child in similar situations were: 'Does that taste good, huh!' 'You like that, don't you?'

When weather permitted, the children played on the porch of their home or in the yard within close range of the porch. When intimate associates were present, approximately 10 percent of the utterances conceivably directed to the nearby pre-schoolers were questions, 75 percent imperatives, 10 percent exclamations, and 5 percent statements (cf. Mitchell Kernan's comments in Slobin 1968:12)[4]. However, Trackton children were exposed to a wide variety of individuals other than their family and neighborhood associates. Friends and kin from other areas of the county came and went often, sometimes temporarily taking up residence in Trackton. These frequent visitors to the community would tease the children, challenging them to particular feats or making statements of fact about the children.

You ever gonna learn to ride 'at tractor?

Can you lemme see you go, boy?

Your momma better come change your pants.

I betcha momma don't know you got dat.

Children were not expected to respond verbally, but to do what any command clearly addressed to them called for. Children were more talked 'at' than 'with.'

A wide variety of strangers – utility servicemen, taxi drivers, bill collectors, and the like – came to the community. They usually acknowledged pre-schoolers, addressing questions such as 'What's your name?' 'Anybody home?' 'Are you out here by yourself?' to the children. Most of the time these were met with no verbal responses. Occasionally when older pre-schoolers answered these questions, they would later be chastised by adults of the community. Children learned very early that it was not appropriate to report on the behavior of their intimates to strangers whose purposes in the community were not known. Likewise, outside the community, when non-intimates asked information about the children's family or living arrangements, they usually got no answer. Thus when school or community service personnel asked questions such as 'How many people live in your house?' or 'Doesn't James live on your street?' the children would often not respond and would be judged uncooperative, 'stupid,' or 'pathetic.'

In Trackton, children did not hold high positions as information-givers or question-answerers, especially in response to questions for which adults already knew the answer. When children were asked questions, they were primarily of five types. Table 2 provides a description of the types of questions used with pre-schoolers in Trackton. The various uses noted here do not include all those evidenced in Trackton, but they constitute the major types used by adults to young children. Crucial to the flexibility in the uses of interrogative forms is their embeddedness in particular communication and interpersonal contexts. In the analysis of types, it should be evident that there is a distinction between what some of these interrogatives mean and what the speaker means in uttering them. Another way of stating this is to say that the questioner using each of the types has a conception, perhaps unique to this particular communication context, of what the appropriate response by a pre-schooler to the ques-

TABLE 2   Types of questions asked of children in Trackton

Types	Responses called for	Examples
Analogy	Nonspecific comparison of one item, event, or person with another	What's that like? (referring to a flat tire on a neighbor's car)
Story-starter	Question asking for explanation of events leading to first questioner's question	Question 1: Did you see Maggie's dog yesterday? Question 2: What happened to Maggie's dog?
Accusatory	Either nonverbal response and a lowered head or a story creative enough to take the questioner's attention away from the original infraction	What's that all over your face? Do you know 'bout that big mud-puddle . . .
A-I	Specific information known to addressee, but not to questioner	What do you want? Juice.
Q-I	Specific piece of information known to both questioner and addressee	What's your name, huh? Teeg.

tion asked will be. In other cultures and in other contexts where different age and status relationships might prevail, these question types might not call for the response noted here as appropriate for pre-school children. For example, in a classroom, a teacher asking questions similar to 'What's that like?' very often has in mind as the answer a specific piece of information assumed to be known to both questioner and addressee.

TEACHER (*pointing to a small circle used on a map to depict a city of a certain size*) What does that remind you of?
EXPECTED RESPONSE That set of circles in our book. (*the set of circles talked about in the social studies book in the section on reading maps*)

Teachers often 'answer' questions to themselves as they ask them, and they expect answers from students to conform to those preconceived in the questioner's mind.

It is important to compare these questions with those which called for analogies from Trackton children. These were the closest thing to 'training questions' Trackton adults had for young children. Children were not asked 'What's that?' but 'What's that like?' 'Who's he acting like?'. Requests that children name objects or list discrete features of objects or events, which appeared in teachers' talk to their pre-schoolers, were replaced in Trackton by questions asking for analogical comparisons. Adults seemed to assume children knew how to compare events, objects, and persons. Adults' use of these questions, as well as their frequent use of metaphors in conversations in the presence of children, seem to underscore their assumption that listeners understood similarities and differences.

You know, he's the one who's got a car like the one Doug useta have.

She's got eyes like a hawk.

You jump just like a toadfrog.

Sue sound like some cat got its tail caught in the screen door.

Young children noticed likenesses between objects, and even pre-verbal but mobile children would, on seeing a new object, often go and get another that was similar. Older children also gave great attention to details of objects; this attention was, however, not expressed as questions but as statements: 'That thing on your belt look like that flower in your blouse.' In parallel situations in teachers' homes, their pre-schoolers would say 'Is that flower like that thing on your blouse?' At early ages, Trackton children recognized situations, scenes, personalities, and items which were similar. However, they never volunteered, nor were they asked by adults, to name the attributes which were similar and added up to one thing's being like another. A grandmother playing with her grandson age 2;4 asked him as he fingered crayons in a box: 'Whatcha gonna do with those, huh?' 'Ain't dat [color] like your pants?' She then volunteered to me: 'We don't talk to our chil'un like you folks do; we don't ask 'em 'bout colors, names, 'n things.'

What these speakers meant in asking questions calling for analogical comparisons was very different from what teachers meant in classrooms when they used the same interrogative forms. At home, Trackton children could provide nonspecific comparisons without explanation. Thus, in the classroom, they were likely to respond to questions of 'What's that like?' with answers which seemed to teachers too broad or totally unrelated to the lesson at hand.

TEACHER (*pointing to a new sign to be used in arithmetic*) What was it we said earlier this sign is like?
EXPECTED RESPONSE The mouth of an alligator. (*an explanation used earlier in the day by the teacher*)
TRACKTON STUDENTS RESPONSE Dat thing up on da board. (*The student looks at a bulletin board for social studies which has yarn linking various cities; the yarn forms a shape like the sign*)

Though the gross outlines of the sign's shape have been recognized by the student, he has made the comparison to a temporary and highly specific representation in the room. He has not envisioned the similarity between the open mouth of an alligator (presumably a permanent symbol in the minds of children familiar with this picture from books) and the mathematical symbol. The comparison is valid, but the teacher's response ('Huh? Uh . . ., I guess that's okay') indicated she considered the answer neither as useful nor as relevant as the one proposed in the lesson.

Another type of question used by Trackton residents was a *story-starter*. These questions were addressed to the oldest pre-school children as well as to older children and adults. In situations which called for these, a person knew a story, but wanted an audience to ask for the story. However, there had to be some way of letting the audience know the story was there for the telling. A frequent technique was to ask what was ostensibly an A–I question: 'Didja hear Miss Sally this morning?' The appropriate response to this question was 'Uh-oh, what happened to Miss Sally?' If the respondent (especially an adult) heard the question as an A–I question and replied 'No,' the questioner would say, 'Well, I ain't gonna tell you nut'n.'

Accusatory questions were also used by Trackton residents. Similar in form to story-starters, they occurred more frequently than story-starters with children. In these questions, the adult or older child asked a question which was known by all to be a statement of accusation; the addressee, if guilty, had only two appropriate responses. One of these was to bow the head, say nothing, and wait for the verbal diatribe which was sure to follow. The other was to create a story or word play which would so entertain the questioner that the infraction would be forgotten. In these responses, the child was allowed to shift roles, to step out of a submissive role, to exhibit behavior which for older children would be judged as 'uppity.' One mother exasperated with her son 3;9 years of age, said 'Whadja do with that shoe? You wan me ta tie you up, put you on da railroad track?' The child responded:

> Railroad track
> Train all big 'n black
> On dat track, on dat track, on dat track.
> Ain't no way I can't get back.
> Back from dat track,
> Back from dat train,
> Big'n black, I be back.

All the listeners laughed uproariously at this response, and his mother forgot about the accusation. Older children could use these playful responses to other children or to certain low-status adults in the community, but they dared not do so with high-status adults, either kin or nonkin.

A–I questions were fairly straight-forward, asking the child to express a preference or desire or to give a specific piece of information he was known to have which the questioner either could not or did not have. Q–I questions, so frequent in the homes of teachers, occurred rarely in Trackton. When they occurred, they usually did not have the purpose which dominated teachers' Q–I questions to their own children at home, i.e., requests for confirmation that the children had an objective piece of knowledge (the name of an object, its color, size, use, etc.). In Trackton, Q–I questions were used to confirm subjective knowledge held between the questioner and the addressee. For example, an adult or older child would accost a pre-schooler with 'Whatcha name, huh?' The pre-schooler would be expected to give as an answer the nickname developed in relations between the questioner and the child, not his given name. In providing the appropriate nickname, the child confirmed the special relationship between him and the questioner.

The creativity of children in language use and their awareness of differences in language use were often displayed in situations where they engaged in self-talk. For example, Mandy, a child 4;1 years of age, was observed playing with a mirror and talking into the mirror. She seemed to run through a sequence of actors, exemplifying ways in which each used questions:

How ya doin, Miss Sally?
Ain't so good, how you?
Got no 'plaints. Ben home?

What's *your* name, little girl?
You a pretty little girl.
You talk to me.
Where's yo' momma?
You give her this for me, okay?

When Mandy realized she had been overheard, she said, 'I like to play talk. Sometimes I be me, sometimes somebody else.' I asked who she was this time; she giggled and said, 'You know Miss Sally, but dat other one Mr. Griffin talk.' Mr. Griffin was the insurance salesman who came to the community each week to collect on insurance premiums. Mandy had learned that he used questions in ways different from members of her community, and she could imitate his questions. However, in imitation as in reality, she would not answer his questions or give any indication of reception of the messages Mr. Griffin hoped to leave with her.

In summary, children in Trackton were not viewed as information-givers in their interactions with adults, nor were they considered appropriate conversation partners, and thus they did not learn to act as such. They were not excluded from language participation; their linguistic environment was rich with a variety of styles, speakers, and topics. Language input was, however, not especially constructed for them; in particular, they were not engaged as conversationalists through special types of questions addressed to them. Occurrences of Q–I questions were very rare, and frequently involved a focus by an adult on speech etiquette when individuals outside the intimate circle of regulars were present. For example, pre-schoolers running through the room where a guest was preparing to leave might cause an adult to ask: 'Didja say 'goodbye' to Miss Bessie?' Other question types addressed to pre-schoolers were also used by adults in conversation with other adults and were in no way especially formed for pre-schoolers. The intent and/or expected response to some of the question types, especially analogy, was sometimes special for pre-schoolers. (When analogy questions were addressed to adults, they were generally A–I, and the answerer was expected to provide information the questioner did not have, e.g., 'What's his new car like?') In general, children were expected to learn to respond to questions which asked them to relate to the whole of incidents and composites of characteristics of persons, objects, and events. Pre-schoolers were judged as competent communicators if they learned when and how to use the various responses, both verbal and nonverbal, appropriate for the various question types.

Interrogatives in the Classroom

Questions teachers used in their homes with their own pre-schoolers were very similar to those they and their colleagues used in school with their students. Both of these were different from those used in Trackton. Therefore, children enculturated into competence in responding to adults' questions in Trackton had to acquire new uses in the school. The early nursery-school experiences of Lem, a Trackton 4-year-old, provide one example of the kind of shift which the acquisition of school questioning strategies required.

Before Lem began attending nursery school, he was a very talkative child by community standards. He was the baby of the family and, for several years, the youngest child in the community, and he was on every possible occasion challenged to respond verbally and nonverbally to others in the community. Lem was particularly fascinated by fire trucks, and in the car he would keep up a chain of questions whenever we passed the fire station.

Dere go a fire truck.

Where dat fire truck go?

What dat fire truck do?

What dat dog do at da fire?

Whose dog dat is?

As soon as answers were given to this series of questions, he began asking others about the sources of information which the participants had.

> How da firemen know where dey going?

> How come dat dog know to stay on dat truck?

At age 4;3, Lem began attending nursery school. It was his first experience in an institutional setting away from family and primary associates of the community. The nursery school was a cooperative run by middle-class parents and taught by a woman from a local church. During the first few weeks in school, Lem said almost nothing except when cookies and juice were passed out and he felt he was not getting a fair share. At other times, he watched and listened, showed strong preference for manipulative toys, and had little patience for talk-centered tasks directed by adults. At the end of the first 19 days of nursery school, in the car on the way home, he saw a fire truck. His sequence of questions ran as follows:

> What color dat truck?

> What dat truck?

> What color dat truck?

> What color dat coat?

> What color dat car?

> What color . . .

My response was: 'What do you mean, 'What color is that truck'? You know what color that truck is. What's the matter with you?' Lem broke into laughter in the back seat, realizing his game had been discovered. During the first weeks of school, he had internalized the kinds of questions which occurred in teacher-talk centered tasks, and he was playing 'teacher' with me. In the next few weeks, Lem's game in the car was to ask me the same kinds of questions he had been asked that day in school: 'What color dat?' 'Dat a square?' 'What's dat?'

During those school activities which focused on giving labels to things and naming items and discussing their attributes, Lem did not participate. He listened and often tried to escape these structured sessions to play with trucks, puzzles, and so forth. He had no interest in looking at books and being asked questions about them, and he preferred to be involved in some kind of activity during story-reading time. He enjoyed activities taught to music, and when new activities were taught, he was the first to learn and always showed irritation with the repetitions required for other children to learn. In those learning tasks in which the teacher showed the children how to do things, rather than talked about the things themselves and what one did with them, Lem was enthusiastic and attentive. It is significant that in these tasks, teachers did not ask questions about the things or events themselves, but said instead: 'Can you do that?' 'Let's try it together. Remember the rope goes this way.' (Compare Goody 1977, which discusses cognitive skills in the learning of manipulative tasks and the role of questions in this learning among the Gonja of Africa.) Once Lem began going to school, he had acquired information and had had experiences of which Trackton adults had no knowledge, and many of their questions became information-seeking ones.

Whadja do today?

Didja go anywhere?

Didja have juice?

Lem rarely answered these questions directly, but he volunteered other information he judged relevant.

Mike got dirty pants.

Joey go over de swing, and fall off de top. She cried, and her mamma had to come. Mrs. Mason tol us not to go on dat swing like dat anymore.

If questions were directed to Lem about this incident, he would answer; however, if other unrelated questions were continued, he would act as though he had not heard the questions. Adults did not pursue their questioning, and they soon turned their attention to other matters.

The types of questions Lem faced in nursery school were very similar to those used in the first grades of elementary school. At this level, teachers asked questions of children to become acquainted with their students and to assess their level of knowledge of the world.

What's your name?

Where do you live?

Have you ever seen one of these?

What color's this?

Can you find the apple in the picture?

These are common and seemingly harmless approaches to acquaintance and judgments of ability. However, children from Trackton either did not respond or gave minimal answers. Increasingly after the first few days of school, when most of the questions were centered around teachers' getting to know their students, the questioning shifted to other topics. Colors, numbers, letters, and elements of pictures in books became the foci of questions. A predominant characteristic of these questions was their requirement that students pull the attributes of objects out of context and name them. The stimuli for such questions were often books or picture cards which represented the item in flat line drawings with no contextual background. Among these items, many of the characters (queens, elves, uniformed policemen) and objects (walnuts, sleds, and wands) were unknown in Trackton. Indeed, to Trackton children, their teachers asked foreign questions about foreign objects.

Research on teacher questions has delineated numerous features of their use in the classroom (for surveys of this literature, see Gall 1970 and Hargie 1978). In studies of classroom language the percentage of questions in comparison to other types of utterances is uniformly shown to be high. Moreover, there are special properties of classroom questions and their use in sequences of units of language arranged to produce interaction (cf. Mehan 1978). In extended interactions, questions consume nearly 60 percent of the classroom talk (Resnick 1972).

Questioning in the classrooms by teachers involved in the study reported here fit the general patterns revealed in research in other classrooms. Questions dominated classroom talk; the predominant type of question used in classroom lessons called for feedback of information included in the lesson; questions which asked for analysis, synthesis, or evaluation of lesson data occurred much less frequently and were used predominantly with top-level reading groups. Of particular importance in this study is attention to types of question used in the classroom as compared with the homes of teachers and students.

In the research literature which attempts to classify question types, little attention is given to questions which do not have directly evident educational objectives, i.e., are not recall, analytic, synthetic, or evaluative questions (Bloom 1956; Gall 1970). In the classrooms of this study, questions which regulated behavior, especially with respect to classroom routines and attention to learning skills, emerged as particularly important (Heath 1978). Many questions asked by teachers were interrogative in form but were imperative or declarative in intent. 'Why don't you hang your coat up, Tim?' was intended to be interpreted as 'Hang your coat up, Tim.' 'What's going on here?' was intended to be interpreted as a declarative ('Someone is misbehaving') and a directive ('Stop misbehaving'). The question 'Didja forget again?' was to be interpreted as 'You forgot again.' Teachers used questions with these meanings with their pre-schoolers at home and continued their use at school. Trackton students had relatively little experience with these indirect directives, viewed by teachers as the 'polite way' of controlling the behavior of others. Of the types of questions used in Trackton, the accusatory were closest to these, and neither of the responses used in Trackton (bowing the head or offering a creative answer) was appropriate in the classroom. Trackton students generally ignored these questions and did not alter their behavior until given explicit directives ('Hang your coat up').

In lessons, teachers often asked questions which required confirmation of certain skills necessary to exhibit knowledge. Attention to appropriate stimuli – the person reading, a letter chart, or a specific page of a book – was tested by questions. Teachers used these in extended interactions with single students, small groups, and the entire class. If directed to a specific student, this question type demanded a response, either by display of the skill or by verbal confirmation. If directed to a group of students or the class, these questions were not to be answered, for they were merely forerunners to questions which would require answers.

Can you point to the short *a*? How do we say it?

Do you see the silent *e*? What does that make the vowel?

As might be expected, most of the questions used in lessons were Q–I questions, in which teachers asked for information which both they and often many students in class had. Trackton students were unfamiliar with questions which asked for labels ('What's the name of . . .?') or called for an account of attributes ('How do we know that's a   ?') They usually did not respond or would parrot the answer given immediately preceding the question directed to them. Their communicative competence in responding to questions in their own community had very little positive transfer value to these classrooms.

The learning of language uses in Trackton had not prepared children to cope with three major characteristics of the many questions used in classrooms. First, they had not learned how to respond to utterances which were interrogative in form, but directive in pragmatic function (e.g., 'Why don't you use the one on the back shelf?' = 'Get the one on the back shelf'). Second, Q–I questions which expected students to feed back information already known to the teacher were outside the general experience of Trackton students. Third, they had little or no experience with questions which asked for display of specific skills and content information acquired primarily from a familarity with books and ways of talking about books (e.g., 'Can you find Tim's name?' 'Who will come help Tim find his way home?'). In short, school questions were unfamiliar in their frequency, purposes, and types, and in the domains of content knowledge and skills display they assumed on the part of students.

Intervention: A Two-Way Path

The task of schools is to transmit certain kinds of content and skills, but much of this transmission depends on classroom questions. For Trackton students to succeed academically, therefore, they had to learn to use questions according to the rules of classroom usage. However, intervention did not have to be one-way; teachers could also learn about the rules for community uses of questions. The choice in intervention was therefore not only to change Trackton students, but also to provide an opportunity for alterations in teachers' behaviors and knowledge.

Teachers were dissatisfied with the lack of involvement and the minimal progress of students from Trackton and similar communities. Teachers felt that questions were important to check on pupil learning and students' memory of skills and lessons, and to discover gaps in their knowledge. Yet questions were obviously not working to help teachers achieve these goals. Several agreed to look at the kinds of questions used in Trackton and to incorporate these, when appropriate, into classroom activities. They found that several types of questions used in Trackton could be considered what education textbooks called 'probing questions' (cf. Rosenshine 1971). These were questions which followed questions, and questions designed to compare the knowledge questioner and addressee had about situations. Interrogatives modeled on some of the types used in Trackton were therefore justifiable in terms of good pedagogy. If used in classrooms, they would not only benefit students of low achievement; education research had shown these kinds of questions could benefit students across ability levels.

For some portions of the curriculum, teachers adapted some teaching materials and techniques in accordance with what they had learned about questions in Trackton. For example, in early units on social studies, which taught about 'our community,' teachers began to use photographs of sections of different local communities, public buildings of the town, and scenes from the nearby countryside. Teachers then asked not questions about the identification of specific objects or attributes of the objects in these photographs, but questions such as:

What's happening here?

Have you ever been here?

Tell me what you did when you were there.

What's this like? (pointing to a scene, or an item in a scene)

Responses of children were far different from those given in usual social studies lessons. Trackton children talked, actively and aggressively became involved in the lesson, and offered useful information about their past experiences. For specific lessons, responses of children were taped; after class, teachers then added to the tapes specific questions and statements identifying objects, attributes, and so on. Answers to these questions were provided by children adept at responding to these types of questions. Class members then used these tapes in learning centers. Trackton students were particularly drawn to these, presumably because they could hear themselves in responses similar in type to those used in their own community. In addition, they benefitted from hearing the kinds of questions and answers teachers used when talking about things. On the tapes, they heard appropriate classroom discourse strategies. Learning these strategies from tapes was less threatening than acquiring them in actual classroom activities, where the facility of other students with recall questions enabled them to dominate teacher-student interactions. Gradually, teachers asked specific Trackton students to work with them in preparing recall questions and answers to add to the tapes. Trackton students then began to hear *themselves* in successful classroom responses to questions such as 'What is that?' 'What kind of community helper works there?'

In addition to using the tapes, teachers openly discussed different types of questions with students, and the class talked about the kinds of answers called for by certain questions. For example, *who, when*, and *what* questions could often be answered orally by single words; other kinds of questions were often answered with many words which made up sentences and paragraphs when put in writing.[5]

Tapes and discussions of types of questions were supplemented by photographed scene sequences showing action in progress. *Why* questions were often the focus of these sequences, because both Trackton students and other students were especially tentative about answering these. Inferencing strategies in reading comprehension depended on the ability to answer *why* questions, making them particularly critical to reading success. The photographed scene sequences depicted a series of events, and students would arrange them in order and explain why they had chosen a particular order. For example, in picture A, a girl was riding a bicycle; in picture B, the bicycle was on the ground, the girl nearby frowning and inspecting her knee; in picture C, the only details different from those in A were a bandage on the knee and a broad smile on the girl's face.[6] Because workbook exercises in the primary grades frequently called on the children to arrange pictures and later sentences in the proper sequence, children had to be taught to verbalize the characteristics of phenomena in and of themselves and in their relations with other things in the environment in order to complete workbook tasks. Teachers and students came to talk openly about school being a place where people 'talked a lot about things being about themselves.' Students caught onto the idea that this was a somewhat strange custom, but one which, if learned, led to success in school activities and, perhaps most important, did not threaten their ways of talking about things at home.

The primary rationale behind the research reported here was simple: if change agents (teachers and parents) were willing and involved, knowledge about language use could proceed along a two-way path, from the school to the community, and from the community to the school. Traditionally, education research has emphasized the need to train parents of children who are not successful in school achievement to conform to school practices.

Knowledge had proceeded along a one-way path from school to 'culturally different' communities. In this research the movement of ideas along that path was made two-way, so that a we-they dichotomy did not develop. In the past decade, research has identified standard English structures and patterns of discourse as 'school talk' and non-standard English as 'at-home' talk. Prescriptions derived from this dichotomy have found their way into parent education programs, encouraging early home initiation of children to 'school talk' and school tasks and ways of thinking. There has been a decided we-they dichotomy, emphasizing how 'we' of the school can enrich the background of the 'they' of culturally different communities.

Moreover, remediation of language skills in classrooms traditionally followed the pattern of slowing down the process used for teaching 'average' children, breaking the pieces of work into smaller and smaller units, presenting them repeatedly, and insisting upon mastery of the skills prescribed for each stage before moving on to the next stages. This breakdown of skills, stages, and units emphasized the use of recall questions, Q-I types for those of low achievement and analytic, evaluative, and synthetic questions with the academically successful. Elaboration and analysis of classroom language, habits leading to academic success, and ways of categorizing knowledge about things often led educators to believe these patterns of behaving had to be transferred to home settings of low-achievers before they could succeed in school. No one, either in teacher training programs or in the daily practice of education, seemed able to tap the uses of language and ways of 'talking about things' of the culturally different and to bring these skills into the classroom.

To do so, at least two components were necessary: first, teachers as inquirers and second, credible data from both the classroom and the students' communities. For teachers to be involved in the inquiring process, they had to want to know what and how they and their students learned in language socialization, and they had to take part in collecting the data to answer these questions. In carrying out research on their own families and in their own classrooms – voluntarily and in situations where their job performance was not being evaluated – they acted from their own felt needs. They learned that their own behavior exemplified patterns which were sometimes contrary to their ideals and principles, or, at the very least, unexpected. Taking part in data collection and analysis gave them opportunity to consider how and why data on everyday behavior – their own and that of others – can be useful in bringing about attitude and behavior changes.

Teacher-training activities, whether workshops, graduate courses, or inservice programs, often involve teachers in the inquiry process. Equally necessary, however, in order to bring about change in response to their felt needs, are ethnographic data from their students' communities. Ethnographic data on communities and institutions of the United States can be used in a wide variety of teacher training and curriculum preparation programs. However, such data are rarely available, and of those studies which do exist, many do not provide either the degree or kind of detail and focus on language and learning needed to inform decisions about formal education changes. It is hoped that as anthropologists increasingly turn their attention to the United States, its communities and institutional settings, the ethnographic data needed will become available in formats appropriate for consideration by educators.

Such ethnographic data from communities and schools shared across participants should insure the exchange of information and skills along a two-way path. Ethnographic data which contributed to changes in teaching materials and methods in the classrooms reported here were not collected with the purpose of proving the ways of one group right and another wrong. They were not used to evaluate the practices of teachers. They were not used to prove to school authorities that they should change the ways in which Trackton residents interacted with their children. Data collected by teachers in their own homes and in their classrooms, combined with data from Trackton, led them to ask questions of their own practices and to admit other practices into their interactions which would not necessarily have emerged otherwise. The long period of time over which these data were collected, the large number of people involved, and the openness of communication among groups insured that the ethnographic research was not pressuring change. Innovations and adaptations emerged in the educational process in accordance with felt needs of the teachers.

Notes

1 The materials reported here on Trackton, teachers' homes, and classrooms are based on research conducted between 1970 and 1975 by myself and by my graduate students at Winthrop College. A full ethnography of communication study, containing data on Trackton and a southern Appalachian-oriented community comparable in socioeconomic class, and schools attended by the young of both communities, is in preparation (Heath, 1983).
2 The teachers whose children are cited in the study of questioning at home were all primary-level teachers; all either were teaching in local public schools at the time of the study or had taught in the academic year preceding the study.
3 The questions and answers quoted from adults and children in this paper are represented in standard orthography rather than in phonetic transcription, since our focus is not on pronunciation. Some contractions and other indications of relaxed casual speech are used for the sake of realism, but they are not intended as exact portrayals of speech.
4 Tape recordings were never made in Trackton; all field notes were written either on the scene or immediately after extended stays in the community. Percentages given here are averages based on analysis of field notes recording language use in play

periods approximately two hours in length one day a week for eight months of each year, 1973 to 1975.

5 The teachers whose classroom data are reported here include those involved in the study of questioning at home plus the teacher in the nursery school and three additional teachers at the upper primary grades who were familiar with the results of the home-questioning study.

6 Based on reading materials prepared by Shirley B. Faile, Rock Hill, South Carolina.

References

BARATZ, JOAN, and ROGER SHUY, eds. 1969. *Teaching Black Children to Read*. Washington, D.C.: Center for Applied Linguistics.

BLANK, MARION, 1975. 'Mastering the Intangible Through Language.' In Doris Aaronson and Robert W. Rieber, eds., *Developmental Psycholinguistics and Communication Disorders*. New York: New York Academy of Sciences, 44–58.

BLOOM, B.S., ed. 1956. *Taxonomy of Educational Objectives: Handbook I: Cognitive Domain*. New York: David McKay Co.

BLOUNT, BEN G. 1977. 'Ethnography and Caretaker-child Interaction.' In Catherine E. Snow and Charles A. Ferguson, eds., *Talking to Children: Language Input and Acquisition*. London: Cambridge University Press, 297–308.

BROWN, ROGER. 1973. *A First Language: The Early Stages*. London: George Allen and Unwin.

COOK-GUMPERZ, JENNY. 1973. *Social Control and Socialization: A Study of Class Difference in the Language of Maternal Control*. London: Routledge and Kegan Paul.

CORSARO, WILLIAM A. 1977. 'The Clarification Request as a Feature of Adult Interactive Styles with Young Children.' *Language and Society* 6:183–207.

ERVIN-TRIPP, SUSAN. 1970. 'Discourse Agreement: How Children Answer Questions.' In R. Hayes, ed., *Cognition and Language Learning*. New York: John Wiley and Sons, 79–107.

ERVIN-TRIPP, SUSAN, and WICK MILLER. 1977. 'Early Discourse: Some Questions about Questions.' In Michael Lewis and Leonard A. Rosenblum, eds., *Interaction, Conversation, and the Development of Language*. New York: John Wiley and Sons, 9–25.

GALL, MEREDITH D. 1970. 'The Use of Questions in Teaching.' *Review of Educational Research* 40: 707–720.

GLEASON, J. BERKO. 1973. 'Code Switching in Children's Language.' In T.E. More, ed., *Cognitive Development and the Acquisition of Language*. New York: Academic Press, 159–167.

GLEASON, JEAN B., and SANDRA WEINTRAUB. 1976. 'The Acquisition of Routines in Child Language.' *Language in Society* 5:129–136.

GOODY, ESTHER. 1977. 'Towards a Theory of Questions.' In Esther N. Goody, ed., *Questions and Politeness: Strategies in Social Interaction*. London: Cambridge University Press, 17–43.

HARGIE, OWEN. 1978. 'The Importance of Teacher Questions in the Classroom.' *Educational Research* 20:99–102.

HARKNESS, SARA. 1977. 'Aspects of Social Environment and First Language Acquisition in Rural Africa.' In Catherine E. Snow and Charles A. Ferguson, eds., *Talking to Children: Language Input and Acquisition*. London: Cambridge University Press, 309–318.

HEATH, SHIRLEY BRICE, 1978. *Teacher Talk: Language in the Classroom*. No. 9, Language in Education Series. Washington, D.C.: Center for Applied Linguistics.

HEATH, SHIRLEY BRICE, 1983. *Ways with Words*. Cambridge University Press.

HOLZMAN, M. 1972. 'The Use of Interrogative Forms in the Verbal Interaction of Three Mothers and Their Children.' *Journal of Psycholinguistic Research* 1:311–336.

HOLZMAN, M. 1974. 'The Verbal Environment Provided by Mothers for Their Very Young Children.' *Merrill-Palmer Quarterly* 20:31–42.

HYMES, DELL H. 1962. 'The Ethnography of Speaking.' In T. Gladwin and W.C. Sturtevant, eds., *Anthropology and Human Behavior*. Washington, D.C.: Anthropological Society of Washington, 13–53.

KOCHMAN, THOMAS, ed. 1972. *Rappin' and Stylin' Out*. Urbana: University of Illinois Press.

LABOV, WILLIAM. 1970. *The Study of Non-Standard English*. Champaign, Ill.: National Council of Teachers of English.

LABOV, WILLIAM. 1972. 'The Logic of Nonstandard English.' In *Language in the Inner City*. Philadelphia: University of Pennsylvania, 201–240. (First published 1969).

LABOV, WILLIAM, et al. 1968. *A Study of the Non-Standard English of Negro and Puerto Rican Speakers in New York City*. Report on Cooperative Research Project 3288. New York: Columbia University.

LEVELT, W.J.M. 1975. *What Became of LAD?* Peter de Ridder Publications in Cognition 1. Lisse, Netherlands: Peter de Ridder Press.

MEHAN, HUGH. 1978. 'Structuring School Structure.' *Harvard Educational Review* 48:32–65.

MITCHELL KERNAN, CLAUDIA. 1971. *Language Behavior in a Black Urban Community*. Monograph No. 2 of the Language-Behavior Research Laboratory, Berkeley, CA.

NEWPORT, ELISSA, HENRY GLEITMAN, and LILA R. GLEITMAN. 1977. 'Mother, I'd Rather Do It Myself: Some Effects and Non-Effects of Maternal Speech Style.' In Catherine E. Snow and Charles A. Ferguson, eds., *Talking to Children: Language Input and Acquisition*. London: Cambridge University Press, 109–150.

NINIO, ANAT, and JEROME BRUNER. 1978. 'The Achievement and Antecedents of Labelling.' *Journal of Child Language* 5:1–15.

RESNICK, L. 1972. 'Teacher Behavior in an Informal British Infant School.' *School Review* 81:63–83.

ROSENSHINE, B. 1971. *Teaching Behaviors and Student Achievement*. Slough National Foundation for Education Research.

SACHS, JACQUELINE, ROBERT BROWN, and RAFFAELA ANN SOLERNO. 1976. 'Adults' Speech to Children.' In W. von Raffler Engel and Y. Lebrun, eds., *Baby Talk and Infant Speech*. The Netherlands: Sevets and Zeitlinger, 246–252.

SHATZ, MARILYN, and ROCHEL GELMAN. 1977. 'Beyond Syntax: The Influence of Conversational Constraints on Speech Modifications.' In Catherine E. Snow and Charles A. Ferguson, eds., *Talking to Children: Language Input and Acquisition*. London: Cambridge University Press, 189–198.

SLOBIN, DON J., 1968. 'Questions of Language Development in Cross-Cultural Perspective.' In *The Structure of Linguistic Input to Children*. Working Paper No. 14. Berkeley, CA: Language-Behavior Research Laboratory, 1–25.

SNOW, CATHERINE E. 1977. 'The Development of Conversation Between Mothers and Babies.' *Journal of Child Language* 4:1–22.

SNOW, C., ARLMAN-RUPP, A., HASSING, Y., JOBSE, J., JOOSTEN, J. and VORSTER, J. 1976. 'Mothers' Speech in Three Social Classes.' *Journal of Psycholinguistic Research* 5:1–20.

STACK, CAROL. 1976. *All Our Kin*. New York: Harper and Row.
WARD, MARTHA COONFIELD. 1971. *Them Children: A Study in Language Learning*. New York: Holt, Rinehart and Winston.
WOLFRAM, WALT. 1969. *A Sociolinguistic Description of Detroit Negro Speech*. Urban Language Series, No. 5 Washington, D.C.: Center for Applied Linguistics.
YOUNG, VIRGINA HEYER. 1970. 'Family and Childhood in a Southern Negro Community.' *American Anthropologist* 72:269–288.

Academic Tasks in Classrooms

W. Doyle and K. Carter

In recent years there has been a growing interest in the study of classroom structures, that is, regularized patterns for conducting work and processing information in classroom environments (see, for example, Bossert, 1978; Doyle, 1979b, 1981; Gump, 1969; Hammersley, 1974; Kounin and Gump, 1974; Mehan, 1979; Sinclair and Coulthard, 1975; Soar and Soar, 1979; Yinger, 1982). In this type of inquiry, attention is directed to questions of how events in classrooms are arranged and interrelated in time and space and how organization affects learning.

Most studies of classroom structures have emphasized social dimensions. One particularly active tradition has centered on 'participation structures,' i.e., the organization of turn-taking in group lessons and the ways in which this organization affects access to instructional resources such as teacher attention or opportunities to practice academic skills (see Au, 1980; Mehan, 1979; Philips, 1972). These studies have shown that students need social or interpretive competence to participate successfully in classroom events. A second cluster of studies has emphasized perceptions of and attitudes toward subject matter (see Anderson, 1981; Bloome, 1981; Blumenfeld, Pintrich, Meece, and Wessels, 1982; Davis and McKnight, 1976; Stake and Easley, 1978). These studies have found that teachers' and students' attention in classrooms is often dominated by concerns for maintaining order and finishing assignments. As a result teachers often concentrate on giving directions for completing and handing in work rather than explaining the substance of assignments, and students frequently have little understanding of the meaning or purpose of the work they do (Brophy, 1982; Duffy and McIntyre, 1982).

These investigations have provided important insights into the nature of schooling, but more needs to be known about the academic work students actually accomplish (see Buchmann, 1982; Confrey, 1982) and how that work is affected by classroom events (Erickson, 1982). The field study reported in this article was a preliminary attempt to examine closely the structure of academic work in classrooms.

Conceptual Framework

The study was built around Doyle's (1979a, 1979b, 1980) conceptual framework for integrating the managerial and academic dimensions of classroom life. A central component of this framework is the concept of 'classroom tasks', a concept derived from recent work in cognitive psychology and cognitive anthropology (see Dawes, 1975; Frederiksen, 1972; Laboratory of Comparative Human Cognition, 1978; Rothkopf, 1976). The term 'task' is used to designate the situational structures that organize and direct thought and action. Tasks contain, in other words, the plans for behavior that are embedded in settings (see Barker, 1963), plans that are a central part of cognition for participants in the setting (see Erickson and Shultz, 1981). The study of tasks, then, provides a way to examine how students' thinking about subject matter is ordered by classroom events.

Tasks organize cognition by defining a goal and providing instructions for processing information within a given setting. A task has three elements:

1 *A goal or product*
2 A set of *resources or 'givens'* available in the situation
3 A set of *operations* that can be applied to the resources to reach the goal or generate the product

Students' Tasks

From this perspective, the curriculum consists of a set of academic tasks that students encounter in classrooms. Students are guided in processing information in classrooms, in other words, by the tasks they are required to accomplish with subject matter. They can be asked, for instance, to recognize or reproduce information previously encountered, apply an algorithm to solve problems, recognize transformed versions of information from texts or lectures, or select from among several procedures those which are applicable to a particular type of problem. Each of these tasks represents a different set of information-processing operations as well as a different level of understanding of the content.

Academic tasks are defined by:

1 The requirements for the products students are expected to hand in, such as an expository essay or a test paper

2 The resources available to students while accomplishing work, such as a model of a finished essay supplied by the teacher or fellow students

3 The operations that are to be used to generate the product, such as memorizing a list of words for a test or classifying examples of a concept for a worksheet exercise

Because academic tasks in classrooms are embedded in an evaluation system, they are accomplished under conditions of ambiguity and risk. *Ambiguity* refers to the extent to which a precise and predictable formula for generating a product can be defined. *Risk* refers to the stringency of the evaluation criteria and the likelihood that these criteria can be met on a given occasion. Risk is closely tied to the accountability system in classrooms. If no answers are required or any answer is acceptable, then there is no risk (and probably no task). A task of memorizing 50 lines of poetry is low on ambiguity – one clearly knows what has to be learned – but high in risk because of the factors that might interfere with a successful recitation on a given occasion. Understanding tasks, i.e., tasks which require students to *construct* rather than *reproduce* answers, are high in both ambiguity and risk because the precise answer cannot be fully specified in advance and constructive processes can sometimes be unreliable. It seems reasonable to expect that the actions of teachers and students in managing ambiguity and risk will affect the nature of the academic work that is accomplished.

Available evidence suggests that students spend a large portion of their time in classrooms thinking about how academic tasks can be accomplished (see King, 1980). In addition, students are known to react strongly to changes in the task system. Davis and McKnight (1976) reported that an attempt to change a math class from a task system based on algorithms to one based on alternate ways of conceptualizing problems was met by considerable student resistance. Academic tasks, in other words, provide a central classroom structure that governs student information processing. A description of such tasks should provide, therefore, insight into how the curriculum is realized on a daily basis in classrooms.

Teachers' Tasks

The academic work students accomplish is, from a teacher's perspective, only one dimension of the task of teaching in classrooms. In addition to structuring academic tasks for students and assisting them in accomplishing these tasks, a teacher must create work settings for a group and attend to the monitoring and pacing of group events (see Clark and Yinger, 1979, on teacher thinking). Teachers encounter classrooms as units of time and as groups of students. In addition, there is a general expectation that classroom events appear to have some connection to the recognized outcomes of schooling. These situational factors define the proximal task of teaching as one of *gaining and maintaining cooperation of students in activities that fill class time* (see Doyle, 1979b). The term 'activity' in this context refers to how groups of students are organized for working, e.g., seatwork, small group discussions, lectures, etc. Other key dimensions of activities include duration, the physical space in which the activity occurs, the type and number of students, the props and resources used, and the expected behavior of students and the teachers (see Gump, 1969; Yinger, 1982). Available evidence suggests that classroom order rests in fundamental ways on the activity system the teacher establishes and sustains (see Doyle, 1979a).

Cooperation in an activity depends upon a number of factors, including:

1 The structure of the activity, i.e., the spatial configuration and interdependencies among participants (Kounin and Gump, 1974)

2 The familiarity of the activity to participants (Yinger, 1982)

3 The rule system and management skills of the teacher (Doyle, 1979b; Kounin, 1970)

4 The students' abilities to do the work and their inclinations to participate in classroom events (Campbell, 1974; Metz, 1978)

Every activity, in other words, contains a definition of roles for participants, such as listening, writing, answering, questioning, etc. For an activity to 'work,' at least some students must be willing to participate, i.e., become involved in the activity, and most students must be willing to cooperate, i.e., allow the activity to continue without disruption. If a large number of students do not cooperate in the activity, then public evidence is available to all students present that the teacher lacks classroom management skills. Such evidence has serious consequences for maintaining cooperation in subsequent activities. Achieving cooperation is an expectation students have for teachers (see Nash, 1976). If cooperation is not achieved, misbehavior increases and cooperation can be lost completely (see Doyle, 1979b; Emmer, Evertson, and Anderson, 1980; Gannaway, 1976).

Academic Work and Classroom Activities

Academic work exists in classrooms as a component of the activity system. This feature of classroom life has two consequences. First, the way work is organized can affect the resources available to students for accomplishing tasks. If problem-solving exercises are conducted in small groups, for instance, some students may be able to copy answers generated by other students and thus never engage in problem-solving operations themselves.

Second, academic work is tied fundamentally to processes of classroom management. If a large proportion of students in a class are unable or unwilling to do the assigned work, then the activity system will eventually break down and order will be lost. Teachers, in turn, may attempt to achieve cooperation in difficult circumstances by adjusting task demands. One strategy for making such adjustments involves reducing risk for answering by accepting all answers as correct (see MacLure and French, 1978). Another involves extensive teacher prompting so that every student can answer correctly (see MacKay, 1978), a technique Lundgren (1977) has called 'piloting.'

The study reported here was focused precisely on the convergence of teachers' and students' classroom tasks and the delicate balances that need to be achieved to sustain academic work in classroom settings. Such an analysis was seen as a useful way to learn more about the nature of the academic work students accomplish and how that work is shaped by classroom events.

Nature of the Study

The study consisted of an intensive case analysis of the academic tasks accomplished in two average-ability English classes (designated A1 and A2) and one high-ability (or honors) English class in a junior high school in a middle-class suburban district in a large metropolitan area in the south-west. All three classes were taught by the same teacher, referred to here as Ms. Dee. Designations of ability levels were based on the school district's tracking system in which the highest and lowest ability students (approximately the top 5% and the bottom 5%) within a school building were placed in separate homogeneous classes. The remaining students were assigned to average-ability classes.

Selection of a teacher for the study was based on two major considerations. First, special attention was given to writing because of its distinctive properties as an academic task. Composing text is often a difficult operation for many students and precise rules for generating compositions are not easy to specify. In McPhersons's (1977) words: 'Good writing is neither mechanical nor formulaic, and thus there can be no absolute formula for producing it' (p. 187). It was anticipated, therefore, that writing tasks would be problematic for both teachers and students and that a description of such tasks would yield rich insights into the processes associated with accomplishing academic work under classroom conditions. Second, emphasis was placed on effective classroom management to increase the chances that a functioning academic task system could be observed in the classes. Previous research, consistent with the conceptual framework of the study, indicated that academic work was often pushed aside in poorly managed classes (see Emmer, Evertson, and Anderson, 1980). The investigators wished to avoid a situation in which establishing and maintaining order was the central pre-occupation of the teacher.

Ms. Dee was nominated for the study by the school district's curriculum coordinator in English. Ms. Dee was described as an effective manager with a reputation for emphasizing the teaching of writing. She had 26 years of experience, participated actively in in-service programs in writing, and conducted workshops for teachers in the region. It seemed likely, therefore, that a variety of writing tasks would be attempted in these classes.

The study was presented to Ms. Dee as an investigation of the assignments students do in English classes. She was told that the study would involve a large amount of observation as well as the inspection of students' work. Finally, she was asked to give a general overview of the assignments she planned to make during the observation period.

Data Gathering

Thirty-three observations were conducted in each class between December 3, 1979, and February 29, 1980. Doyle was the observer for one of the average-ability classes (designated here as A1), and Carter was the observer for the high-ability class and the second average-ability class (A2). Each observation was conducted for a full class period (55 minutes) and consisted of a running account in narrative form of events occurring during the session. For the first two and one half weeks of the study, classes were observed daily. After this initial period, observations were conducted twice each week. In addition, the investigators examined samples of student work and copies of assignment sheets, handouts, and tests. Finally, the investigators talked informally with Ms. Dee on a regular basis to clarify assignments and other information related to academic tasks.

The immediate practical problem of observation was to devise a way to describe academic tasks in the classes. This problem was solved by focusing observations on the products students handed in to the teacher for a summative grade, e.g., paragraphs, worksheets, exercises, tests, and the like. During observations, the investigators paid special attention to instances in which work was handed in or graded and to information potentially contributing to the accomplishment of this work, e.g., directions for assignments, remarks that students were to write something down for later use, etc. Attention was also given to the prompts, resources, and formulae available to students while they were working on assignments and to what students did to manage the nature and quality of requirements. Finally, the observers kept time logs so that events could be analyzed for duration and sequence and made general estimates of student engagement.

The investigators worked closely together prior to conducting observations to develop a common descriptive language. A formal reliability analysis was not conducted because observations were not made simultaneously in the same classes. However, a comparison at the level of specific task descriptions, which were written independently, showed a high degree of agreement between observers.

Analysis

The analysis reported here is based primarily on the 15 observations made in each class during the first two and one half weeks of the study, i.e., December 3 to December 19. This period was selected for primary attention because it was found that a daily record was needed for monitoring tasks. When observations after the Christmas holidays were made only twice a week, considerable information about specific tasks was lost. These later observations were used primarily for estimating the general stability of patterns related to task systems in the classes.

The analysis of observational data consisted of going through the narrative records to identify occasions when tasks were completed and to trace the events leading up to them. Two steps were involved in this process. First, the general events that took place for each class session were listed and occasions when products were handed in were noted. For example, on 12/10/79 the session in class A1 was devoted to:

1 Preparation for vocabulary test 2
2 Work on a two-paragraph assignment; handed in
3 Introduction to the short story, *Mateo Falcone*

Second, each completed assignment was extracted from the list, given a brief title, and described in terms of the number of sessions devoted to introducing or working on the assignment and the estimated amount of classroom time spent on the assignment. For example, the assignment completed on 12/10/79 in class A1 was described as follows:

> *Title*: Two-paragraph assignment comparing Christmas in Capote's story, *A Christmas Memory*, with Christmas today.
> *Sessions*: 3 (12/6/79; 12/7/79; 12/10/79).
> *Estimated time*: 105 minutes.

Once all completed assignments (whether they consisted of writing or not) had been identified and briefly characterized, they were sorted into three categories:

> 1 Major assignments, i.e., those that were specifically designated by the teacher as major (e.g., worth 1/4 of the grade for the term or used more than 10% of the total class time)

2 Minor assignments, consisting of one-day assignments and quizzes
3 Exercises, consisting of brief assignments (ten to 12 minutes) for part
of a daily grade.

See Table 1 for a listing of academic tasks accomplished in class A1 from
12/3/79 to 12/19/79.

The next step in the analysis consisted of writing more complete descriptions of the major tasks and selected minor tasks. The topics for these more thorough descriptions were:

1 The assignment, i.e., a description of requirements stated by the teacher for the final product and any changes that occurred in these requirements during the time spent working on the assignment;
2 Time spent introducing the assignment, getting started to work, and actually working on the assignment in class;
3 Prompts and resources given by the teacher or otherwise available to the students during class sessions;
4 Accountability, i.e., how the teacher talked about grading during class sessions and how the assignment was actually graded after it was handed in;
5 A general description of how the task was accomplished by the teacher and students with special attention to duration, sequence, changes in task requirements, and student engagement.

These task descriptions were then used to identify general patterns asso-

TABLE 1   Academic tasks accomplished in Class A1 from 12/3/79
to 12/19/79

Tasks	Date handed in	Sessions	Time
Major tasks			
1 Two-paragraph assignment comparing Christmas in Capote's story *A Christmas Memory* with Christmas today	12/10/79	3 (12/6, 12/7, 12/10)[a]	105 minutes: 20% of total task time[b]
2 Short story report on a story not read in class	12/17/79	3 (12/3, 12/12, 12/14)	87 minutes: 16% of task time
3 Six descriptive paragraphs with illustrations	12/19/79	4 (12/3, 12/12, 12/17, 12/18)	84 minutes: 16% of task time

Minor tasks

4 Descriptive paragraph based on the story *A Christmas Memory*	12/5/79	2 (12/4, 12/5)	40 minutes: 7% of task time
5 Revision of paragraph based on the story *Flower for Algernon*	12/4/79	(Revisions done for homework)	None during observation period
6 Vocabulary test	12/7/79	3 (12/3, 12/6, 12/7)	30 minutes: 5% of task time
7 True-false test on *A Christmas Memory*	12/5/79	1 (12/5)	8 minutes: 1% of task time
8 Word study combined with a paragraph of reason based on the short story *Mateo Falcone*	12/11/79	1 (12/11)	26 minutes: 5% of task time
9 Vocabulary test combined with a paragraph to compare two things	12/17/79	2 (12/10, 12/17)	51 minutes: 9% of task time
10 Grammar exercise on clauses	12/13/79	1 (12/13)	40 minutes: 7% of task time

Exercises

11 Journal writing	12/6/79	1 (12/6)	10 minutes: 2% of task time
12 Paraphrase of two quotations	12/13/79	1 (12/13)	13 minutes: 2% of task time
13 Literature notes on Poe presentation	12/19/79	1 (12/19)	39 minutes: 5% of task time
14 Two sentences on why people enjoy being terrified	12/19/79	1 (12/19)	13 minutes: 2% of task time

[a] Refers to the number of sessions in which some time was spent either introducing the task or actually working on it.
[b] Refers to the total time spent introducing the task and working on it. All times are approximate.

ciated with the academic tasks accomplished in Ms. Dee's classes. The results
of this analysis form the content of the present report.

Results

During the two and one half weeks of continuous observation, 14 academic
tasks were accomplished in each of the three classes (see Table 1). The
teacher placed considerable emphasis on writing during this period. Each
class session contained either an introduction to a writing assignment or
actual writing time. Moreover, of the 14 academic tasks accomplished, ten
involved some form of composing, ranging from paraphrasing a quotation
to writing six descriptive paragraphs and illustrating them with drawings or
pictures taken from magazines. In addition to emphasizing writing, Ms. Dee
was, as expected, an efficient and businesslike classroom manager. During
the observation period, there were no serious student disruptions and very
few incidents of minor inappropriate behavior. In other words, student
misbehavior was never a serious threat to academic work in these classes.

There was a remarkable similarity in the task systems across the classes.
The only major difference was in the amount of work sometimes required of
students in the high-ability class. For example, Ms. Dee doubled the number
of weekly vocabulary words and typically doubled the number of specified
grammar elements included in writing assignments for the high-ability class.
At a general structural level, however, the same tasks were introduced in all
three classes, little variation was noted in the time allocated to tasks, and
similar problems were encountered in installing and managing tasks. The
analysis was directed, therefore, to common patterns across the three classes
and differences are noted as necessary to clarify task dimensions.

General Features

Ms. Dee was very careful and thorough in explaining assignments. Although
she sometimes became frustrated by requests to repeat directions, she
usually tried to clarify requirements and to assist students in getting their
work done. She also reminded students frequently that she was available
after school for extra help.

Accountability for work was a prevalent feature of the classes. The
teacher frequently talked about grades and the importance of getting good
grades, even when giving examples to illustrate grammar rules or concepts in
literature. Students received a daily grade in addition to test grades and
grades on major projects. For some assignments, specific portions of the term
grade were indicated: vocabulary work and a descriptive paragraph assign-

ment were worth 1/4 of the grade for the six-week term. Assignments were typically graded and returned the next day, and every assignment returned was to be corrected by the students and placed in folders that were checked periodically by the teacher.

Accountability was affected by an elaborate point system. Points could be earned for volunteering to answer 'bonus' questions in class and these points could be allocated by students to assignments of their own choice. In addition, if the local professional football team won their game that week, all students received bonus points equal to the team's score. Bonus points could not be used to substitute for incomplete parts of assignments but could be used to compensate for mistakes. Finally, Ms. Dee sometimes made 'progress checks' in which students' work was inspected to see if they were getting as much done as expected. Points could be lost for insufficient progress.

In sum, Ms. Dee was a lively and energetic teacher who emphasized writing and who kept student attention focused on academic tasks and their accomplishment.

Character of Major Tasks

There were three major academic tasks accomplished during the observation period, accounting for approximately 1/2 of the class time devoted to academic work. All three tasks involved writing. In order of occurrence, these tasks were:

> 1 A two-paragraph assignment comparing Christmas as depicted in the story, *A Christmas Memory*, with Christmas now, handed in on 12/10/79
> 2 A report on a short story not read in class, handed in on 12/17/79
> 3 A collection of six descriptive paragraphs with illustrations, handed in on 12/19/79

Task 1

The first major task was a two-paragraph writing assignment. For this assignment students were to write two paragraphs, the first showing similarities between Christmas as depicted in Truman Capote's short story, *A Christmas Memory*, and Christmas today and the second showing differences. In the average-ability classes, *five* active verbs were to be used and underlined in the two paragraphs, each paragraph was to contain *one* compound sentence that was to be underlined, and transition words were to be circled. In the high-ability class, the teacher required *two* compound sentences per paragraph and told students not to circle transition words.

The content of the assignment consisted, then, of facts about Christmas as presented in the story and Christmas today, with specified grammar elements, and the operations to be performed on that content consisted of writing a comparison and a contrast between these two versions of Christmas and designating the grammar elements.

Portions of three sessions were allocated to this task. The task was introduced on Thursday, December 6, and students were given time in class to write first drafts to be handed in for grading at the end of the period. In her introduction, Ms. Dee described the nature of the assignment, discussed the meaning of comparison and contrast, offered several bonus point questions, and promised ten bonus points for a 'creative' title. In addition, she suggested several possible comparisons and contrasts and gave an example on the chalkboard of an introduction to the first paragraph, although students were told not to copy this example for their first paragraphs. The transition to actual work time on the assignment was slow as students asked Ms. Dee to repeat part or all of the assignment. These questions persisted as students began to work and Ms. Dee began to rove around the room to comment about the students' work.

The next day, Ms. Dee redistributed drafts with her corrections to the students. She indicated to the class that she had not graded their work because it was their first attempt to write a two-paragraph assignment. After a brief introduction, she gave students time to revise their paragraphs. During work time, students continued to ask questions about the assignment, and the teacher actively inspected and commented on papers. Papers were handed in at the end of the session for final grading. On Monday, December 10, however, the teacher returned the paragraphs without grades. She told the students that they would be working on a two-paragraph assignment over the next several weeks and directed them to revise this one again with a particular focus on the specified grammar elements and her labeling requirements. With her instructions, she handed out a model she had written of the assignment and a list of common errors made by the students.

Especially on the first two days of this task, students' questions about requirements and procedures were quite frequent during work time. In class A1, for example, 11 public questions about the assignment were asked during work time on the first day, and 12 such questions were asked on the second day. By the third day the teacher's instructions were very explicit, and the time necessary for getting started was very short and only a few private questions about the assignment were asked. The teacher often refused, particularly on the first day, to repeat information which had just been given. Directions were repeated for the total group as part of the initial presentation and later if the contact was fairly private. But public questions, especially by students who tended not to pay attention and frequently asked for information to be repeated, were often ignored. This strategy was not always successful, however, because the students often became louder in their requests for information or turned to fellow students for answers. On such occasions, the teacher was required to attend to student conduct and the activity system became difficult to manage.

Ms. Dee provided a large number of prompts for accomplishing this task, and these prompts became increasingly explicit over the three sessions devoted to this assignment. The teacher provided feedback on two occasions and offered numerous suggestions for possible similarities and differences in ways of celebrating Christmas, including a model of two paragraphs she had written. In addition, during public interactions with students, suggestions frequently became requirements and general rules were often narrowed to precise directions. For example, on December 7 in class A2, Ms. Dee responded to a student's question concerning paragraph length by saying:

> Forget about how many sentences. I will not accept a two sentence paragraph, for heaven's sake, nor will I accept 12 to 15. Hit a happy medium. Five is a good number.

The accountability system for this task was complex and the teacher adjusted it several times during the course of working on the task. On the first day, students were told that their rough drafts would be graded for content and mechanics. First drafts were not graded, however, and the 'final' copies turned in on the second day were then returned for another revision before a grade was assigned. In addition, the accountability system contained a surplus of bonus credit to bolster final grades. Bonus points could be earned for answering questions during discussions of the assignment on all three days, and an extra ten points could be earned for a 'creative' title. The teacher also reminded students several times of the bonus points available from the winning score of the local professional football team. Finally, it can be noted that in all three classes the content grade was consistently higher than the mechanics grade.

Ms. Dee's comments to the classes and to the observers indicated that she was dissatisfied with the final products of this task and thought that the students were probably not ready yet for a two-paragraph writing assignment. (A two-paragraph assignment was achieved later in the year – on 1/23/80 – by the use of a sentence-combining exercise in which clusters of simple sentences were given on the board, and the students were required to combine sentences within clusters to form sentences that were arranged into two paragraphs. This assignment was quite successful but required a minimum of composing energy on the part of the students.)

Task 2

The second major task also involved writing: a report on a short story not read in class. Areas to be covered in the analysis were: (a) point of view; (b) tone; (c) plot structure; (d) characterization methods; and (e) theme. They were to include the following grammar elements: (a) five compound sentences; (b) one compound subject, verb, direct object, predicate nominative, predicate adjective, objective of a preposition; and (c) five transition words to be circled. The final product was to contain five paragraphs, the last paragraph being a conclusion paragraph pulling together the major points of the analysis.

A brief description of this task was given on December 3 in the average-ability classes and on December 10 in the high-ability class as advanced warning related to their grades for the trimester. On December 12, the assignment was explained in detail to all three classes and the teacher placed special emphasis on the importance of this assignment for their grades. Directions were very explicit and examples were numerous. In addition, the teacher commented that this was the last short story report, so presumably most of the requirements had been explained before. Throughout the explanation of this task, the teacher exhorted students to take notes because she would not repeat the information, but few students appeared to follow this suggestion. Finally, the teacher suggested that students should have a rough copy of their assignment with them when they came to class on December 14, the session set aside for writing the final copy of the report.

On December 14, Ms. Dee reviewed requirements once again (although only briefly in the high-ability class) and gave students the remaining class time to write. As work began, several students asked questions about requirements and procedures. Although Ms. Dee attempted to hold to her promise not to repeat the directions and requirements, she yielded when students were not working or turned to each other for assistance. Students persisted with public questions and also solicited the teacher's help privately at her desk or podium. When she repeated instructions for one student, several others followed up with additional questions. In the end, the teacher repeated instructions several times during the start-up period and during seatwork. After class the teacher commented that it was difficult to enforce the rule of not repeating directions. Finally, Ms. Dee spent the last 20 minutes checking papers and suggesting corrections before they were handed in, and she extended the deadline to include the weekend for them to finish their reports.

The teacher's original accountability proposals described on December 12 also did not endure. Inspection of the grade book indicated that these reports received a check mark, a minus sign, or a zero but that no letter or numerical grades were recorded. In other words, the final product was not actually graded but simply checked in if students completed it.

Task 3

The final major task consisted of a set of descriptive paragraphs, each with its own illustration designed by the student. Students in the average-ability classes were to have *six* descriptive paragraphs, three based on ideas from the journals that they regularly kept. In the high-ability class, *12* paragraphs were required, six which were derived from in-class short story readings, and six which could be traced to journal entries. (In the average-ability classes, it was possible to do 12 paragraphs for extra credit, but only six were required.) For the paragraphs based on stories, persons and places were to be emphasized, and each paragraph in the collection was to have a title which showed 'originality'. Each of the paragraphs, together with matching illustrations, were to be placed in a new folder, the cover of which also was to be decorated by the student. Those students 'not artistically blessed' could use magazine illustrations supplied by the teacher. Construction paper, tape, and scissors were also supplied for the students during work periods. Students were not required to label grammar elements. However, active verbs were to be used in the paragraphs rather than linking verbs. Students were also admonished against using cliches, contractions, informal expressions, and such phrases as 'there are' and 'I think' or 'I feel.' In addition to these requirements, very explicit directions were given for the coversheet, the table of contents, and each page containing a descriptive paragraph. Similarly, explicit directions were given for mounting illustrations.

In all three classes, portions of three days were allocated to defining this assignment. During the introductory sessions, Ms. Dee explicitly detailed requirements by referring to characters and scenes in short stories, which would easily lend themselves to description, by quoting descriptive events from her own journal, by providing students with an example of a descriptive paragraph that she had written after reading *So Much Unfairness of Things*, and by drawing on the chalkboard a chart of the content and sequence of the pages to be included in the final product. She also emphasized that this assignment was worth 1/4 of their grade for the trimester.

December 18 was identified as the day that would be devoted entirely to working on this task. The pattern of working on this assignment was similar to that observed in conjunction with the other major tasks. The period opened with a review of the requirements for the assignment, and Ms. Dee attempted to resist repeating directions already given but gave several explicit suggestions about how to get a high grade. The students took several minutes to get started working on the paragraphs, and during this time numerous questions were asked concerning requirements and procedures. Questions persisted during the work session as the teacher went around to check their progress. Ms. Dee was especially active in monitoring work on this task and frequently commented publicly and privately about mistakes that were being made. In particular, she emphasized that their paragraphs were to be descriptive rather than expository. At the end of the period students were allowed to consult with one another to check finished products, and the teacher inspected students' work and gave corrective feedback before it was handed in. Finally, several opportunities to earn bonus points were provided, and the teacher reminded students that 35 points were available from the winning score of the local professional football team.

Even with bonus points, Ms. Dee later commented to the investigators that she was not pleased with students' grades for this assignment. An inspection of the papers revealed that most paragraphs were expository rather than descriptive and that most of the teacher's comments centered on the quality of the illustrations and the mechanics of the assignment.

Summary

The major assignments, all of which involved writing, seemed to follow a pattern of lengthy explanations, relatively long transitions from explanations to actual working on the assignment, and frequent student questions during transitions and working times. In addition, prompting was extensive over the several class sessions devoted to each major task, and directions often became increasingly explicit as the students requested that the teacher re-explain the assignment. In other words, the activities during class sessions devoted to working on these tasks did not run smoothly and required extensive teacher energy and action for successful management. Finally, few students actually met all the requirements of the task, and the teacher was not satisfied with the performance of the class as a whole.

Minor Tasks

Minor Writing Tasks

Two minor writing tasks that occurred during the first three weeks of observation serve as usful comparisons to highlight the special features of the major tasks. Both of these minor tasks involved one-paragraph assignments and were combined with vocabulary exercises.

On December 11, the first of these tasks was introduced and completed within a single class session. Students were asked to write a 'paragraph of reason' in conjunction with a word-study exercise that followed the text of the short story, *Mateo Falcone*. The paragraph of reason consisted of defending a sentence written on the chalkboard: 'According to the code of Corsican peasants, Mateo Falcone was justified in shooting his son'. The word-study portion of the assignment involved choosing the correct word from a two-response choice of vocabulary words located at the end of the story. Students in all three classes were given a full period to complete the assignment and most finished early.

In contrast to the major tasks, this assignment was accomplished with relative ease. For one thing, students could do the word-study section efficiently. In addition, the instructions for the writing portion of the assignment could be encapsulated into a formula. The teacher's directions to the high-ability class illustrate this feature of the task:

> You are writing a paragraph of reason . . . Now you're basing your comments on the selection. Begin with a transition of time or enumeration in this case. 'First . . .' then first reason, then 'Second . . .,' then put your second reason, etc. Then you've got any number of transitions to show your conclusion like 'consequently,' etc. (12/11/79, high-ability class).

With this formula available, students could begin work quickly and in all three classes they did. Student questions and call outs were infrequent in comparison to writing sessions for major tasks, and the teacher's monitoring was less obvious and vigilant.

A second minor assignment also involved paragraph writing and was joined to the weekly vocabulary test, a routine event in the classes. For the writing part of this assignment, students were asked to write a paragraph in which they compared two things. The topic and length were left up to the students. The activity went smoothly and students began work soon after the teacher's explanation. In addition, nearly all students accomplished the assignment successfully and grades were relatively high (the average grade in class A1, for example, was *B*+). It appeared that the established routine of a weekly vocabulary test served to delay and reduce the total number of student questions about the writing assignment and to mitigate the problems of student resistance to task involvement.

Grammar Tasks

In general, grammar tasks observed over the course of the study were characterized by a similar expediency. On December 11, for example, Ms. Dee introduced adjective clauses and dictated 10 main clauses while the students wrote an adjective clause to complete each sentence. By the end of the period she had secured products from students that showed a high level of proficiency.

Journal Writing

In comparison to major tasks, journal writing tasks, which received only minor emphasis in calculating student's grades, were especially easy to accomplish in the classes. Introductions for journal writing occasions were brief and transitions to work were almost immediate. In addition, no questions about the requirements for the assignment were asked during the work period. Two factors probably affected the smoothness of this activity. First, journal writing was an established routine in this class, and such routines typically operate with ease and are resistant to disruptions (see Yinger, 1982). Second, the grading was based solely on content rather than grammar and the actual grades were very high. (Indeed, content grades for all writing tasks were typically high.) It was likely, therefore, that students could succeed on this task.

Summary

Minor tasks, i.e., tasks that carried only a small amount of 'weight' in the grading system of the classes, were typically accomplished within a single class period. In addition, minor tasks were usually accomplished with recurring and routinized procedures or, in the case of the two short writing assignments, in close association with familiar assignments. Finally, minor tasks were accomplished efficiently: instructions were explicit, few students asked questions about content or procedures, and most students were successful in doing the work accurately. It is important to note, however, that minor tasks were *algorithmic*. That is, minor tasks could normally be accomplished by using a standardized and reliable formula or routine.

Discussion

The patterns of academic work identified in this study would seem especially useful for understanding tasks that require students to exercise higher-level cognitive processes, i.e., to construct products by assembling information and making executive level decisions about its use, rather than by simply reproducing information seen previously or applying a reliable formula to a set of problems to generate answers. In the classes studied, higher-level tasks (i.e., the major writing tasks) were unstable. When first introduced, these tasks were given an important place in the accountability system. In addition, the teacher defined the tasks initially to provide many openings for students to exercise judgment and express their own ideas and impressions.

There was, in other words, a degree of intentional ambiguity built in to writing assignments to allow students to practise composing processes. As work on the assignments progressed, however, there was a clear drift toward greater explicitness and specificity concerning the nature of the final products and a narrowing of the range of judgments students were required to make on their own. In other words, the teacher gradually did an increasing amount of work for the students by clarifying and specifying the features of an acceptable product. Furthermore, accountability was softened through the use of bonus points, the extension of time to finish the work, and the generous awarding of credit for content of paragraphs. In the end, the tasks that were accomplished were substantially different from the tasks that were announced.

The pattern for minor tasks, which typically involved clearly defined and reliable algorithms for generating products, were quite different. In the case of grammar tasks, instructions were brief and explicit, few questions were asked to clarify work requirements, accountability was strict, and the task definition remained stable throughout the work session. Similarly, minor writing assignments that were attached to routinized vocabulary exercises were conducted efficiently and were characterized by a high degree of specificity and stability. Journal writing exercises also ran smoothly but in this instance accountability was quite loose. Any answer was acceptable as long as the student tried to write.

The processes through which the transformation of higher-level tasks occurred were themselves interesting. In essence, drift toward greater specificity was affected by students in both direct and indirect ways. Students influenced task demands directly by asking public and private questions about content and procedures. In some instances, especially in the high-ability class, students would offer guesses or provisional answers to elicit clarifying reactions from the teacher. Although only a few students typically asked most of the questions, they were quite persistent, and all students were able to benefit from the teacher's answers. Students consistently sought, in other words, to reduce ambiguity and risk by clarifying task demands and obtaining feedback concerning the quality of their provisional writing efforts.

Indirect pressure on the task system was created by slowing down the pace of classroom events. Students were slow to begin working on the major writing tasks, and transitions and working periods were frequently punctuated by questions. The teacher typically responded to this slow pace by providing suggestions and repeating instructions. The teacher often warned students that information would not be repeated and occasionally became impatient with students who appeared to be inattentive. However, her refusal to answer students' questions only slowed the pace even further and gave students a public excuse for not working. Moreover, some students became quite adamant in their demands for clarity, and others turned to their classmates for help. On such occasions, order began to break down and the normal smoothness and momentum of the classes were restored only when the teacher provided the prompts and resources the students were requesting. The teacher was pushed, in other words, to choose between preserving conditions for students' self-direction and preserving order in the classroom. In most instances she reduced ambiguity to establish or sustain work involvement.

At least two additional factors contributed to the transformation that occurred in major writing tasks. First, these tasks typically took several days to introduce and to accomplish. Thus, there were many opportunities for students to elicit information about how the task could be accomplished. Second, the tasks were clearly quite difficult for many of the students. As a result, getting started and working independently were not easy. In addition, the final products for many students fell below the standards outlined by the teacher during her initial presentations. The teacher responded to this performance deficit by offering bonus points, giving feedback and additional opportunities to complete the assignments, and using generous grading policies for the content of writing assignments. It appeared, in other words, that the teacher reduced risk in order to encourage students to continue working on writing tasks. Grades for grammar elements and mechanics (spelling and punctuation) were typically lower, but these areas were easier to define explicitly. It is interesting to note that students often appeared to be more concerned about clarifying grammar elements than with eliciting suggestions about content. They apparently were aware of the differential weight assigned to grammar on writing assignments.

In the end, the teacher's efforts to have students engaged independently in the composing process met with only limited success. This outcome was not attributable to deficiencies in general management skills or to a lack of enthusiasm for writing instruction. The teacher was well organized and efficient and devoted considerable energy to designing writing assignments, providing background and definitions for topics and themes, and explaining how tasks were to be accomplished. Indeed, she was selected for the study precisely because she had demonstrated these attributes in the past. The difficulty stemmed, rather, from tension within writing assignments between the teacher's emphasis on latitude for exercising composing skills and the students' concern for guidance and predictability in an evaluative situation. As the teacher pushed for independence and the students pushed for specificity, the precarious balance of forces within the work setting was threatened. The various efforts of the teacher to encourage students to attempt writing assignments and to keep order and momentum in the work setting eventually led to fundamental changes in the nature of the composing tasks students accomplished.

The results of this analysis raise important questions about the realization of higher-level curriculum objectives in classroom environments. Are workplace tensions inherent in the use of tasks that require students to exercise judgment rather than simply to reproduce information or apply reliable algorithms? Do teachers' attempts to resolve these tensions actually short circuit students' higher-level processing of curriculum content? Do teachers circumvent these tensions by excluding higher-level tasks during planning or by treating them as algorithmic tasks? What can be done to help teachers translate curriculum into workable task systems and develop the skills necessary to manage the social contingencies that shape how these tasks are ultimately experienced by students?

One of the central contributions of the present study would seem to be the development of a language with which to describe curriculum dimensions of the teaching process, an area that has often been neglected in research on general teacher characteristics and behaviors. The development of this language beyond its present rudimentary stage should not only promote inquiry into the curriculum in classrooms but also establish a foundation for building practical knowledge about managing academic work.

Notes

Data gathering for this study was supported in part by a grant from the North Texas State University Organized Research Fund. Support to the senior author during the writing of this report provided in part by the National Institute of Education Contract OB-NIE 80-0116, P2, Classroom Organization and Effective Teaching-Project. The opinions expressed herein do not necessarily reflect the position or policy of the NIE and no official endorsement by that office should be inferred.

References

ANDERSON, L.M. *Student responses to seatwork: Implications for the study of students' cognitive processing*. Paper presented at the annual meeting of the American Educational Research Association, Los Angeles, April 1981.

AU, K.H. Participation structures in a reading lesson with Hawaiian children: Analysis of a culturally appropriate instructional event. *Anthropology and Education Quarterly*, 11 (1980): 91–115.

BARKER, R.G. On the nature of the environment. *Journal of Social Issues*, 21 (1963): 17–38.

BLOOME, D. *Reading and writing in a classroom: A sociolinguistic ethnography*. Paper presented at the annual meeting of the American Educational Research Association, Los Angeles, April 1981.

BLUMENFELD, P.C., PINTRICH, P.R., MEECE, J., and WESSELS, K. The formation and role of self-perceptions of ability in elementary classrooms. *Elementary School Journal*, 82 (1982): 400–420.

BOSSERT, S.T. *Activity structures and student outcomes*. Paper prepared for the

National Institute of Education Conference on School Organization and Effects, January 1978.

BROPHY, J.E. How teachers influence what is taught and learned in classrooms. *Elementary School Journal*, 83 (1982): 1–13.

BUCHMANN, M. The flight away from content in teacher education and teaching. *Journal of Curriculum Studies*, 14 (1982): 61–68.

CAMPBELL, J.R. Can a teacher really make a difference? *School Science and Mathematics*, 74 (1974): 657–666.

CLARK, C.M., and YINGER, R.J. Teachers' thinking. In *Research on teaching: Concepts, findings, and implications*. Edited by P.L. Peterson and H.J. Walberg, Berkeley: McCutchan Publishing Corporation, 1979.

CONFREY, J. Content and pedagogy in secondary schools. *Journal of Teacher Education*, 33(1) (1982): 13–16.

DAVIS, R.B., and MCKNIGHT, C. Conceptual, heuristic, and S-algorithmic approaches in mathematics teaching. *Journal of Children's Mathematical Behavior*, 1(Supplement 1) (1976): 271–286.

DAWES, R.M. The mind, the model, and the task. In *Cognitive theory* (Vol. 1). Edited by F. Restle, R.M. Shifrin, N.J. Castellan, H.R. Lindman, and D.B. Pisoni. Hillsdale, New Jersey: Lawrence Erlbaum Associates, 1975.

DOYLE, W. Making managerial decisions in classrooms. In *Classroom management*. 78th yearbook of the National Society for the Study of Education, Part 2. Edited by D.L. Duke. Chicago: University of Chicago Press, 1979. (a)

DOYLE, W. *The tasks of teaching and learning in classrooms* (R&D Rep No. 4103). Austin: The Research and Development Center for Teacher Education, University of Texas at Austin, 1979. (b)

DOYLE, W. *Student mediating responses in teaching effectiveness* (Final Rep., NIE-G-76-0099). Denton, Texas: North Texas State University, 1980.

DOYLE, W. Research on classroom contexts. *Journal of Teacher Education*, 32(6) (1981): 3–6.

DUFFY, G.G., and MCINTYRE, L.D. Naturalistic study of instructional assistance in primary grade reading. *Elementary School Journal*, 82 (1982): 14–23.

EMMER, E., EVERTSON, C., and ANDERSON, L. Effective classroom management at the beginning of the school year. *Elementary School Journal*, 80(5) (1980): 219–231.

ERICKSON, F. Classroom discourse as improvisation: Relationships between academic task structure and social participation structure in lessons. In *Communicating in the classroom*. Edited by L.C. Wilkinson. New York: Academic Press, 1982.

ERICKSON, F., and SHULTZ, J. When is a context? Some issues and methods in the analysis of social competence. In *Ethnography and language in educational settings*. Edited by J.L. Green and C. Wallat. Norwood, New Jersey: Ablex, 1981.

FREDERIKSEN, C.H. Effects of task-induced cognitive operations on comprehension and memory processes. In *Language comprehension and the acquisition of knowledge*. Edited by J.B. Carroll and R.O. Freedle. Washington, D.C.: V.H. Winston, 1972.

GANNAWAY, H. Making sense of school. In *Explorations in classroom observation*. Edited by M. Stubbs and S. Delamont. London: John Wiley, 1976.

GUMP, P.V. Intra-setting analysis: The third grade classroom as a special but instructive case. In *Naturalistic viewpoints in psychological research*. Edited by E.P. Willems and H.L. Raush. New York: Holt, Rinehart and Winston, 1969.

HAMMERSLEY, M. The organization of pupil participation. *Sociological Review*, 1 (1974): 355–367.

KING, L.H. *Student thought processes and the expectancy effect* (Research Rep. No. 80-1-8). Edmonton, Alberta: Centre for Research in Teaching, University of Alberta, 1980.

KOUNIN, J.S. *Discipline and group management in classrooms*. New York: Holt, Rinehart and Winston, 1970.

KOUNIN, J.S., and GUMP, P.V. Signal systems of lesson settings and the task-related behavior of pre-school children. *Journal of Educational Psychology*, 66 (1974): 554–562.

LABORATORY OF COMPARATIVE HUMAN COGNITION. Cognition as a residual category in anthropology. In *Annual review of anthropology* (Vol. 7). Edited by B.J. Siegel, A.R. Beals, and S.A. Tyler. Palo Alto, California: Annual Reviews, Inc., 1978.

LUNDGREN, U.P. *Model analysis of pedogogical processes*. Stockholm, Sweden: Department of Educational Research, Stockholm Institute of Education, 1977.

MACKAY, R. How teachers know: A case of epistemological conflict. *Sociology of Education*, 51 (1978): 177–187.

MACLURE, M., and FRENCH, P. Routes to right answers: On pupils' strategies for answering teachers' questions. In *Pupil Strategies*. Edited by P. Woods. London: Croom Helm 1980.

MCPHERSON, E. Composition. In *The teaching of English*. 76th yearbook of the National Society for the Study of Education, Part 1. Edited by J.R. Squire. Chicago: University of Chicago Press, 1977.

MEHAN, H. *Learning lessons: Social organization in a classroom*. Cambridge, Mass.: Harvard University Press, 1979.

METZ, M.H. *Classrooms and corridors: The crisis of authority in desegregated secondary schools*. Berkeley: University of California Press, 1978.

NASH, R. Pupils' expectations of their teachers. In *Explorations in classroom observations*. Edited by M. Stubbs and S. Delamont. London: John Wiley, 1976.

PHILIPS, S.U. Participant structures and communicative competence: Warm Springs children in community and classroom. In *Functions of language in the classroom*. Edited by C.B. Cazden, V.P. John, and D. Hymes. New York: Teachers College Press, 1972.

ROTHKOPF, E.Z. Writing to teach and reading to learn: A perspective on the psychology of written instruction. In *The psychology of teaching method*. 75th yearbook of the National Society for the Study of Education, Part 1. Edited by N.L. Gage. Chicago: University of Chicago Press, 1976.

SINCLAIR, J., and COULTHARD, M. *Towards an analysis of discourse: The language of teachers and pupils*. London: Oxford University Press, 1975.

SOAR, R.S., and SOAR, R.M. Emotional climate and management. In *Research on teaching*. Edited by P.L. Peterson and H.J. Walberg. Berkeley, CA: McCutchan, 1979.

STAKE, R.E., and EASLEY, J.A., Jr. *Case studies in science education* (Volumes I and II). Urbana, Illinois: Center for Instructional Research and Curriculum Evaluation and Committee on Culture and Cognition. The University of Illinois at Urbana-Champagne, 1978.

YINGER, R.J. A study of teaching planning. In *Focus on teaching*. Edited by W. Doyle and T. Good. Chicago: University of Chicago Press, 1982.

PART THREE
Teacher Typifications and Expectations

Research into Teachers' Expectations and Their Effects

C. Rogers

The social world in which each of us lives is marked by great complexity and variety. All of us interact at various times with people whose behaviour differs markedly from each other. The behaviour of any one person with whom we interact will vary, perhaps considerably, as time passes and the interactions move from one situation to another. If we entered each of these interactions with no idea at all as to what was to happen then the reasonably smooth social interactions that most of us enjoy most of the time would be rare events indeed.

Typically we enter into interactions with others with a variety of expectations as to what will happen. These expectations make it possible for us to predict the behaviour of other people and, in turn, to make appropriate adjustments to our own behaviour. These expectations will have a variety of sources which can be classified under two broad headings. First, expectations deriving from things which we believe to be true about certain individual people. We might expect a particular acquaintance to be difficult to talk to as we know them to be shy. Second, expectations are derived from the social settings themselves and the roles occupied by people within them and can be applied to the people we interact with within those settings even though we may know nothing about them personally. A judge in court is expected to behave in a sober manner and a car salesman to speak highly of the cars in his show-room. Such expectations are so thoroughly learned that we typically only notice them if they are disconfirmed. It is the car salesman who refers to one of his models as 'a rusty heap' that we remember [. . .]

Given that we are generally unaware of the expectations that we hold for

159

others, it follows that we would not typically check the truth or falsity of these expectations before putting them to use in predicting and interpreting the behaviour of other people. It may well be the case then that we will enter into social interactions with other people taking with us expectations for their behaviour that are actually false. If this happens though, surely we would quickly notice that the expectations with which we have started were incorrect and begin to amend them in the light of experience?

Often this will indeed be the case, but not always. In our interactions with other people we respond not so much to what the other person does but to the interpretation that we place upon it, the meaning that we attribute to it. The behaviour itself may be perfectly clearly perceived but its interpretation may be ambiguous. The teacher observes her class and notices that one pupil has put down his pen and is gazing out of the window. What she has seen is perfectly clear, but what does she make of it? The pupil could have finished the work set and be quietly waiting for further instructions. He could be carefully thinking over a problem he has encountered in his work and still be actually working hard or he could have decided that the work was either too difficult or too boring (or both!) and started to day-dream over his favourite pop star or girl-friend. If the teacher knew absolutely nothing of the pupil, or his class, she would be unable to select any of these or other interpretations as being more probable than any of the others. Rarely, though, would this be the case. Teachers will know their pupils, if not through their own past dealings with them, then by reputation. The interpretation placed upon the behaviour of the pupil will be influenced by the teacher's expectations [. . .]

The Self-fulfilling Prophecy

In 1968 Rosenthal and Jacobson published their book, *Pygmalion in the Classroom.* Like the more recent *Teaching Styles and Pupil Progress* (Bennett, 1976) and *Fifteen Thousand Hours* (Rutter *et al.*, 1979), this book quickly captured the attention and often the imagination of its readers. Robert Hutchins, writing in the *San Francisco Chronicle*, 11 August 1968, was not atypical in writing the following: 'Here may lie the explanation of the effects of socio-economic status on schooling. Teachers of a higher socio-economic status expect pupils of a lower socio-economic status to fail.' The clear implication was that these expectations of teachers of 'higher socio-economic status' were in some way actually responsible for the lack of success experienced by some pupils, and the success enjoyed by others.

This claim regarding the nature of the causal relationship between teachers' expectations for the success or otherwise of an individual pupil and the actual level of attainment experienced by that pupil lies at the heart of the continuing debate over the 'teacher-expectancy effect'.

It has been established (e.g. Dusek and O'Connell, 1973) that teachers will sometimes be able to predict the future level of performance of their pupils. That the expectations of teachers for their pupils should correlate with their pupils' performance is fairly unremarkable and for the most part non-controversial. A good teacher, like a good horse-racing tipster, should be able to make reasonably good predictions on the basis of their expert knowledge of the performance capabilities of their subjects. But while the good horse-racing tipster will be admired for an ability to predict accurately the outcome of races, should it be suspected that the tipster's predictions are actually having a causal effect on the outcome of the race the reaction of the horse-racing public would be quite different. Exactly the same applies to teachers. If a teacher were quite unable to tell us which of her pupils was currently performing well and which poorly, and if she were quite unable to predict future levels of performance, we could well consider this sufficient ground for casting doubt upon her level of professional competence. But quite different considerations would apply if the expectations of the teacher were believed to be actually determining levels of performance amongst her pupils. It is the latter case that has become known as the teacher-expectancy effect.

In order then to demonstrate the existence of a teacher-expectancy effect at least two things have to be established. First, that teachers' predictions or expectations are reasonably accurate. Second, that this accuracy is not simply due to the predictive powers of the teacher, but due rather to these predictions having a causal effect on actual pupil performance.

The first condition can be fairly readily investigated. All one has to do is measure expectations or predictions at various points in the school year and then correlate these with measures of actual performance at various later points in the school year. High positive correlation, especially if found in a number of studies over different types of school populations, would show that the pupils expected to do well by their teachers actually did so and that those expected to do badly actually did badly – and that is all that it will show!

It is not always clearly appreciated by readers of social science that causality cannot be directly and simply inferred from correlational data. Many events may be correlated but not be in any way causally related. If each morning both the postman and the milkman called at your home you could keep a record of times of arrival and analyse these data to see if these times are correlated. A high positive correlation would show that if the postman arrived early so too would the milkman, and if the postman was late so too would be the milkman. It is clear in this case that this does not demonstrate that something about the postman's behaviour is causally determining the behaviour of the milkman. In this instance the claim that one regular caller at your front door is determining the behaviour of another is not 'obviously' correct and so we would immediately call for further evidence to substantiate such a claim before being prepared to accept it.

It the case of teacher expectation and pupil performance the claim that these two variables are causally related is, to many, extremely plausible and the demands for further substantiating evidence have perhaps not always been as clear and as emphatic as they should have been. But what type of further evidence could be made available? For many social psychologists the answer to this question has been clear – experimental evidence.

Let us briefly return to the postman and milkman. One way of determining the truth or falsity of the claim that the behaviour of one determines the behaviour of the other is to intervene experimentally in the situation. If you intercept the postman one morning before he had reached your house, you would be experimentally controlling one of the variables you were interested in – the time of arrival of the postman. The second variable, the time of the milkman's arrival, would still be free to vary. If the postman did determine the milkman's behaviour, then your experimental intervention should have an effect on the milkman – he will be very late completing his round. If there was no direct causal relationship then the milkman's time of arrival would be unaffected.

This, in essence, was the strategy adopted by Rosenthal and Jacobson (1968). They attempted to control experimentally the expectations of teachers so as to be able to assess more directly the effects these expectations had on pupils' levels of performance.

Pygmalion in the Classroom

Interventionist methodologies of the type discussed above had already served Rosenthal well in his earlier research into 'experimenter effects' (the way in which an experimenter's expectations can actually affect the results obtained in various types of psychological research – see Rosenthal, 1966) and it seemed only reasonable to adopt them when switching the focus of attention to educational matters.

The Californian school chosen for the study (referred to as 'Oak School' in the report) was duly visited and pupils were assessed on Flanagan's Test of General Ability (TOGA), a test purporting to measure 'basic learning ability'. The test was selected as one that would be previously unknown to the twenty schoolteachers (two of whom were male) to be included in the study and was presented to them as the Harvard Test of Inflected Acquisition. The results of this test, or so the teachers were told, would enable the researchers to pick out the 20 per cent of the schoolchildren who would be likely to 'bloom' or 'spurt' during the coming academic year. The teachers then were led to expect these top 20 per cent to improve more than the rest of their pupils. In fact, the researchers had selected the 20 per cent entirely at random – there was no reason to believe that they would perform any differently from the others, unless the teachers' expectations brought this about.

Just one year after the initial testing had taken place, and eight months after the teachers had been supplied with the information about the potential bloomers, the children were retested on TOGA. An additional retest was conducted after a further year had passed. What is of interest, then, are the relative gains made by the children identified as bloomers and those not so identified, the controls.

Over the first year the control children gained on average, 8 IQ points while the bloomers gained 12, the difference between the two being statistically significant. However, when the results were analysed by grade level it was only the youngest children (those in first and second grade, aged about 6–8 years) who demonstrated the expectancy effect (i.e. bloomers showing significantly greater gains in IQ than controls).

As well as using the apparently objective data provided by TOGA, Rosenthal and Jacobson also obtained various ratings from the teachers concerning the pupils' academic performance and details of their more general behaviour. It is interesting to note at this stage that while these results show that the teachers have rated the two groups of children differently in some respects, they were unable to recall which particular children had been earlier identified as bloomers.

For the ratings of academic performance only one of the eleven school subjects considered revealed a significant difference between bloomers and controls. Teachers maintained that the bloomers had performed better in reading. The significance of this, however, is enhanced by the knowledge that the children were assigned to tracks (or top, middle, or bottom streams) primarily on the basis of teachers' assessments of reading ability. At the end of the year, but not at the beginning, teachers also rated their pupils on a number of behavioural criteria. Bloomers were considered significantly more curious, interesting, appealing and happy, to have a greater chance of future success and to be less in need of approval.

Rosenthal and Jacobson report more detailed results, looking independently at boys and girls, older and younger, and more and less able children, and the ethnic origins of the child (primarily Mexican and others), but these need not be of concern (here). What should be already clear from the results referred to above is that the effect apparently found by Rosenthal and Jacobson was by no means applicable across the board. For example, by the end of the first year only the two youngest age groups showed an expectancy advantage, while after the retest conducted two years after the initial testing only fifth graders showed an expectancy advantage.

In spite of this, the immediate reactions seem to have been swift and clear. Researchers had apparently provided hard evidence to show that teachers' expectations had determined levels of pupil performance. While obvious ethical considerations had restricted these experimentally induced expectations to positive ones (the children identified as bloomers would improve in the future), the implication was clearly drawn that teachers' negative expectations would similarly depress pupils' performance.

A more critical reaction to the study was not long in coming. The majority of these criticisms concerned alleged weaknesses in the design and analysis of the Oak School experiment. The interested reader can see an excellent collection of these critical and detailed reviews in Elashoff and Snow (1971).[1] [. . .]

Replications of Rosenthal and Jacobson

Most of the research studies carried out into teacher-expectancy effects have not been strictly speaking replications of the original Pygmalion study. As the limitations of the original study became more widely appreciated so later researchers attempted to ensure that their own studies avoided these particular pitfalls. It has also been the case that other researchers have been interested in particular parts of the expectancy process and have accordingly carried out research studies with somewhat different foci of attention from that found in Pygmalion [. . .] (Here) attention will be limited to those studies that have sought to directly test forms of the hypothesis that teachers' expectations of their pupils will affect their own behaviour and in turn the behaviour of their pupils so as to bring into effect their initial expectation.

These studies can be classified along two different bipolar dimensions. First, one can differentiate between studies that have investigated possible workings of the expectancy effect within the classrooms in which the teachers themselves work, and those which create a new, and usually controlled environment for the teacher to work in (although it can be noted at this point that studies of this latter type have also frequently used people other than real teachers and pupils). The former group then can be referred to as classroom studies and the latter as analogue studies as they involve the use of specially created analogues of real classrooms.

The second dimension that can be used to classify teacher-expectancy studies makes reference to the nature of the expectations that are at the centre of the investigations. Rosenthal and Jacobson created artificial expectancies for the teachers in their study by supplying them with false information regarding the potential of some pupils. It will be remembered that this was done so as to enable the researchers to make statements concerning the causal connection between expectations and performance. If the expectations induced by the researchers were determined on a random basis, then any relationship that may have developed between expectation and pupil performance could not have been due to the pupils' earlier levels of performance giving rise to the expectations. In spite of this, however, other researchers, as we will be seeing below, have argued that such artificially induced expectations can tell us little, if anything, about the effects of the expectations that teachers form for themselves as they go about the job of teaching pupils. Induced-naturalistic expectations form the second dimension.

Four main types of study can therefore be identified. Classroom studies using induced expectations, analogue studies using induced expectations, classroom studies using naturalistic expectations and analogue studies using naturalistic expectations. This final type of study has only very rarely been used and will not feature prominently in the following discussion. The original Pygmalion study is an example of a classroom study using induced expectations and the most direct replications of Rosenthal and Jacobson will also be therefore of this type.

Classroom Studies Using Induced Expectations

One of the best known and most frequently cited classroom studies using induced expectations, following Pygmalion, is that reported by Claiborn (1969). Claiborn followed essentially the same strategy as Rosenthal and Jacobson. He attempted to induce expectations in some teachers by telling them that the TOGA scores indicated that certain of their first-grade pupils were potential bloomers, and then tested the children at a later stage to see if these expectations had had an effect upon the children's IQ scores. They did not. Claiborn could find no significant differences between experimental and control groups. However, his study differed from Pygmalion in a number of important ways.

The expectations in Pygmalion had been induced at the beginning of the school year, before teachers had had much direct experience of the children for themselves. This would have meant that for the youngest children (and it was here the significant expectancy effects were mainly found) the induced expectations would be less likely to have to compete with any other already established expectations of the teachers for those children. In Claiborn's study the expectations were induced one month into the second semester (half) of the school year. Teachers would therefore have already had plenty of time to form their own expectations for each child in their class, and, perhaps, be more likely to disregard the information provided by the researcher. Further, Claiborn's study was only two months in duration. The induced expectations were not given very long to operate. In Rosenthal and Jacobson's study, measurement of IQ taken halfway through the one-year experimental period revealed no significant expectancy effects for over-all IQ scores.

Claiborn's study also differed from Pygmalion in that he obtained observational data in addition to pre- and post-experimental period IQ data. This observational data was collected to test the hypothesis that teachers' behaviour towards bloomers would differ from that towards non-bloomers. No such differences were found.

Another often quoted expectancy study is that reported by Fleming and Anttonen (1971). Fleming and Anttonen's study, as Claiborn's, differs from the original Pygmalion in a number of ways. The final sample of 1,087 second-grade (7- to 8-year-olds, approximately) pupils were drawn from their total of twenty-two schools, half of which were classified as being comprised of predominantly middle-class pupils and half predominantly of pupils of lower socio-economic status. The authors took care to ensure that their own expectations did not affect the results obtained (an accusation often levelled at Rosenthal and Jacobson) by delivering their instructions and collecting their data through an intermediary blind to the true purpose of the study.

The purported intention of the study was to compare the effectiveness of various types of intelligence test in predicting school performance. At the beginning of the school year the teachers received data of various kinds relating to the measured intelligence levels of 75 per cent of their pupils and no data on the remaining 25 per cent. In actuality, four different types of data were presented. Just 50 per cent of the pupils, randomly selected like all the others, had their true intelligence levels reported to teachers but these were equally divided between two different tests which resulted in scores of a different type but with essentially similar implications. For a further 25 per cent no information was passed on, while the final 25 per cent had their true IQ scores inflated by sixteen points before the data were made available to teachers. This information was given to teachers at the beginning of the school year and pupils were tested for IQ and attainment between five and eight months later. Over an extensive range of measures, including objective attainment tests and the grades awarded in different school subjects by teachers, no systematic effects were found related to the various types of information supplied to the teachers [. . .]

While their own attempted manipulations of teachers' expectations failed to have any effect Fleming and Anttonen did find that those teachers who had a positive attitude towards the usefulness of IQ data produced more and greater improvements in both IQ and attainment than did those teachers who had a low opinion of the usefulness of such data.

In evaluating this study and comparing its results with those reported by Rosenthal and Jacobson (1968), the differences between the two studies need to be kept carefully in mind. Remember, first of all, that while the Pygmalion study only used one school covering a low socio-economic status area, the Fleming and Anttonen study employed twenty-two schools covering a range of pupil social-class backgrounds. This could be argued to give the latter study a greater amount of generalisability and therefore be the more significant of the two. While both studies allowed approximately an equal period of time for the created expectancies to have an effect, Fleming and Anttonen gave a 'weaker' form of expectancy inducing information. Whereas Rosenthal and Jacobson had specified certain pupils as bloomers (and by implication had labelled the others as plain ordinary), Fleming and Anttonen simply gave intelligence scores relating to 75 per cent of the pupils, one-third of which had been inflated. Teachers did not have their attention drawn to these latter pupils. In order to accept that differential expectancies had been established, one has to assume that the teachers would be sufficiently attuned to the full meaning of the intelligence score and capable of adjusting their expectations on the basis of this type of data. Although the inflated IQ scores were increased by the equivalent of one standard deviation (sixteen IQ points) on the test involved, it is still quite possible that many of those pupils with inflated IQs would still appear to have lower IQs than the more intelligent of those pupils with 'accurate IQs'. In other words, the inflated IQ group in Fleming and Anttonen's study had not been identified as having any particular, as yet, undeveloped potential as strongly as had been the case with Rosenthal and Jacobson's bloomers. Regrettably, Fleming and Anttonen made no attempt to check (independently of their search for an expectancy effect) the success of their attempt to manipulate teachers' expectations. Admittedly, Rosenthal and Jacobson had only done this by asking if teachers could recall the bloomers' names one year after having been given them – and had found that they could not.

A further study by José and Cody (1971) arrived at a similar conclusion to that of Fleming and Anttonen. José and Cody kept close to Rosenthal and Jacobson's design but limited the experimental period to seventeen weeks and added classroom observation designed to assess the interactions (both verbal and non-verbal) that took place between teachers and pupils. Only children in grades one and two were studied. No expectancy effects were found either with respect to intelligence scores, attainment scores or to data obtained from the observational study. Although it is not clear here exactly when the induced expectations were 'planted', the authors do speak of the teachers having prior expectations.

Not all studies in this category, those conducted in the classroom but with artificially induced expectations, fail to support Rosenthal and Jacobson. Meichenbaum, Bowers and Ross (1969) identified six adolescent girls (out of fourteen) in a training school for young offenders. All four teachers of these girls were given the expectation that the six would bloom. As the study only covered a five-week period the focus of attention was on the nature of teacher-pupil interaction rather than on intelligence or attainment gains. However, gains of the latter type were found to be greater for the bloomers than for the controls (but only on objective tests, not on subjective ones) and these may have been related to the changes observed in the teacher-pupil interactions. The quality of interaction overall did not seem to be affected but there was a net shift towards more positive interactions with the bloomers. Some teachers obtained this by increasing the positive contacts, while another decreased negative ones (one teacher in contradiction to this general trend decreased positive contacts with the bloomers). Due to the atypical nature of the school used for this piece of research, however, the impact of these findings is necessarily limited.

On balance, findings from studies that have used essentially the same basic design as Pygmalion have failed to support the original claim – that teachers' expectations have the power to become self-fulfilling and actually alter the behaviour and performance of pupils. However, all of the studies mentioned above have weaknesses in design, analysis or reporting that make clear interpretation very difficult. Many factors vary between the studies also. Age and social-class background of the pupils, type and number of schools, type and number of teachers involved, time of onset and duration of the study and the type of information given to teachers in experimenters' attempts to induce the expectancies. Any one, or any combination of these factors, could be having a critical influence on the operation (or non-operation) of an expectancy effect. In a study conducted in already established classrooms where only so much disruption by researchers can be tolerated by teachers and school administrators, full control over all these factors will only very rarely be possible.

In order to try and simplify matters some investigators had moved away from the original grand scale of Rosenthal and Jacobson's study and have carried out smaller scale pieces of research with less ambitious aims. These are the analogue studies as classified above.

Analogue Studies of the Expectancy Effect

The studies to be discussed below are representative of studies that have employed a number of different designs and techniques. The one similarity is that they have all attempted to set up analogue models of full-scale classroom, in whole or in part, and to investigate within this simplified context certain aspects of teacher and pupil behaviour. These studies have typically employed induced expectations.

An extreme form of an analogue design is illustrated by studies by Cooper

(1979) and Finn (1972). In both cases 'teacher' and 'pupils' never came into contact with each other. Cooper conducted his research in the context of contemporary concern about the effects of the record cards that most schools keep on their pupils. If such record cards establish expectations in the teachers regarding the pupils' future performance, and these expectations acquire self-fulfilling properties, then the child who begins her school career badly may rapidly be condemned to continue it in a similar vein. Cooper did not undertake to investigate this possibility by studying the actual effects of real record cards in real schools, but instead established an analogue situation. One advantage of such an approach is that exact control can be exerted over the detail included in the expectancy inducing information (the analogue school-record cards in this case) and over other aspects of interactions that may take place. One disadvantage is that one cannot know whether or not any effects found in the analogue study would take place in the real school settings.

Just 100 university students were used as 'teachers' (the majority of which Cooper assumes to have had either an intention to become a teacher or actual teaching experience) and each of them was given a booklet of information on a hypothetical junior-school pupil. This booklet was worked through section by section by the 'teacher' (from now on to be referred to more accurately as the subject). First, the subject received information about the child's ability (high, average, or low) from one of a number of sources ranging from those rated as relatively inaccurate (the child's physical characteristics) to the relatively accurate (objective test results). These subjects then predicted their pupil's performance on a spelling test and indicated the extent to which they believed their own expectation to be accurate. Further information was then provided giving details of actual performances by the child on reading tests and subjects were again asked to indicate their expectations and the accuracy they attributed to these.

Cooper's results showed that these subjects did indeed form differential expectations on the basis of the information supplied to them and in addition that they did not moderate expectations for either very good or very bad performance when these were based on information from less accurate sources. Further, he demonstrated that these initial expectations continued to have an effect, although not a direct simple one, on the later expectations based on an illustration of actual performance.

Finn (1972) used real teachers in his study, drawn from urban and suburban schools. Like Cooper, however, he only exposed these teachers to information about the pupils and not to the pupils themselves. Finn's teachers assessed essays that they believed to have been written by pupils who were either black or white, male or female, and of high or low IQ and attainment. While in the suburban schools essays were rated regardless of race, sex or ability information, this was not true for the urban teachers who gave higher scores to essays supposedly written by the 'better' pupils. This difference between urban and suburban teachers alerts us to the fact that teachers are different and that the expectancy effect, given that it operates at all, may well not operate in the same ways for all teachers in all schools. Further illustrations of differences of this type are given below.

In studies like Rosenthal and Jacobson's in which attempts are made by researchers to induce expectations and to measure the effects of these on pupils' performance, ethical considerations require the induced expectations always to be positive in direction and predicted effect. That is, it is generally considered to be ethically acceptable to select a child randomly and label her as a potential bloomer, but unethical to label the child randomly as a 'wilter' – a child whose performance will show a relative decline over the coming year. As the most worrying consequences of the teacher-expectancy effect in real life are concerned with cases where a teacher's negative expectancies may stunt a pupil's educational development, such an ethical limitation is a serious one.

Under analogue conditions, however, the same ethical problems do not necessarily arise. Studies can be designed in which the actual life chances of individuals are left quite unaffected by the study. Mason (1973) conducted such an analogue study. Here teachers observed video recordings of individual pupils taking a test after the teachers had been primed with either positive, negative or neutral reports on the child. Teachers were asked to watch carefully for any errors the child might make on the test and then to predict end-of-year performance. The results clearly indicated that the negative reports had a greater effect than either the positive or neutral ones in influencing the teachers' predictions [. . .] Mason's study alerts us to the possibility of negative expectations having a greater effect than the positive ones usually investigated in experimental classroom studies.

Other analogue studies have established both negative and positive expectations in teachers who then actually come into contact with the pupils to whom the expectations relate. Two such studies (Rothbart, Dalfen and Barrett, 1971; Rubovits and Maehr, 1971) were concerned with investigating the effects of teacher expectations on the actual interactions that took place between teacher and pupils. Rosenthal and Jacobson have suggested that the effects of teacher expectations on pupil performance will be mediated by the quality, rather than the quantity, of the teacher-pupil interactions that take place. Both Rothbart and Rubovits and Maehr tested this suggestion by having undergraduate students lead discussions with groups of four school pupils, two of whom they expected to be bright and two relatively dull, pupils actually having been randomly allocated to these two groups.

Rubovits and Maehr found that over the 40- to 60-minute sessions, their 'teachers' made significantly more requests of the 'brighter' pupils and praised them more often, but the total amount of attention received by the two groups was essentially the same. Rothbart's study produced somewhat different results in that here 'teachers' did not differ in the extent to which they provided positive and negative reinforcement to the bright and dull pupils but did give more attention to bright students who in turn talked more during the discussion session. This last point is of potential significance as it illustrates how a teacher's initial expectations can quickly set off a chain of events that lead to their fulfilment.

Neither of these studies, however, provides data on what was actually learnt by the pupils; indeed neither involved any instruction on the part of the teacher at all. In a further form of an analogue study Beez (1968) investigated just this.

Beez had sixty graduate students (some of whom had teaching experience) teach the meanings of a series of pictorial signs. Each teacher worked with one 5- to 6-year-old pupil and had a faked psychological report to read on the child beforehand. In the report the child, who in each case was a participant in a Head Start programme, was either described as being of normal intelligence and, due to various personality characteristics, expected to benefit from Head Start participation, or described as being of 'low average' intelligence, and having characteristics that would make school adjustment difficult.

The results were clear enough. Teachers of 'high-ability' children attempted to teach nearly twice the number of signs as the teachers of the 'low-ability' children. High-ability children also learned a significantly greater number of signs with 77 per cent of the high-ability group learning five or more signs compared to only 13 per cent of the low-ability pupils. High-ability children were also rated by their teachers as being more intelligent, more socially competent and having a high level of attainment.

Under conditions of one-to-one contact for a strictly limited period of time, and no prior contact between teacher and pupil, Beez supplies data that show a dramatic expectancy effect. It is worth noting at this stage that the expectancy inducing information supplied to teachers included not only IQ data but data regarding the children's behavioural characteristics as well. The 'high-ability' children were described as being open and friendly, smiling readily, being well motivated and so on. 'Low-ability' children were described as being carelessly dressed, unresponsive and sulky. Studies discussed at a later stage will also indicate the importance of such 'social' expectancies, particularly for children in this age range (5 to 6 years).

Over all, the analogue studies show clear effects of induced expectancies. However, for the most part these studies are limited to demonstrating that the behaviour of teachers, or people 'role-playing' teachers will differ according to the expectations they might have for their pupils. Only a very limited number of studies (e.g. Beez, 1968) have shown that the pupils' learning is also affected. Analogue designs are potentially useful in that they enable careful control to be exercised over specific variables. However, by the same token they are limited to demonstrating that these variables may have a potential effect upon the behaviour of teachers and pupils in real classrooms. To see if the expectations naturally formed by real teachers do influence the performance of their pupils it is necessary to study those real expectancies directly.

Naturalistic Classroom Studies

The final category of expectancy effect study to be examined here is that which includes the studies that have attempted to investigate the effects of naturally occurring expectations in a classroom setting. While these studies share this basic similarity, the examples to be discussed below represent a number of different strategies and techniques. As has been the case with the studies discussed above, each of these variations tends to have its weaknesses as well as its strengths. It is necessary to look at the overall pattern as well as the details of particular studies.

A series of studies reported by Pidgeon (1970) differ from most others in that they do not in some ways attempt to assess expectations and then try to follow through to the study of the effects of these but rather attempt to establish that effects occur under conditions where Pidgeon, at least, would be prepared to argue that the expectations of teachers must have been at least partly responsible.

Two of the studies reported by Pidgeon illustrate this approach. The first of these took advantage of a naturally occurring allocation of school pupils to two different types of schools. For various administrative reasons a group of primary-school children whose birthdays fell at a certain time of year were kept in their primary schools while their classmates moved on to secondary school. Prior to this move all the children had taken a battery of intelligence and attainment tests and some of these children took a similar, second battery of tests a year later. It was possible therefore to compare changes in test scores between those who had had a year of secondary schooling with those who had had a further year of primary schooling (remembering that the two groups had been established according to date of birth, not ability or attainment levels).

These comparisons showed that the children who had had an extra year of primary schooling consistently made gains in test scores, while those who had had a year of secondary schooling consistently made losses. As Pidgeon points out there are many possible reasons for this effect, for example the stresses associated with the transition from primary to secondary school may in themselves depress performance. However, Pidgeon's preferred explanation lies in the differences he believes to exist between the teachers in the two types of schools with regard to their interest in, attitude towards and expectations for the future development of their pupils.

A second of Pidgeon's studies is employed by him to support his argument that curricular decisions, sometimes taken at an administrative level above that of the individual school, reflect general expectations for pupil performance that become self-fulfilling. A cross-cultural study compared the level of performance displayed by 10- to 11-year-old pupils on tests of arithmetic. The test showed a marked superiority for a group of English and Welsh children over a group from the USA. Again, while recognising the problems involved in interpreting these results, Pidgeon concludes that 'it . . . demonstrates how children of a given age in one education system can produce a markedly lower level of performance than in another, when no higher level is expected from them' (p. 123).

None of the studies reported by Pidgeon clearly demonstrate expectancy effects at work, all the effects he discusses could be explained without making reference to expectancy effects as such. However, these studies are important and useful in that they demonstrate that the type of effects one would expect to see taking place if self-fulfilling prophecies did occur in educational settings do actually take place. For instance, Pidgeon reviews a number of studies that show that only a very small proportion of children are transferred from higher to lower streams, or vice versa, and that an even smaller proportion are transferred between grammar and secondary-modern schools. These actual transfer rates are much lower than the known adequacy of selection procedures would predict. In other words, placement into a certain stream or type of school establishes expectations for a child that can become self-fulfilling. Such studies, however, only show that expectancy effects may be operating, not that they actually do.

Dusek and his colleagues (Dusek and O'Connell, 1973; O'Connell, Dusek and Wheeler, 1974) draw a distinction between teacher-bias and teacher-expectancy effects. Expectancy effects here refer simply to a correlation existing between teachers' predictions and the actual level of pupil attainment. A teacher-bias effect would only be claimed if a causal relationship was found in which attainments are actually determined by expectancies. The former study measured teacher expectations by asking teachers to place in rank order the sixteen best pupils in their class. A bias effect was then encouraged by the experimenters giving additional information to the teachers that reportedly showed that eight of these sixteen would show marked improvement in the coming year. These eight had been, of course, selected at random. The second study followed the children aged initially between 8 and 11 years, through into a second school year.

The results show no bias effect in either the first or second year, the randomly induced expectations did not influence levels of pupil attainment. In both the first and second years of the study, however, teachers' rank orderings related closely to actual level of performance. Dusek and colleagues conclude 'that teachers do not bias either the intellectual development or achievement of children of elementary school age' (O'Connell *et al.*, 1974, p. 327). They prefer to see naturally occurring teacher expectations as being accurate predictors of their pupils' levels of performance, not causal determinants of them.

Palardy (1969) reports details of a study that seems clearly to indicate the existence of the self-fulfilling prophecy when naturalistic expectations are studied. Following preliminary testing of a larger group, Palardy selected two groups of teachers of 6-year-old pupils who differed from each other with respect to their views of the learning abilities of boys and girls. The first group of teachers believed that, at this age at least, boys and girls had essentially equal ability when it came to learning to read. The second group believed girls to have a higher level of this particular ability. Prior to teaching commencing in September, the pupils of these teachers were tested for reading readiness. The test scores revealed no systematic differences between the sexes. By March, the actual reading attainments of boys and girls were equal only if they had had teachers who believed that boys and girls did have equal ability in this respect. The boys whose teachers believed them to be less capable apparently became so, showing a decidedly lower level of performance than the girls and the boy pupils of the first group of teachers.

As in Rosenthal and Jacobson's study using induced expectations, Palardy's study did not include an observational element so as to enable some statements to be made about the processes involved in teachers' expectations becoming 'translated' into pupil behaviour. Brophy and Good (1970) help to redress this imbalance by observing teachers of 6-year-olds in interaction with pupils who they (the teachers) had placed either at the top or bottom of their class in respect to the pupils' achievements. Pupils from the 'top of the class' tended to initiate for themselves a greater number of contacts with teachers but did not consistently receive a greater number of teacher-initiated contacts. However, clear differences in the quality of pupil-teacher interactions did emerge between the two groups of pupils. Teachers were more likely to praise their 'successful' students for giving correct answers to questions, but were more likely to criticise their 'less successful' pupils for giving wrong ones. Teachers failed to give any feedback at all to responses from successful pupils only 3.3 per cent of the time, compared to 14.8 per cent of the time for the less successful ones. These results are similar to those of Rubovits and Maehr (1971) who in an analogue study with induced expectations also found that it was the quality rather than the quantity of teacher-pupil interaction that seemed to be affected by teacher expectations.

One of the best-known teacher-expectancy studies (Rist, 1970) concludes that both the quality and quantity of teacher-pupil interactions are affected by naturalistic expectations. Rist's study is primarily concerned with the detailed observation of one kindergarten teacher throughout the school year with the pupils also being observed somewhat less extensively for parts of the next two years to provide follow-up data. The kindergarten teacher was observed twice weekly for one and a half hours on each occasion. Initial interest was in the way in which the teacher grouped the pupils into three working groups and then in the ways in which her relationships developed with each group.

While the teacher had claimed that children had been grouped into fast, medium and slow learners, Rist argues persuasively that her groupings could as readily be explained in terms of the degree to which pupils corresponded to her ideal pupil. Importantly, this ideal type contained a number of elements that bore no necessary relationship to the children's actual academic capabilities. Children at the top table were cleaner, better dressed and better behaved than those in the middle who were in turn generally 'nicer' than those on the bottom table. By the end of the year, Rist's observations showed that the teacher was virtually limiting her teaching to the top table, the others being increasingly ignored. The follow-up study showed that the effects seemed to last. In the following year, no children from the middle and bottom first-year groups were placed in a second-year top group. The second-year top group contained all the first-year top group. Similar effects occurred following the transition from second to third year.

Rist argues that at the beginning of their school career these children are type-cast according to criteria that have no necessary implications for their levels of attainment. The effects of this early grouping, however, are such that when, in later years, groups are established on the basis of past educational attainments, the groups tend to remain the same. Rist equates this process with a caste system that allows for no upward mobility.

In sharp contrast to Rist's study (carried out in the USA), Murphy (1974) studied teachers in a British primary school and concludes that 'the self-fulfilling prophecy premised as it is on 'inaccurate' and 'intransigent' teacher appraisals appears as incongruous in light of the accurate and malleable expectations and typifications of teachers in this study' (p. 338).

Murphy argues that teachers employ two distinct modes of appraisal in respect to their pupils. One mode is concerned with the pupil's academic ability. This, Murphy argues, is seen by the teachers as being relatively fixed, a pupil either has it or not and teachers are not therefore likely to attempt to induce change. The second mode refers to the child's social and moral behaviour. It is the well behaved and presentable child who is preferred by the teachers. While not supplying full details Murphy does supply some data that show that these preferences of teachers are positively correlated with a child's academic ability (as reflected in a child's position in the class) but not as highly correlated as is the pupil's IQ. In other words, Murphy's claim is that while teachers have preferences for 'nice' pupils, these preferences do not lead to higher levels of academic attainment as argued by Rist.

As both Rist and Murphy develop their arguments by selecting examples of teacher comments and behaviour to illustrate their various points it is difficult to compare their apparently conflicting claims. Crano and Mellon (1978), in the final study to be discussed here, present details of a quite different study that also examines the effects of teacher expectations for both their pupils' social and academic behaviour.

Crano and Mellon used data collected earlier in Barker Lunn's (1970) study of streaming in English and Welsh primary schools. Three basic sets of data were available. A group of first-year junior schoolchildren aged over 7 were assessed for aspects of reading and arithmetic performance as well as for IQ in that first year and for the next three years. In addition to this, the teachers of these children provided, each year, data that was indicative of their expectations for each child in two domains. The first domain concerned academic ability, with teachers giving their opinions of the child's capabilities in reading, arithmetic, and an overall assessment of the child's general ability level expressed in the form of a prediction of a child's chances of obtaining a grammar-school place. The second domain relates to one which might be called the teacher's social expectations. Teachers gave their views on the child's attitudes towards school, the child's general level of obedience within the school and, finally, on the extent to which the child was considered to be a pleasure to have in class. Unfortunately, data relating to the academic expectations held by teachers for the youngest pupils were not available.

Crano and Mellon's contribution was in the analysis of the data. By employing cross-lagged panel analysis (see Crano and Mellon, 1978; Campbell and Stanley, 1963 for details) they are able to make statements concerning the existence, or otherwise, of causal relationships between expectations and attainments, without having to employ the experimental procedures of the type employed by Rosenthal and Jacobson and others. The study thus has the advantage of using naturalistic expectations while retaining the ability to investigate causal relationships.

The results are most interesting. The clearest finding to emerge was that the social expectations of first-year teachers were causally predominant over the attainments of the same pupils in their second year. Two points need to be kept in mind here. First, as is mentioned above, no data were available regarding the academic expectations of these first-year teachers, so it is not possible to determine whether, for these teachers, academic or social expec-tations are the more potent as possible determinants of later pupil perfor-mance. Second, the methods employed by Crano and Mellon only permit statements about the relative strength of causal relationships to be made. Their data indicate that in eight of the twelve cases investigated the social expectations of first-year teachers had a greater effect upon the later perfor-mance of those pupils in their second year than did the performance of first-year pupils upon the expectations of second-year teachers. In the remaining four cases this was reversed, the performance of first-year pupils having a greater effect upon second-year teachers' expectations than did first-year teachers' expectations have upon second-year pupils' performance.

The position advocated by Crano and Mellon then is one in which causality operates in both directions. The earlier expectations of teachers can affect the later performance of pupils, but these expectations are, in part, determined by earlier pupil performance. Their results, however, suggest that, particularly with social expectations held by teachers for young children, the expectations have a relatively greater effect upon the attainments than vice versa, and that overall expectations tended to determine performance.

Summary

One thing is clear from this discussion of just some of the studies that have a direct bearing upon teacher-expectancy effects – they do not produce results that provide an immediately obvious and consistent picture. Some show the expectancy effect, some do not. Some show effects only with younger children, some only with older ones. Some show effects with urban teachers, but not suburban. Some show quantitative but not qualitative effects on teacher-pupil interactions, while others show the exact opposite. Most of the studies can be criticised for problems in their design and on balance they indicate that expectancy effects, certainly the type investigated by Rosenthal and Jacobson, do not seem to happen [. . .] There is certainly now available sufficient evidence to demonstrate that teacher-expectancy effects will sometimes take place. It is not claimed that all teachers have expectations for their pupils which will always determine pupil performance – only that this can sometimes happen.

As yet we do not know enough to be able to say under which conditions expectancy effects will occur and under which they will not. The closest we can come to this at present is in saying that such effects are far more likely to take place with younger than with older children and probably when teachers have 'social' expectations for their pupils (Rist, 1970; Crano and Mellon, 1978). As Murphy (1974) argued it is the social aspect of pupils' classroom behaviour that is seen by teachers as being alterable rather than their academic potential [. . .]

Another reasonably clear conclusion to emerge is that it has proven to be particularly difficult to replicate the type of study reported by Rosenthal and Jacobson (1968), that is studies carried out within the classroom using induced expectancies. More often than not, these induced expectations fail to have any effect. This, however, would seem to tell us more about the usefulness of various research strategies than it does about teacher expectancies and their effects. One explanation for the failure of these studies to produce effects is simply that the induced expectancies are relatively unimportant in comparison to the naturalistic ones. Dusek's research (Dusek and O'Connell, 1973; O'Connell, Dusek and Wheeler, 1974) provides evidence to suggest just this.

As argued at the beginning of this chapter, expectancies are a part of everyday social life, outside of the classroom and within it. It is perhaps quite unrealistic to expect a few manipulated test scores and the associated comments of researchers to override, or even add to, the expectancies already held by teachers that might have their origins in many years of teaching experience.

Rosenthal and Jacobson are to be thanked for provoking interest in the possible biasing effects of teacher expectations but their contribution is limited to this by their chosen methodology. If further progress is to be made, we need to begin to investigate in earnest the sources of naturalistic expectancies held by teachers and the dynamics of the processes involved in a possible translation of these expectancies into different levels of actual pupil performance [. . .]

Notes

1 An interesting personal anecdote is relevant here. A few years ago I was preparing a course for undergraduates that was to examine the teacher-expectancy effect literature. As I had only just been appointed to the university in which I was working I needed to check the library catalogue to ensure that the texts needed for the course were available. Some very well-used copies of Rosenthal and Jacobson (1968) were there, but no copy of Elashoff and Snow (1971), which is highly critical of the former. The immediate success (in publishers' terms at least) of *Pygmalion in the Classroom* has been claimed to be due to the way in which it said exactly what people at that time wanted to hear. Decisions regarding the purchase of books for the University Library seemed to support this. Incidentally, while I could readily order and obtain extra copies of Rosenthal and Jacobson, the book by Elashoff and Snow was out of print and unavailable!

References

BARKER LUNN, J.C. (1970). *Streaming in the Primary School*. Slough, National Foundation for Educational Research.
BEEZ, W.V. (1968). 'Influence of biased psychological reports on teacher behaviour and pupil performance', Proceedings of the 76th Annual Convention of the Maerican Psychological Association, No. 3, 605–6.
BENNETT, N. (1976). *Teaching Styles and Pupil Progress*. London, Open Books.
BROPHY, J. and GOOD, T. (1970). 'Teachers' communication of differential expectations for children's classroom performance: some behavioural data', *Journal of Educational Psychology*, 61, 365–74.
CAMPBELL, D.T. and STANLEY, J.C. (1963). *Experimental and Quasi-Experimental Designs for Research*. Chicago, Rand McNally.
CLAIBORN, W.L. (1969). 'Expectancy effects in the classroom: a failure to replicate', *Journal of Educational Psychology*, 60, 377–83.
COOPER, H.M. (1979). 'Some effects of pre-performance information on academic expectations', *Journal of Educational Psychology*, 71, 375–80.

CRANO, W.D. and MELLON, D.M. (1978). 'Causal influence of teachers' expectations on children's academic performance: a cross-lagged panel analysis', *Journal of Educational Psychology*, 70, 39–49.

DUSEK, J.B. and O'CONNELL, E.J. (1973). 'Teacher-expectancy effects on the achievement test performance of elementary school children', *Journal of Educational Psychology*, 65, 371–7.

ELASHOFF, J.D. and SNOW, R.E. (eds.) (1971). *Pygmalion Reconsidered.* Worthington, Ohio, Charles A. Jones.

FINN, J.D. (1972). 'Expectations and the educational environment', *Review of Educational Research*, 42, 387–410.

FLEMING, E.S. and ANTTONEN, R.G. (1971). 'Teacher expectancy or my fair lady', *American Educational Research Association Journal*, 8, 241.

JOSE, J. and CODY, J. (1971). 'Teacher-pupil interaction as it relates to attempted changes in teacher expectancy of academic ability and achievement', *American Educational Research Association Journal*, 8, 39–49.

MASON, E. (1973). 'Teachers' observations and expectations of boys and girls as influenced by biased psychological reports and knowledge of the effects of biases', *Journal of Educational Psychology*, 65, 238–43.

MEICHENBAUM, D., BOWERS, K. and ROSS, R.A. (1969). 'A behavioural analysis of teacher expectancy effects', *Journal of Personality and Social Psychology*, 13, 306–16.

MURPHY, J. (1974). 'Teacher expectations and working-class under-achievement', *British Journal of Sociology*, 25, 326–44.

O'CONNELL, E.J., DUSEK, J.B. and WHEELER, R.J. (1974). 'A follow-up study of teacher expectancy effects', *Journal of Educational Psychology*, 66, 325–8.

PALARDY, J.M. (1969). 'What teachers believe – what children achieve', *Elementary School Journal*, 69, 370–4.

PIDGEON, D.A. (1970). *Expectation and Pupil Performance.* Slough, National Foundation for Educational Research.

RIST, R.G. (1970). 'Student social class and teacher expectation: the self-fulfilling prophecy in Ghetto Education', *Harvard Educational Review*, 40, 411–51.

ROSENTHAL, R. (1966). *Experimenter Effects in Behavioral Research.* New York, Appleton-Century-Crofts.

ROSENTHAL, R. and JACOBSON, L. (1968). *Pygmalion in the Classroom.* New York, Holt, Rinehart and Winston.

ROTHBART, M., DALFEN, S. and BARRETT, R. (1971). 'Effects of teachers' expectancy on student teacher interaction', *Journal of Educational Psychology*, 62, 49–54.

RUBOVITS, P. and MAEHR, M. (1971). 'Pygmalion analysed: towards an explanations of the Rosenthal-Jacobson findings', *Journal of Personality and Social Psychology*, 19, 197–203.

RUTTER, M., MAUGHAN, B., MORTIMORE, P. and OUSTON, J. (1979). *Fifteen Thousand Hours.* London, Open Books.

A Theory of Typing

D.H. Hargreaves, S. Hester and F. Mellor

[. . .] How does [a child] come to be defined as a deviant person? i.e. how do teachers make the transition from X pupil is a person who commits Y deviant act(s), to X is Y type of deviant person? For there is an important difference between recognizing (knowing) that Jones is telling a lie and claiming (knowing) that Jones is a liar. What is the link between deviant acts (talking, cheating, fighting) and deviant persons (chatterbox, cheat, bully)?

Our thinking prior to the beginning of the research suggested that this topic of pupil identity in the eyes of the teacher was of crucial significance – and not merely for a 'labelling theory' approach to deviance in school. Other approaches to the study of classroom life also suggested that the identity the teacher imputes to the pupil has important consequences for the analysis of teacher-pupil interaction and the development of pupil careers. Perhaps the most striking parallel for us is the work of Rosenthal and Jacobson (1968) on 'self-fulfilling prophecies' in the classroom, which generated considerable interest as well as further research. The close relationship between labelling theory and self-fulfilling prophecy theory can be clarified by reducing them to a schematic summary.

Self-fulfilling Prophecy Theory

    1 Teacher believes X about a pupil (e.g. that he is very intelligent).
    2 Teacher makes predictions about the pupil (e.g. that he will make outstanding academic progress).
    3 Change in teacher attitude and behaviour towards the pupil.

4 Change in pupil self-conception and behaviour in line with the teacher's attitude/behaviour.

5 Fulfilment of the prediction.

Labelling theory:

1 Pupil commits X deviant act.

2 Teacher labels the act or person as deviant.

3 Problems experienced by the pupil as a result of the labelling.

4 Commission of further deviance by the pupil as a means of resolving such problems.

It is interesting to speculate why these two approaches, which have so much in common, have tended to remain as separate strands in the literature. We think that the main reason is because Rosenthal's work was concerned with positive self-fulfilling prophecies. It is true that there has been considerable interest in negative self-fulfilling prophecies (e.g. Rist, 1970), but if the research is experimental, as was true in Rosenthal's pioneering studies, then there are good ethical grounds for taking an interest in the positive rather than the negative self-fulfilling prophecies. For who would dare mislead teachers into believing that certain pupils were likely to deteriorate academically, and risk bringing about such an effect, merely to demonstrate that negative self-fulfilling prophecies can occur? Labelling theory, on the other hand, is part of deviance theory and therefore neglects the consequences of the labelling by teachers of pupils and their acts as 'conformist'. Yet these two approaches have a common theme: how do teachers come to formulate pupils as being certain kinds of persons, and what are the consequences of such formulations?

To bring the two together requires the development of a 'theory of typing'. In attempting this we shall be predominantly concerned with deviant typing, but we believe that our conceptual scheme has a more general applicability to the typing of pupils. In Rosenthal's original study, the teachers were given information about pupils' academic potential 'from the outside', that is, from the judgments made by psychologists on the basis of tests administered to the children. This gives us no indications of how teachers make their own judgments in the natural situation where psychologists do not intervene with the provision of expert opinion. Similarly, other studies, which will be referred to shortly, tell us how teachers type pupils at a particular point in time, but fail to explain how the teacher came to such judgments. In other words, these studies offer a static analysis, whereas we are concerned to develop a dynamic or process theory which examines what happens between the point when a teacher says 'I don't know Smith' or 'I know Smith by sight, but that's all I know about him' and the point when the teacher confidently states 'Smith is a troublemaker' [. . .]

Our first data on pupil typings, collected in school A, derived mainly from our interviews with teachers. These interviews were of two kinds. The first involved asking teachers for commentaries on events or verbal statements (usually deviance-imputations) that had occurred in lessons observed by the researchers. The second involved asking teachers directly about individual pupils. Sometimes the two kinds of data were collected in the same interview, when the discussion of an incident led to a fuller discussion of the pupil(s) involved in that incident. It was clear in this material that these teachers had over the years developed highly elaborate typifications of pupils and that these typifications formed part of the teachers' commonsense knowledge of pupils and their acts in classrooms. Whilst we asked teachers to reconstruct their acquisition of this knowledge from the first time they had met a particular pupil – and such reconstructions are very significant data – such material gives little insight into how the teachers actually developed their conceptions during a much earlier period. For this material we turned to school B, where we followed first year pupils and their teachers during the early days of these pupils in the secondary school. Our theory will present the data in an order which reverses the order of its collection, and which also reverses the order in which we developed the theory.

Before embarking on this, an important caveat is in order with reference to our use of the term *typing*. This concept in its popular, everyday usage has distinctly pejorative connotations. If one were to ask teachers directly, 'How do you type your pupils?' many would reply that they do not think of their children as types but as individuals or as persons. In saying this teachers are asserting that they do not think of pupils merely in terms of labels such as 'bright', 'lazy', 'highflyer', or 'troublemaker' which fail to do justice to the complexity and individuality of the children they know. We do not wish to make any assertions to the contrary. We recognize that teachers do develop highly complex conceptions of their pupils, and we hope that our theory does justice to that complexity. Teachers do, of course, use terms or labels to think or talk about pupils – but that, as the teachers rightly claim, is only part of the story. For us, then, the concept of 'typing' is synonymous with the concept of 'person formulation'[1] Our theory of typing must analyze how teachers come to recognize each pupil as a complex individual who is utterly unique. Whilst our theory is concerned with how one group of persons, teachers, comes to type another group of persons, pupils, and especially deviant pupils, there is also in our work an implicit general theory about how any person comes to type any other person. What teachers are doing with respect to children is not a phenomenon confined to schools; it is a phenomenon common to all people in all places at all times. Our present concern is simply one limited aspect of a universal practice.

One of the most basic ideas within the symbolic interactionist perspective is that man understands things (objects, persons, events) by naming them. The names we use are categories. A person can understand or know what is the round green object I have in my hand, when he has learned the category 'apple', which is a single name that is applied to a whole range of objects with certain characteristics. 'Apple' as a category is also understood in relation to other categories, such as 'fruit' and 'edible' as well as 'round' and 'green'. The ability to name the object is to understand it. These names or categories are evaluative; since we are creatures who need to eat, for an object to be described as 'edible' or 'tasty' is to make a positive value-judgment upon it. These names also direct our action towards the object; when we are hungry, we look for tasty, edible things to eat. So it is with persons. We use names or categories – or constructs, or labels, or types – with which we make sense of others. The names are evaluative, since some of these characteristics are held to be desirable, and they direct our action. We avoid 'obnoxious' people just as we avoid 'poisonous' fruits. To type other people – to name them, categorize them, label them – is an inherent part of understanding them. In itself, it is not something one should or could dispense with.

Labelling theory considers this process of naming or typing others in a particular way. It asserts that the naming of certain kinds of persons – 'deviants' – and the treatment that often accompanies such naming, can have particular consequences. Implicitly it also asserts that these consequences are either unintended or undesirable (which is a value-judgment), and, paradoxically, these consequences can reinforce, strengthen or increase the deviant conduct which the labelling is perhaps intended to punish, diminish or remove. In this sense it is clearly utterly absurd to argue that labelling theorists are saying that we should never label, or even that we should never label deviant acts: that would be an impossibility [. . .]

It is part of the liberal ideology of teaching that teachers should look at the 'whole child'. Be that as it may, teachers are still teachers and the child is still a pupil. People always encounter and interact with other people within specific role-relationships, of which the teacher-pupil relationship is but one example. A role-relationship is a way of saying that the encounter is governed by particular interests and purposes, takes place in particular settings, and is structured in particular ways. This is not the place to give a detailed account of this relationship, which has been analyzed by many sociologists and social psychologists interested in education. We merely wish to re-assert the simple idea that teachers tend to perceive pupils in particular ways and act upon them in particular ways. It has been argued elsewhere (Hargreaves, 1972) that teachers have two prime interests in regard to pupils. The first is an academic interest, for teachers have the task of ensuring that pupils learn. The second is a disciplinary interest, for teachers have the task of ensuring that pupils conform to the rules and regulations which aim to maintain social order in the classroom. These two tasks or interests are, of course, closely interwoven. The outcome is that many of the names or labels applied to pupils reflect those interests. It is in terms of these labels that teachers can understand and make sense of pupils. Naturally, teachers do not see children in school exclusively in terms of their teacher interests; they also have a much more general reaction to their charges. For instance, they make a general evaluative reaction to children in terms of their 'likeability', which is an aspect of almost all human encounters, whatever the particular nature of the role-relationship. But even this more generalized reaction takes place within the role-relationship. There is, quite naturally, a tendency for teachers to like those pupils who cause them the least trouble in realizing their interests. This has been amply demonstrated in the literature, and shows itself in the present analysis.[2]

The theory proposes that pupils are typed or formulated by teachers in three stages. The first stage, that of 'speculation', begins when the teacher first comes to know about and/or to meet the pupil for the first time. The third stage, that of 'stabilization', marks the point at which the teacher has a relatively clear and stable conception of the identity of the pupils. He 'knows' the pupil; he understands him; he finds little difficulty in making sense of his acts and is not puzzled or surprised by what he does or says. The second stage, that of 'elaboration', stands between the other two stages.

As will be made clear later, these stages should not be regarded as highly discrete or distinct stages that can easily be distinguished. Although the stages do occur in a sequence, they do not refer to distinctive periods of time. A stage is characterized by certain problems and processes. The stages fuse into each other, both in the sense that they can overlap in time and in the sense that processes from different stages can and do occur at the same point in time.

When we talked to teachers in school A, it was evident that they 'knew their pupils well'. They spoke confidently, unhesitatingly and at length about them. But we had no access to the ways in which they had come to know them. This was the result of two things. First, our interviews with staff were mostly about third or fourth year pupils who had already acquired a stabilized deviant typing. Second, though eventually sensitized to the need for study of teachers' reactions to new pupils, we had arrived at the school half-way through the school year and thus had no opportunity to study the ways in which teachers had 'got to know' pupils new to them. We therefore decided that we would go to school B at the start of the school year to observe and talk to teachers in relation to the first year pupils who had just arrived in the school. Our theory is thus not derived from a longitudinal study of one set of children. Subsequent research may reveal the consequential weakness of our theorizing.

When pupils arrive at their secondary school, they do not normally know their teachers and the teachers do not know them. It is tempting to think that as far as their new teachers are concerned, these eleven-year-old pupils are simply 'blanks', bare canvases that can only be filled in by the passage of time, or perhaps hidden pictures whose detail will be revealed by the passage of time. Yet this is not, in fact, the case. Certainly it is true that the teacher does not know them as individuals; at the first meeting they are pupils without names. But each teacher does know quite a lot about them in general or as a collectivity. They all have a history for the teacher, but it is a typical history, not an individual one.

In the first place, he knows that they are first year pupils. They have a common age-range; they come from a local area; they have recently left a primary school. If he has some experience as a secondary school teacher, he will have encountered first year pupils before. He knows what first year pupils have been like in the past, so he knows something about what to expect from this particular intake. Indeed he will probably use his past experience as a standard against which to judge these newcomers, and will soon be saying:

> 'They're the worst first year form I've ever had.'
> 'They're not settling down very quickly this year.'
> 'They're much more docile than the lot I had last year.'

He knows something about the school's catchment area. He knows that some pupils come from the 'better' districts, residential areas for professional people, and that others come from areas noted for 'problem' families. He knows something about the primary schools that 'feed' his school; that one school gives its pupils a 'traditional' education, whilst another is perhaps experimenting with highly 'progressive' methods. All this he knows from his typifications of schools and neighbourhoods, even though as yet he cannot attach particular pieces of information to any individual pupil.

If the teacher has record cards from the primary schools at his disposal, he may read them and discover the proportions of pupils coming from particular schools or areas – though it fact he is unlikely to do this unless he is the 'form-teacher'. (He may even have met the pupils on a visit to the primary school.) He may see a surname that he knows, and so realize or guess that this may be a brother or a sister of a pupil he has taught in the past. He may have some accidental information about a pupil. For instance, he may live in the same street as the pupil, or he may be a personal friend of one of the primary school teachers who has passed on some information.

So on the first day of term, when the teacher meets his pupils for the first time, he knows little about the vast majority of them. Over the next few weeks, he will 'get to know' them. He will learn to put names to faces and each pupil will emerge as a unique individual with his own personality and characteristics. Yet this formulation of pupils as persons is not a creation ex nihilo. Rather, each pupil is matched against some other material. First, he is matched against any pre-information he has of the pupil, which includes, as we shall see, any information that is passed to him by other teachers. Second, he is matched against the teacher's conception of the typical first year pupil, which is an anonymous abstraction derived from all his previous experience of first year pupils. Third, he is matched against his peers – all the other first year pupils. The first two or three pupils to emerge as individuals serve as a kind of yardstick against which an emergent individual can be matched; a pupil is described as being 'similar to' or 'the opposite of' or 'not at all like' those pupils who have already acquired a degree of individuality. In the teachers' terms, within the first few days one or two pupils begin to 'stand out' from the rest, who remain temporarily 'unknown quantities' precisely because they do not stand out.

To discover what it is that leads a pupil to 'stand out' is to discover some of the important forms or terms in which a pupil is typed by teachers. Their early descriptions, or more accurately their 'first impressions' of pupils, reveal the constructs they use to formulate pupils. We approached this problem in two ways. We asked teachers after two weeks of term which pupils had made any impact on them; and we also provided teachers with a list of pupils and asked them to comment on each name. Teachers, of course, varied in the speed with which they 'got to know' the pupils. Doubtless some teachers made a more active effort to do this than others. But more important, some teachers had special responsibility for certain groups of pupils, as tutors or form-teachers, and so made special efforts in this direction. Further, some teachers taught the pupils more often than others, and so naturally made more rapid progress.

The main constructs (or terms or 'labels') to appear in the early descriptions provided by the teachers are of five kinds.

1 *Appearance*: Naturally teachers noted facial appearance, size, dress and demeanour in their first impressions. Indeed, teachers often recalled a boy not by his name but by some appearance characteristic. They would ask us, 'Isn't he the little boy who sits at the back?' Amongst the constructs used were: tall, short, fat, thin, nice-looking, attractive, untidy, elfish-looking, athletic build, a vague look in his eyes.

2 *Conformity to discipline role aspects*: Common constructs were: awkward, difficult, truculent, resentful, cocky, cheeky, rude, hostile, disruptive, chatterer, talkative, noisy, sulks, familiar, fusspot, messes about, doesn't toe the line, quiet, polite, co-operative, no problem behaviour-wise.

3 *Conformity to academic role aspects*: Common constructs were: intelligent, bright, clever, brainy, hard worker, eager to learn, keen, diligent, slow, dim, lazy, sleepy, lethargic, inattentive, time-waster, poor reader.

4 *Likeability*: This concerned a general positive feeling of liking that many teachers expressed. It was commonly mentioned, though the terms are almost always the same – 'a likeable lad', 'a pleasant lad', 'a nice lad'.

5 *Peer group relations*: Whilst these were fairly infrequent at this early stage, they did appear occasionally: leader, ringleader, bully.

Two other groups of constructs were in evidence. The first might be called 'personality' constructs, such as aggressive, easy-going, extrovert, friendly, helpful, perky, shy, self-confident, withdrawn. An examination of their original context of utterance suggests that these terms are used to make indications which relate to one or more of the five main categories. The second group consisted of a set of highly general 'deviant' labels, such as nuisance, pest, naughty, fool, nutcase, trouble-maker, disturbed. We shall consider these in more detail later. Two other terms were used – 'normal' and 'average'. At this stage these terms were used in a particular sense, to indicate that the pupil concerned did not as yet 'stand out' in any striking way, either positively or negatively. They were not used in the more narrow psychological sense of 'normal' as compared with 'disturbed' or 'abnormal'; rather they implied that the teacher simply knew little about the pupil: 'He doesn't really stand out as far as work or anything – he's just an average boy in the form.'

Our findings are clearly in line with earlier investigations[3] using very different methods for collecting and analyzing data. After two or three weeks these teachers were able to provide brief portraits of individual pupils. Sometimes these are based upon a single incident or a single occasion when the pupil came to the teacher's attention.

> 1 T: I know him because when I was teaching him he was in such an agony trying to learn the school prayer. He worked so hard and was the first boy to try and say it, and he didn't succeed. But he's a lovely boy.

> 2 T: He emerged yesterday in the lesson. He's very good. A very pleasant, well-mannered boy.

Sometimes the teacher's knowledge is focused on limited aspects of the pupil, i.e. on one of the five types of construct.

> 1 T: He's a very small, very cocky little lad, who would take on the whole world, and he's inclined to provoke other boys by annoying them in silly little ways. For instance, he'll catch hold of a boy behind the back of the neck and throw him down the bank of the stream, and then be surprised that the boy retaliated.

> 2 T: Yes, in his case it's his size that will be his biggest problem. I think to some extent, without making it obvious, he's going to have to be protected a little bit because it's no good boys treating him like that. All right, they're not hitting him, I don't think they are intentionally harming, they're just picking him up and playing with him . . . he's just a plaything more or less.

> 3 T: He has stood out because he's generally one of the first ones to finish and again he's one of the first with his hand up.

4 T: Now he's very quiet, very quiet lad. He seems very shy to me, and a bit frightened. Doesn't like to ask me anything and seems almost to apologize before he asks permission to do anything . . . I think he's a little bit shy, doesn't like to put up his hand in class, doesn't like to answer.

5 T: It's because he's a poor reader that I remember him, and he's a bit absent-minded. A bit of a dreamer most of the time. If you tell every-body, then you have to tell him a second time. He looks absent-minded, he looks as if his mind's not on what he's doing at all, ever. He does – he looks as if he's never paying attention, anyway. His eyes look vague, dreamy and vacant all the time.

6 T: Whenever I look at him I think he's going to burst out crying. I don't know why. He's just got that expression on his face. Seems a bit frightened and a bit nervous.

More typically the characterization of the pupil draws on several types of construct and is based, like some of the cameos given above, not on a single isolated event but on multiple observed events which cumulatively contrib-ute to the impression made. It is because the pupil repeatedly behaves in a particular way that he is assumed to be a particular type of person.

1 T: He stands out from the rest in the fact that he's a nice looking boy, he's an athletic build. He works hard in lessons and I think he's about the best boy in the class.

2 T: I have a feeling from his work that he can't express himself at all. I think he's a poor reader and this reflects in his work output. His behav-iour's all right.

[. . .] Many of these characterizations have qualifications built into them: 'I have a feeling that', 'he seems', 'possibly', 'at first impressions'. The teachers are very aware that their characterizations are built upon fairly slender evidence. The single incident may be atypical; an appearance factor may be misleading; even repeated incidents may be nothing more than part of 'settling down' in the new school. This 'first impression' can be no more than a temporary working hypothesis, whose validity will be tested by subse-quent events.[4]

1 T: To me they are the only two to stand out at this stage as being sort of extroverts, that's all . . . they both seem intelligent kids, but I don't know if they are well above average at this present time. These two seem to me to be quite bright, and that's about all I can tell you at the moment.

2 T: He's another. A bit of a mystery at the moment. He's been away and I just don't really know him. He's no problem, or he hasn't been

yet, discipline-wise. Behaviour is good. I wouldn't like to say about him really.

[. . .] Although the teachers are often aware that the evidence on which the pupil is assigned a provisional typing is somewhat tenuous, the resulting speculative hypothesis points both to the past and to the future. The initial typing is used to make sense of what the pupil has done so far, but it also points forward in time by suggesting the kind of person the pupil will perhaps turn out to be. It is for this reason that we call this the speculative stage.

1 T: Very bright and seems a very nice lad. Now I think more than any of them he will go into the upper band in a couple of years quite easily . . . He is very confident . . . without saying, you know, 'I'm the greatest.' He seems to be self-confident. . . . Mm, you find many in a class that you get to like by the end of the year. By like, I mean as you pick out someone you really like yourself. I reckon at the moment he could be one of the nicest lads I've taught, but then again that's the impression because he does his work, he doesn't fuss about you, you know, he doesn't make a big show of things, he gets on and does it well, yet you don't have to force him to answer and things like that. And that for me is just about – plus the fact that he is a good footballer, and stuff like that – that is just about the ideal, you know, and I think he'll be a good lad.

2 T: I get the impression he hasn't really settled into the class, that he's still a bit apart. Ability-wise he does not seem to be that good, but there again . . . I wouldn't like to say. I don't know, I don't think he'll be any trouble, but he has to be jumped on over books and work and forgetting homework and things like that.

[. . .] Once the teacher has made a working hypothesis about a pupil, then the typing process moves into the elaborative stage. This consists of several processes, the most basic of which is that of 'verification'. There is an attempt made by the teacher to find out if the pupil 'really is that sort of person'. It is concerned with the confirmation of the 'impression' or 'feeling' held by the teacher in the speculative phase. Like a good scientist, the teacher puts his working hypothesis to the test and attempts to verify it. It represents a movement from 'He may be, then again he might not' to 'He is'. But the teacher does not have to set up a special experiment for this; the hypothesis of the speculative typing can be tested against the successive revelations of subsequent events as they naturally occur in classroom life [. . .] It is assumed that 'time will tell' whether or not the teacher is right. So verification is concerned with the compatibility between what is hypothesized and predicted, against what is observed or revealed. It is not so much that very specific events or acts are anticipated. Rather, the teacher anticipates certain kinds of events or acts that are compatible with the provisional typing, i.e.

events or acts that can be made sense of by the typing. If this occurs, then the typing is verified.

In effect this means that the teacher is specially sensitive to the repetition of the acts on which the original typing was based. If the initial basis for the typing was a single incident, then if that same (or more strictly, a similar) incident recurs, then this will be used as evidence for verification. If the original typing was based on repeated incidents ('he tends to . . .' or 'he's always . . .') then that conduct must persist if the original typing is to be substantiated. Additionally, the teacher can look for variations rather than repetitions of acts. If the teacher's original typing is that the pupil is 'lazy', based upon careless and untidy written work, then many subsequent acts can be seen as variations upon, and verification of, that typing – his tendency to come late to classes, the brevity of his homework, the inconsistent standards of his work, his unwilling attitude, and so on.

Should repetition and variation not occur, then the working hypothesis is likely to be falsified. The absence of typical acts, i.e. acts which can be made sense of by means of the imputed typing, challenges the validity of the provisional typing. In other words, the pupils must be 'de-typed'. This can be accounted for in a variety of ways. The teacher may believe that he simply made the wrong judgment in the first place – 'I was wrong about him.' This is particularly so when the original typing was based on appearance and looks rather than on acts, or when it was based on a rather vague impression. In the light of subsequent evidence, the speculative hypothesis is rejected or modified.

> T: Now his written work is very good and his exam and tests were very poor, so although he's been doing good written work, it's not been going in . . . I liked him immensely at first, but now I'm a bit doubtful. He can write nicely so he enjoys writing, but if they don't learn the work and you have to tell them off, then he seems very miserable and unhappy. I was surprised because I suggested that he should be pushed up a class, incidentally, until these tests and then I found out that it was all written, it wasn't knowledge.

Alternatively, the teacher may believe that the original typing was in some sense correct at the time, but that it must now be rejected or modified, not because the teacher's understanding has changed in the light of evidence, but because the pupil has in fact changed.

September interview
T: Ronald. I've never seen a lad whose work was so neat and level. His presentation is marvellous.

January interview[5]

T: Did I mention any good ones last time? The ones that I would say are fitting in well with the system? Did I mention Ronald last time?
I: Yes, briefly.
T: Well, he was working dead hard when he first came into the school and you thought that here's a lad who's really setting out to do well here in this school. You know, a fresh start and so on. And yet since then – I don't know if he's sensed that he's in a low stream or not, but somehow he's lost the zest for work that he had when he first came here, and it's real shame. It might alter again next year . . . but you feel that if he carries on the same way he is doing now, then he'll really be working below his potential. . . . You can see somehow this loss of zeal from the initial few weeks . . . The light has gone from his eye and that being the case I would detect that as a danger signal for that child.

There exists a hidden dimension to this pupil change. Part of the teacher's commonsense knowledge consists of knowledge of what we might call the 'newcomer status'. It is generally assumed by teachers that coming to a secondary school is for many pupils, and to varying degrees, a traumatic experience. They realize that pupils are entering a new world, with new teachers, new subjects, new rules and routines. Their 'senior' status at the junior school has given way to the lowly status of 'new boys' or 'first year kids'. It is therefore expected that many pupils will experience 'problems' in this process of 'settling down' in their new school. Most pupils, it is assumed by the teachers, experience nervousness and fear when they are newcomers.

T: First of all they are in sheer terror of this place. Most kids come into secondary school in sheer terror of what they come into. They would have been hearing fearsome stories of what happens in secondary schools from their older brothers and so forth. They will have to find their feet and after half-term they will probably be finding out how far they can go with the staff.

Thus a teacher can argue that a pupil has now 'settled down' or 'found his feet' and that the provisional typing was based on pupil conduct which was unrepresentative of him because he was in this abnormal and transient state of adjusting to his new environment. A teacher may claim, 'I thought he was quiet, but he's really quite a chatterbox' thus reading the provisional typing as 'quiet' as misleading and temporary, but justified at the time, because the pupil was too nervous and apprehensive to be his 'real' self. Similarly a pupil may prove to be 'troublesome' as part of this 'settling down' but later turn out to be 'a very nice boy really'. It is assumed that different pupils react to their newcomer status in different ways, which need not be representative of the type in whose terms they will ultimately be formulated. When they lose their newcomer status, with time, then they come out 'in their true colours', which other boys, whose original typings are verified, have shown all the time.

September interview

T: Gavin is more inclined to stand back once he's got a fracas going on and watch it. He's an inciter to action. . . . The three of them together could be a formidable gang if they were allowed to.

I: Although you've lumped the three together, are there any differences between them?

T: [The other two] are ready to help in class. They'll ask me if there is anything I want doing and they'll do it, but Gavin is inclined to sulk if you tell him off about anything. He withdraws into himself and then his whole approach to anything is that of a sulky nature. He's not prepared to co-operate. If you tell him he's done something wrong, he won't apologize. The other two will say they're sorry and be sorry, but Gavin doesn't. He rather harbours a grudge against you. . . . Several times I've had pupils complaining of being bullied and these three had their names given to me. Gavin is the one who resents being told. The other two will accept the fact that they have been accused of bullying and that's the end of it, but with Gavin he always seems to be saying, 'You're picking on me again.'

I: Does he actually say this?

T: It's the impression you get. You know, he shrugs his shoulders at you and he says, 'Well, I wasn't the only one' kind of thing.

I: You say he shows resentment? What are the signs of this?

T: Withdrawing into himself. He won't take an active part in an oral lesson. If he's speaking and you tell him to be quiet and get on, he'll withdraw into himself completely and take no further part in the lesson . . . He's anti-discipline at the moment.

January interview

T: Gavin's a nicer character now than when I first had him. He's not really stirring up like he was before. He used to be the main stirrer up then he'd sit back and watch the trouble that he'd caused, but now he seems to have settled down much more than he had before. . . . I think he's been channelled into lines where he's not looking for trouble. He's more sort of – well, he's fitting into the community of the school better than he did, or than I thought he would. He really was very definitely antagonistic to everything when he first came here, but now he seems to be working much better and has settled in. I wouldn't say that he was 100 per cent for school. He'll still on occasions stand up and say, 'Well, why do we have to do such and such a thing?' He's not anti-social now, except on the odd occasion when he feels he's been put on for some reason or another . . . Now he's joining in things more . . . Since then he seems to have become more like a normal school boy . . . He's even volunteered to do things, which came as a great surprise to me to begin with . . . I've changed my opinion completely . . .

A pupil may be de-typed because he has changed directly as a result of the teacher's treatment of him during the early weeks.

T: Now these two boys were inclined to be a bit silly, so I punished them.
I: When you say 'silly' do you mean chattering?
T: Well, giggling as well, you know a bit of sniggers. I know this boy will do this occasionally and you'll overlook it, but if it gets too much then I will say something about it and I thought they were going to develop so I gave them a punishment last week. Well, since then . . . they've been quite well-behaved and worked well.

On the other hand, some teachers expect pupils to change quite unaccountably.

T: I find that a naughty boy is a good boy next day for no apparent reason and that they've developed into another stage and it's possible that they could come along and be absolute saints through no effort on my part or anybody else's. It just happens in their development.

Clearly, if a pupil is 'de-typed', then he must be 're-typed'. The two processes occur simultaneously, for as the provisional typing fails to find verification, the teacher is creating new hypotheses to account for the pupil. As the pupil is de-typed, no elaboration can take place and instead the teacher must re-type by returning to the speculative stage. But it must be remembered that the provisional typing often consisted of several elements, and that some of these may be verified whilst others are falsified. This is one of the reasons why the idea of stages should not be taken to refer to discrete periods of time. With one element of the typing the teacher may be in the elaborative stage, whilst with another element the teacher may be in the speculative stage.

Sometimes the speculative typing itself contains contradictory elements which will, the teacher trusts, be resolved by subsequent events. In such cases the teachers seem to recognize the conflict inherent in their initial typing.

1 T: If I just look at him, if I had to look round the class and from faces alone say who was going to be the poorest one, I would think of him. Yet his work is quite reasonable. It's a puzzle with him.

2 T: He is very quiet, yet he gives you the impression that he is not quiet really, you know, that he's just biding his time, sort of thing, or as soon as I am out of the way, you know – I don't know – he just does

not look the way he behaves. It's a very prejudiced thing to say, I suppose, it's only my opinion. I just don't know, I wouldn't like to put him in any category at the moment. We'll just have to wait and see about him.

[. . .] Normally, one part of the typing is verified and the other part is rejected to give way to a re-typing.

An important process in the elaborative stage is that of 'type-extension'. The provisional typing based on a single characteristic or cluster of characteristics now leads into a more extensive and wide-ranging constellation of 'multiple typings'. As the teacher sees more of the pupil, doing many different acts in many different situations, it becomes more difficult to understand the pupil – retrospectively, currently or predictively – in terms of merely one or two typings. The more the teacher learns about the pupil, the more he must resort to further types. Only a selection of the pupil's conduct can be used as part of the verification process. Some of the additional knowledge cannot be coded under the provisional typings, and is, in Schutz's (1932) phrase, 'type-transcendent', i.e. cannot be made sense of in terms of the imputed typing. New types must therefore be hypothesized to make sense of the conduct that falls outside, or is residual to, the provisional typing. These new types begin the process again at the speculative stage. [. . .]

As the typings are becoming more extensive, they are also becoming 'idiosyncratized', that is, related to a particular unique individual. This is much more than simply developing a typing which consists of a unique cluster of typings – for that was often evident in the speculative stage. Idiosyncratization refers to the process by which the teacher is able to specify the manner in which, and the conditions under which, a pupil exhibits typical (i.e. type-related) conduct. The teacher learns how a pupil commits his typical acts, for each pupil has his own way of 'being cheeky', or 'acting aggressively' or 'playing the fool'.

> 1 T: If he comes in in a nice quiet mood, he will remain that way all the lesson and I won't have to say a word to him, but if he's acting the clown with [another pupil] at the beginning of the lesson, he never seems to settle down for the rest of the lesson.

> 2 T: If you leave him alone to get on with the writing at his own speed, he's quite a friendly little chap. If you try to hurry him or push him at all, then of course he'll do absolutely nothing.

[. . .] Whereas idiosyncratization specifies how the pupil commits typical acts, motive elaboration is concerned with the question of why he commits them. Schutz (1932) has distinguished two kinds of motive. The 'in-order-to motive' which refers to the purpose, end or object which is to be accomplished by the act. From the point of view of the actor, the reference is to the future. Thus when a teacher says that a pupil lied to avoid getting into trouble, the teacher is imputing an in-order-to motive to the pupil. The 'because-motive' refers to the past experiences of the actor which have determined or predisposed him to act in a particular way. Thus when the teacher says the pupil lied because he comes from a bad home where he is not brought up to tell the truth, the teacher is imputing a because-motive to the pupil. As we shall see later, both kinds of motives are imputed to pupils as part of the typing, since both contribute to the elaboration of the typing. Because-motives help make sense of a pupil's typical act by explaining how the pupil comes to be that type of person who commits typical acts for typical in-order-to motives. Teachers, with their knowledge provided by sociologists of education, commonly see the home background of the child as a source of because-motives and what we might call the 'causal structure' which explains how a pupil has come to be a certain type.

In the speculative stage there is evidence that on occasions the teachers speculate about the motivational aspect of the provisional typings. For reasons we shall see shortly, these normally refer to because-motives, not to in-order-to motives.

> 1 T: I think that he must have been very spoilt, at home and in primary school, because he thinks he's so much better than anyone else.

> 2 T: I think he feels insecure and I also believe that he has an inferiority complex because of his home.

[. . .] Since our particular interest is in the typing of deviant pupils, we must now analyze this aspect in greater depth. What we as social scientists call 'deviant' pupils are, in the speculative and elaborative stages, described by the teachers as pupils who are, and/or who are likely to become, 'a problem' or 'difficult'. What is it that leads some pupils to 'stand out' from the rest – the 'normal' pupils – in this way and to be given such a typing? It is not simply that these pupils break rules, although that is true. It appears that there are several other factors which lead pupils to 'stand out' at an early point, which in themselves have no necessary relation to deviance, but which nevertheless play a very important role in the 'standing out' of deviant pupils.

The first of these factors we call the 'sibling phenomenon'.[6] When a teacher meets his new pupils for the first time, he is aware that some of his pupils may be the younger brothers or sisters of pupils he is currently teaching or has taught in the past. That a pupil is this other pupil's brother or sister makes him 'stand out' automatically. If a teacher recognizes a new pupil's name, or if he notices a facial resemblance, then he checks immediately if there is a family relationship. If so, he tends to remember that pupil. When we provided the teachers with a list of the new pupils in a class for commentary, teachers would remark: 'Well, of course, immediately the ones that strike me are the ones whose brothers I already know.' Or as teachers were going through the list, they would say: 'Yes, I know him. He's got a brother here.'

So a newcomer pupil with a known sibling is likely to find his name learned by the teacher very quickly. But the sibling phenomenon extends far beyond this. If a pupil has an older sibling, then the older brother (or sister) acts as a yardstick or model against which the new pupil can be matched, which is quite unlike the case of the newcomer without a sibling, who can be matched only against the teacher's conception of a typical first year pupil or against other first year pupils. In the case of pupils with siblings, it is assumed by teachers that the newcomer will be like the older brother as much in 'personality' and conduct as in physical resemblance. Whereas the sibling-less newcomer has to provide positive evidence of his typing, the newcomer with a sibling is expected to be like the elder brother unless he gives negative evidence to the contrary. So not only does the teacher get to know the newcomer with a sibling very quickly, but he also tends to speculate and elaborate more quickly, because the older brother provides a constant source of comparison and contrast – and teachers are naturally rather curious to discover the extent to which they are alike.

> 1 T: You know, you could almost do a study of how much does your attitude affect how you look at boys who have got brothers further up the school.
> I: Do you think it does?
> T: I think it does yes, especially in the case of ⎯⎯ who looks so much like his brother.

> 2 T: Again, his brother is in my class, so that's why he comes to my notice. But he is extremely – I noticed a sort of difference in their attitudes, you know. [The elder brother] who is in my class is very loud. He's always seeking attention, shouting out, you know, 'I did this', or 'I did that', and this chap, he's only a little lad – he must be about three foot odd – apparently some people had been bullying. He seems very reserved, very loath to say anything at all . . . He just sits there, he's content to go along, whereas his brother is always chattering, and is always moving about – and this is in third year – moving about, you know, and trying to take the mickey out of other people who are stronger than him.

[. . .] One important effect of the sibling phenomenon is that if a new-comer with a 'good' sibling shows signs of being 'difficult', then this can be interpreted as 'settling down' problems, on the assumption that he will ultimately turn out to be like the elder brother. On the other hand if the new-comer has a 'deviant' sibling, then early conformity may be interpreted as a temporary part of 'settling down' and any later deviance will demonstrate what he was 'really like' all along – his brother.

1 T: I should think he'll probably turn out the same way as [his brother]. Yes, probably once this trouble is behind him, he will go the same way as his brother, because his brother was exceptionally keen on drama and that sort of thing.

2 T: This is the first year one. He's got a brother in the second year who's been in a little bit of trouble now and again and I just wonder whether in fact that this is rubbing off on the younger one now, because he seems to be getting a little bit cocky. That's my opinion anyway. Apart from that I think that we'll have to keep our eyes on him. That may develop, I don't know. [. . .]

A second factor is staff discussion. Occasionally a teacher may know about a newcomer from a primary school teacher.

T: I had a letter from his primary school teacher about him. The father has a family of children and the widow he married has a family, so there are two families in one house. This boy in the primary school put years on his teacher and she felt terribly sorry for him. She wrote to me that when he came here I might take a particular interest in him.

Much more common is the discussion of teachers in the staffroom where teachers often 'compare notes' about pupils they teach. Teachers may seek confirmation or validation of their provisional typings in the opinions of their colleagues – and in the case of 'deviant' pupils some added consolation.

1 T: I don't know why they're like this, but they're not just like this with me. This is a general thing with all the teachers that they have. I know, because we talk in the staffroom.

2 T: I noticed him only because his work was better than others. I asked [a colleague] about him and he said he seemed quite bright so I think that he'd be one that we'd watch and see about getting him put in the other stream, because he does seem to be quite a good worker.

Naturally teachers gossip about 'good' pupils as well as 'deviant' pupils, but it is our impression, as former teachers as well as researchers, that there is more talk about the 'deviant' pupils, probably because such talk is simply more interesting. Inevitably, teachers hear these discussions and remember them even when they do not teach or know a pupil and an important source of pre-information is provided.

1 I: Did you know anything about her at that time?
T: No, but amongst the staff we discuss particularly the new arrivals. You can see after they've been here only a few weeks they start showing their teeth and it's something you watch coming, yet you can't do anything about it. It's like a slow-moving lava bed, if you like, of trouble.

    2 T: I am suspicious of them anyway from mostly more of what I have heard than seen myself . . .

[. . .] Such pre-information may well serve as a pre-typing, a second-hand provisional typing which the teacher can take over, actively searching for validation as if the speculation were his own.

    1 T: I'd heard his name mentioned, but he hadn't in fact stood out in my class. Then this morning we were going over some sentences and he said that 'his' should have a capital letter. So I looked at the sentence and I said, 'No, I'm afraid you're mistaken there.' And he said, '*You're* making the mistake, it should have a capital.' It was his manner – telling me, not asking me, 'Shouldn't it have a capital letter?' You know, I thought, 'Oh . . .' So I said, 'What's your name?' and he told me and I thought, 'That's right, I've heard about you.'. . So that's how he stood out, because he definitely resents being told.

    2 T: He can be a nuisance. He never has been, but I can see . . . I'd heard his name and I didn't even know who he was. Now I noticed this boy who'd start being giddy if Gavin did something . . . I'd heard his name mentioned in the staffroom, so whether he——Mrs——said he was one of those who'd start trouble when they were on the corridor . . . I think he will always need watching and yet you see at first I hadn't noticed him. It was a long time before I noticed that he was like this . . . I know he got off to a bad start with other teachers, and because I heard his name I thought, 'Who is this lad?' And I had a list with their names and where they sat and so I sort of looked and thought, 'Oh, that's him, is it?' but he hadn't done anything in my class.

This is not to say that teachers always accept the typings provided by colleagues. They may have developed their own typing before hearing the judgments of their colleagues or they may find that a pre-typing that is taken over from others fails to be verified.

    1 T: I knew some of them, not by person, I knew them from repute, you know. I mean I've got a form this year, I've heard some of their names bandied about amongst the teachers before I ever met the boys. But mind you, I don't pre-judge. I wait and see what they do with me. But all the same, you can't help but bear it in mind. You know, you wait and see how they behave for you. I don't believe in branding them – they may react differently to another teacher – but all the same it is at the back of your mind. You know you're only human.

    2 T: He's not a noisy individual. He's crafty to a large degree, but he's been quite an industrious boy as far as I'm concerned and hasn't caused me any undue worry. He's done all that I've asked him and worked well, producing good results and his behaviour is quite satisfactory.

From time to time I've heard different members of staff mentioning his name, and yet I can't line up my own experience of him on the same lines as theirs. I don't know whether to put it down to the fact that he likes maths. He does like maths, you see.

[. . .] Pupils are aware of this staff discussion, either through overhearing it or being directly informed by the teachers. Inevitably, perhaps, they see things in a somewhat different light from the teachers.

1 I: Let me put it to you that teachers are always picking on you because you are always doing things wrong?
P: It's mostly what they've heard all the time. They go off other people, other teachers. Like they'll say, 'I've heard this in the staffroom about you today. Do anything in my lesson and you've had it.'

2 P: He [teacher] always picks on me because I'm always taking the piss out of him. Spicer's always taking the piss out of him but Spicer's his pet because he's in the soccer team. Spicer's his pet. He'd get away with murder with [teacher]. I heard [teacher] talking to some other teachers in the gym when they were playing volleyball, and he said to them that Spicer's not as bad. I mean [teacher] is at it, 'He's not as bad as he's made out to be', but he's worse than us lot put together. He's a back-stabber. He'll get you to do something then he'll say, 'Sir, look what he's just done.' He's a dick. He's a poof.

A third factor which may lead a pupil to 'stand out' at an early stage is that the child may have some particular problem about which the school is informed and which becomes widely disseminated among the teachers. A good example is when the pupil suffers from some disabling medical condition. One pupil had a kidney complaint, and teachers were told about this so that they would know that his frequent requests to go to the toilet were legitimate and necessary. Another instance was the pupil who suffered from epilepsy.

In summary, a pupil may 'stand out' at a very early stage if he has an older sibling, and/or is discussed among the staff, and/or if he has a medical condition. But that in itself does not, of course, make him a 'deviant pupil'. What does a pupil do to make himself 'stand out' in this way? Is it perhaps because he breaks the rules in a highly dramatic way in a single incident? In this research we came across only one such case.

The teacher was adopting his jocular manner with the pupils, and there had been no problems in the previous three-quarters of the lesson, no disciplinary events. The teacher was pressing the pupil to tell him the word that they had to remember – 'conscientious' – and the pupil was obviously reluctant to do so, not because he didn't know it, but because he just didn't want to – in my opinion. Just prior to this the teacher had made a pun on his (the pupil's) surname, an innocuous one, pointing out his witticism to the rest of the class. The teacher did get him to say it, but only in a very quiet voice and he had to pull the pupil's hand away from his mouth as he was saying it. He then pushed the pupil further, firstly in trying to get him to say it out loud, which he wouldn't, and then by trying to make him spell it. The teacher indicated that the pupil was being a bit dull, because all he had to do was spell it from the board. At this point the pupil's control snapped and he lifted his fist to the teacher and said: 'Leave me alone or I'll bat you in the mouth!' The teacher was taken aback and just stood there. After four or five seconds the pupil said: 'You're always making fun of me and saying I'm stupid. You'd better stop it!' Throughout all this the pupil kept his fist raised. The teacher had to make a rapid decision. This he did by telling the whole class to say the school prayer out loud again. He made no comment and took no action at this time.

(Observation notes)

In a later interview the teacher commented:

T: When I spoke to him the other day, when he came, I thought devil-possessed, I was just trying to be friendly and I made a pun on his name . . . and instead of accepting it as a joke, he came as if he resented being spoken to and I think he must be – well, I know he is unhappy at home, but it seems to me that after that he resents any type of discipline or being co-opted in and he's lost his sense of humour and I shan't forget him. I tell you, I prayed for that lad last night and this morning because it's really such a pathetic state. I've seen [headmaster] but personally I think he should see a psychiatrist. . .
I: Had there been anything in the previous three weeks to indicate that this sort of thing might happen?
T: Nothing in the room at all, except that he was a Biggs, Terry's brother. I just knew that he was a Biggs and that you'd have to be reasonably careful, but I thought he was coming on reasonably well. He didn't show resentment. Something may have happened at home that we don't know anything about. I find that when a child is like this he's not well. It's quite likely that he'll be ill. But I've taught two murderers and I hope that I'm not teaching a third. It's a bit depressing for an RE Department, isn't it?

This incident is of interest, because it shows how a pupil, on the basis of a 'dramatic' incident, can be re-typed as 'mentally ill' and as a potential murderer, incorporating the sibling phenomenon, a speculative motivation, and new predictions into the re-typing. Yet this is not the way most deviant pupils become typed.

Very large numbers of pupils break a variety of rules when they are newcomers and such rule-breaking is perceived by the teachers as 'normal' and 'natural'. In part this is because the teachers cannot be sure that the pupils know, or have formed the habit of conforming to, the rules of this particular school. The 'settling in' period is regarded as one of rule-teaching and rule-learning. Pupil conduct which technically breaks the rules is interpreted as possibly 'accidental' or 'unintentional'.

> T: In the first week I made a big point of stressing to all of them that this is not a primary school any more and they are to be taught in a different way, and won't be allowed to run about as freely and behave as freely as they were at primary school. And particularly that talking in class and moving about in class, which is a big problem. You know, I would never have dreamt of getting up in the middle of a lesson but at junior school these boys have been allowed to walk about and they just do it now and you can tell them off about it, and they do it unintentionally. They are just used to doing it, and without permission they will suddenly just get up and go and borrow a pencil off somebody.

So when pupils break such rules when they are newcomers, they are reminded of the rule, reproved in a mild way, but not punished. Such 'deviance' is accepted and tolerated as part of the newcomer status. The teachers do not need to find motives for such conduct, for there are typical motives (ignorance, poor memory, accident) which derive directly from their typing (newcomers). Further, it is expected that a certain amount of 'deviance' will spring from fear, nervousness and anxiety, which are additional newcomer typical motives. But once the pupils are no longer accorded newcomer status, it is assumed that they have now learned the rules and that they are no longer nervous and apprehensive: they have 'settled in'. Rule-breaking acts which are treated as normal during the newcomer period now become defined as deviant.

> T: They have had – what? – a month to settle in, it's not so new to them now. This is normally when you start to find out any potential troublemakers, or which boys are going to be good, the sort of boys you put in plays and that sort of thing, you know. About this time, yes I think so. Just after they settle in, they get a bit of confidence and they think, 'I know where everything is now, I can start to be myself', sort of thing. If they are going to . . . I think between now and Christmas is the time you find out.

'Normal' pupils 'get over' their 'normal' deviance in the newcomer period; 'deviant' pupils do not.

> I: Are there any others you see as problems?
> T: Well, there's only giggling Roger. He's silly. He's a really silly little boy. He gets himself into trouble for laughing all the time. He can work

really well when he sets his mind to it, one of the best in the class, but he always has to laugh and hee-haw like a donkey all over the place. If he settles down I think he'll be all right but the fact that he is so silly influences quite a few people in the class. . . . I wonder if really when he first came to the school he felt very insecure, you know, being in a school of this size, and his reaction to that was to giggle and to laugh to cover up the fact that he was feeling very insecure. But it's gone on, you see. It's not been eradicated even though he's been in the class for nearly a term. He's still giggling now and at times he can be really offensive with his giggling.

Many children who are regarded by the teachers as deviant are not typed with a label that refers to a specific deviant act such as 'giggler', 'chatterbox', 'bully' or 'insolent', nor do they come to the teacher's attention because they break particular rules. In the average lesson in schools there are many pupil acts which strictly speaking can be defined as deviant, but a large proportion of these are not overtly defined by the teacher as deviant by a verbal deviance-imputation. There are many reasons for this [. . .] Teachers often do not take action against pupil acts they privately define as deviant, because the deviant acts are often very minor, breaking relatively minor rules; the acts sometimes 'peter out' naturally within a short period; the status of the act as deviant is somewhat ambiguous. We can, then, distinguish two kinds of deviant act; those which result in an overt deviance-imputation of some sort and those which are simply ignored by the teacher, even though the act is defined as deviant or probably deviant. We shall call these 'reactional deviance' and 'subreactional deviance' respectively.[7] Whilst one particular pupil may commit just one or two subreactional deviant acts in a lesson, another pupil may commit many subreactional acts which break a variety of rules. In this case, we can say that the pupil commits multiple and variegated subreactional deviance. Our argument is that some of the pupils who become typed as deviant do not commit isolated 'dramatic' deviant acts, or even repeated deviant acts of a specific kind (as with Roger and his giggling). Rather, they commit multiple and variegated subreactional deviance. In addition, they commit some reactional deviant acts, but these acts in isolation are never regarded as serious because they tend to break minor rules. This subreactional and reactional deviance is not 'compensated' by any outstanding or noticeable acts of conformity, which might counterbalance the deviance. The cumulative result is that the teacher is left with a 'vague impression' that the pupil is deviant, even though he cannot 'pin it down to any one incident'. Often, he cannot in fact remember what the pupil has done, precisely because subreactional deviant acts and minor reactional acts are simply forgotten. A second result is that because the deviant conduct is variegated, no specific label is entirely appropriate to the pupil. In consequence he tends to be given a general or diffuse deviant typing, such as 'difficult', 'a problem', 'a pest', 'nuisance' or 'troublemaker'. None of these labels gives any clear indication of the acts that the pupil commits, whereas 'chatterbox' and 'bully' do. Specific labels may be used to talk about the pupil in detail, but it is the diffuse label which most adequately summarizes the teacher's conception of him. In practice, the teacher may not assign him one of these diffuse labels at an early stage, but expresses a feeling that he is likely to become such a pupil.

Although many of our teachers made statements from which we derived these ideas, one teacher in particular gave a highly explicit and articulate account [. . .] The interviewer was asking the teacher to expand on a comment that he had made in an earlier interview to the effect that he thought the pupil 'could be bothersome later on' but this was 'purely a feeling'.

> T: Well, it's rather like driving a car with the seat of your pants, really. In your perception of children I'm sure there's a lot you don't note consciously, and yet all the time you're absorbing details of their behaviour at all times without this really registering. You're forming opinions even though you may say, 'Look, I can't say that I've had a big emotional upset with the boy', or anything like that. In fact, it's easier if you can say that, because at least you've got some really concrete evidence and this can always be used against the child later on. You start basing impressions of them on the basis of a lot of stimuli from them, and you make a note of it, subconsciously perhaps, and then you'll give an opinion on that child that is based on what? On an accumulation of little bits and pieces here and there.
>
> I: Can you think of any particular incidents?
>
> T: None, except that we know his name. Of all the children in the class there aren't many that you know the name of at this stage. Yet his name has come to the fore, and not for anything academic or otherwise really. It's just that you do know him. Yet there has been no incident where you could say, 'Look. Dreadful boy', and there's been no incident where you could say, 'Lovely lad', and yet you do know him all the same. I reckon it's an accumulation of incidents that have brought his name to notice . . . It's the little incidents that you don't sort of note but which you sum up in the end to making this kind of judgment about him.
>
> I: It's these sort of incidents I'm interested in.
>
> T: But there's nothing really. It's the things that are just not big enough to step into. Nothing there that you could say, 'Here's something that needs intervening over.'

We have now covered the main processes of typing in the speculative and elaborative stages, the factors which can lead a pupil to 'stand out', and the concept of subreactional deviance [. . .] The teachers' typings of first and second year pupils are [. . .] qualified typings. The characterizations may be made with a degree of confidence and the teachers are willing to make predictions about pupils, but normally there is also an element of doubt that remains. The teachers accept that their typings may be wrong or incomplete, and show themselves willing to revise their typings in the light of subsequent developments. As 'time will tell' they can afford to 'wait and see'. Yet this is not a passive period of waiting for teachers; they have a 'working hypothesis', however provisional, which is constantly tested against events. The very fact that the teachers are unsure about the potential deviant puts him in a special category. No doubt there is the equivalent category of the pupil who is potentially 'very good', but provided that such a pupil is not presenting the teachers with any current problems, they do not need to worry about him. They can afford to 'wait and see' passively and optimistically. The special status of the potential deviant resides in the fact that he typically presents current problems, albeit minor ones, which if the teachers' predictions are correct will grow into major ones. So the teachers are actively concerned to avert such an eventuality. It is this determination to find preventive measures wherever possible that makes the teachers suspicious of the potential deviant. In its turn this suspicion results in an active surveillance, for unless the teachers watch the pupil and events closely they may not notice the small incremental steps which constitute 'getting worse', nor will they be able to take preventive measures. They therefore 'keep an eye' on the potential deviant [. . .] As a result of this special surveillance, the potential deviant is elaborated more quickly than 'normal' pupils and the elaboration is in terms of the provisional deviant typing. Thus an appropriate biography and motivational backcloth is constructed for him and such information (having a certain kind of home background, having a deviant elder brother) can, should the speculation be confirmed, be used by the teachers as an explanation of him. They will be disappointed if he turns out to be a deviant, but they will not be surprised.

Over time these doubts and speculations diminish – though they rarely fade completely away – and the typing has entered the stage of stabilization. Essentially, it is a progression from 'he may be this kind of pupil, but then again he may not' to 'he *is* this kind of pupil'. This stage overlaps and fuses with the elaborative stage in that certain elements in the typing may stabilize fairly quickly whilst other elements are being elaborated or are being rejected and reformulated in the processes of de-typing and re-typing [. . .] We must emphasize that type stabilization is not the same as type permanence. In the speculation stage the teachers make hypotheses which may then become confirmed and treated as commonsense 'facts' in the stabilization stage. But such 'facts' too can change. In other words, the stabilization stage can give way to yet a fourth stage, namely the stage of type transformation in which one stabilized type is transformed into a different stabilized type. Our impression is that most pupils are stabilized by the second or third years. The teachers see such a stabilized pupil as changing as he gets older, and as they get to know him better, but these changes are perceived as 'natural developments', that is, as congruent with the way 'he always was'. Other pupils change more radically after stabilization. Pupils who were seen as 'difficult' in the first two years [. . .] sometimes 'improve', for it is part of teachers' commonsense knowledge that there is a long-term version of 'settling down' apart from the adjustment that is typically made immediately following the newcomer status. Equally, other pupils originally stabilized as 'good' may 'deteriorate' or become 'unsettled', either temporarily (where stabilized typing can be retained) or more permanently (where type transformation takes place). There are many explanations teachers can use to explain type trans-formations in either direction – changes explicable by age (especially adolescence); changes due to the influence of friends and peer relations; changes in home circumstances; and changes in school, such as liking/disliking a subject or teacher, or the proximity of examinations, and so on. We witnessed no type transformations in school A, but that does not mean they were not taking place. All the deviant pupils we studied were in the stabilization stage. It is possible that type transformations are unusual in the case of deviant pupils, partly because teachers see such type transformations as unlikely before the pupil leaves school, and partly because when the deviant pupil sees himself as being thus stabilized in the eyes of the teacher, he sees little point in attempting such a type transformation because he believes that the teachers will be unwilling to give up the stabilized deviant typings.

1 P: I hate him. He's always picking on me. If anything goes wrong in the class he always picks on me or [another pupil]. [Another pupil] was going to give me something and he [the teacher] said, 'Don't give it to him you can't trust him.'
I: Why did he say you can't be trusted?
P: It's 'cos I've been in the nick that's why. There's more than him hates me because of that. Mr——does. This girl were coming down the corri-dor and she stuck her shoulder out, this would be when I'd only been here about four or five weeks, so I twisted her arm up her back and he were on the corridor and he said, 'You'll be ending up on another long holiday if you keep doing that Grimes.' It got me mad that. I didn't like it. I didn't tell nobody but I'm waiting for him to say it again. I just want to forget about it, but people like teachers keep bringing it up. If there's any trouble in the school they think it's me.

2: I Do you think that you should start with a clean sheet each year?
P: I'm not particularly bothered. It would be all right if we could in our last year start with a clean sheet, but some teachers don't give you that chance. Something happens and they'll say, 'Come here. Have you done such and such a thing? Do you know anything about it?' You've got a reputation. . . . I know that I'm a troublemaker, but it's the times that you get into trouble for the things that you haven't done that gets

you down. I'm getting blamed for this and I'm getting blamed for that.

[. . .] Once a pupil is predominantly typed in a stable form, a number of important processes are set in train. At this point we need only mention the two basic characteristics of the stage of stabilization. The first of these, 'type fusion', refers to the fact that the teacher's knowledge of the pupil is woven into a complex and relatively coherent whole. The outcomes of the elaborative stage – the multiple typings, the specification of the conditions under which typical acts occur, the elaboration of motives – are brought together into a coherent and clear characterization. At this point the teacher is able to talk about the pupil at considerable length and may find it very difficult to 'summarize' the pupil in a few words or in a short description. The second element in this stage is 'type centralization', where some aspects of the typing are made more central to the pupil than others. The typings are ordered into a hierarchy of significance for the understanding of the pupil, some typings being treated as of central significance and others being regarded as peripheral. For instance, two pupils may commit very similar acts of a deviant nature but one pupil is regarded as 'really difficult' and the other as 'difficult, but he's O.K. underneath really'. The first pupil is regarded as centrally, pivotally or essentially deviant,[8] whilst the second pupil is seen as peripherally deviant and centrally 'normal' or 'conformist'.

Our particular interest is in 'deviant' pupils who have reached the stage of stabilization. [. . .] Such 'difficult' pupils appear to have three characteristics. The first is that their deviant conduct is of variegated form. That is, they commit a wide range of deviance. More specific labels or typings are used to describe the detail of their deviant conduct, but it is the sheer range of deviance which drives the teacher into using a diffuse typing whenever he wishes to make a summary statement about the pupil. The second characteristic is the persistence of the deviant conduct. It is not regarded as a temporary phenomenon, as in the case of newcomer deviance or in the case of those pupils who are seen as 'passing through a difficult phase'. The deviant conduct is seen as a relatively permanent and central feature of the pupil; it continues now as it did in the past and as it will probably do in the future. The third characteristic, related to the second, is that the deviant conduct is irremediable; there is little the teacher can do about it. The teacher is concerned to remedy the deviant conduct both in the short-term and the long-term. In the short-term, the teacher's objective is to handle each deviant act at its point of occurrence in such a way that it is stopped immediately and a recurrence in the immediate future is inhibited. In the long-term, the teacher's aim is to cure the pupil of his deviant behaviour and to convert him to being a 'conformist' or 'good' pupil. A pupil is irremediable when the teacher fails in both objectives, but especially in the second. That is to say, the teacher may manage some degree of short-term control but never manages to eradicate the deviance. Teachers, of course, vary in their ability to achieve short-term control. It is rare for a teacher to find one of these pupils utterly beyond control, but whilst one teacher may find him extremely difficult to handle from lesson to lesson, another teacher may have worked out sufficiently successful short-term strategies which at least allow him 'to cope' with the pupil. Yet all the teachers agree that these deviant pupils are impossible to change.

[. . .] Although deviant pupils may be classified together under the diffuse label of 'troublemaker', there is nevertheless a uniqueness about every typing when pupils are considered as individuals. Deviant pupils emerge as distinct individuals, each with his own methods of deviating on particular occasions and for particular motives. Yet they are all 'trouble*makers*' for they all present the teacher with practical problems. There is a certainty and confidence to the teacher's knowledge of these pupils which, based on multitudinous events a few of which are remembered but most of which are soon forgotten, has been built over time into a coherent and resistant characterization. The hesitancy, the tentativeness and the ambivalence that was so marked in the earlier stage of speculation has been succeeded by the conviction of stabilization. It is this complex stabilized typing which can be readily used by teachers in the evidencing of deviant acts. Since the typing is an integral part of the teacher's commonsense knowledge of the classroom and the pupils, he can use it in ambiguous situations to 'fill in' what the pupil is doing and for what motives. In the same way, this commonsense knowledge constantly informs the ways in which teachers formulate methods of handling or responding to deviant acts.

Notes

1 There have been three major approaches to this topic. The phenomenologists have drawn extensively on Alfred Schutz's work on types and this has been linked with the sociological/phenomenological approach to motives (Blum and McHugh, 1971). Social psychologists have approached the topic in the form of person perception, where there have been some major phenomenological contributions (Heider, 1958; From, 1971). Heider provided the foundations for attribution theory in social psychology (Jones, 1972). The third approach is based on the work of George Kelly (1955) on personal construct theory. Each strand has been developed with a quite astonishing neglect of the other two. The relationship between these three strands is far too complex to analyse in a note. In this [article] we have drawn most heavily on the first of the three approaches.
2 For some references, see Hargreaves (1972), pp. 156–8.
3 Our findings here come as no surprise; they fully support the literature. We shall take two of these many studies. Hallworth (1961, 1962), in a psychometric study, analysed teachers' personality ratings of their pupils. Two main factors emerged. The first factor, based on the teacher's implicit question, 'How does this child get on with me?', is called the factor of conscientiousness and reliability. It includes traits such as emotional stability, trustworthiness, persistence, co-operation with

teacher, and maturity. The second factor, which arises from the teacher's implicit question, 'How does this pupil get on with other pupils?', is called the factor of extraversion, and includes such traits as cheerfulness, sense of humour and sociability. From our point of view this pioneering study has one important failure: it imposes certain constructs or terms in the rating schedule given to the teachers, and tells us little about the teacher's natural or everyday constructs that he uses in his own thinking or conversation. This fault is remedied in Nash's (1973) study, using Kelly's repertory grid test, which elicits the teachers' own constructs in the form of bipolar opposites. With an extremely small sample of secondary school teachers, he showed that the main constructs are:

bright	– dull
lively	– lumpish
likeable	– less likeable
well-behaved	– less well-behaved
sociable	– less sociable

There is clearly a heavy overlap with Hallworth's findings. Nash claims that his approach is phenomenological, but this is a claim we would dispute. Having obtained the constructs from the teachers, Nash then makes comparisons between teachers without checking that the constructs have the same meanings for the teachers, and he also quantifies the constructs in a highly dubious way. More important from our point of view, Nash shows no interest in how these constructs are arrived at by the teachers, but instead spends a whole chapter reporting his own interpretive observations of pupils in the light of the constructs elicited from the teachers. 'The child in the classroom was observed as objectively as possible and . . . his behaviour was reinterpreted as it seemed to be perceived by his teacher' (pp. 29–30). Apart from the inherent absurdity of such a practice, it simply does not help us to discover either the teacher's meanings of the constructs or the way in which they were generated. Nash compounds and confuses his own commonsense knowledge with that of the teacher, instead of attempting to explicate the teacher's commonsense knowledge by analysing the meanings of, and grounds for, as well as the relationship between, the teacher's constructs. Since our interest was in providing a dynamic and process theory of typing, we used the interview method, which seems more appropriate to that purpose than the time-consuming and cumbersome repertory grid technique.

4 This clearly draws upon George Kelly's (1955) notion of the layman as an 'incipient scientist'.

> As a scientist, man seeks to predict, and thus control, the course of events. It follows, then, that the constructs which he formulates are intended to aid him in his predictive efforts . . . each construct represents a pair of rival hypotheses, either of which may be applied to a new element which the person seeks to construe.

A much more extensive treatment of this notion is provided in the work of Garfinkel (1967).

5 We had a serious methodological problem here in that we were unable to make very frequent checks on teachers' developing typings without taking the risk that our questions might actually affect the process of typing. Teachers are not normally subjected to such questions and we were anxious not to create a special research-effect by regular or repeated interviews about these first year pupils. We confined ourselves to two interviews, one in September and one in January, and we did not warn the teachers in September that we would repeat the process in January.

6 Seaver (1973) shows that what we call the sibling phenomenon can create self-fulfilling prophecies with respect to academic attainment.

7 This distinction rests upon a distinction between the covert definition of an act as deviant and the overt reaction to that act.

8 This notion is a common one in labelling theory. Becker (1963) draws upon Everett Hughes's (1945) distinction between 'master' and 'auxiliary' characteristics. Lofland (1969) writes:

> One of the clustered categories is singled out and treated as the most important and significant feature of the person . . . being dealt with. It is seen as defining the character . . . That is, there comes to be a *pivotal category* that defines 'who this person is' . . . The phenomenon of humans adopting a category as pivotal and scrutinizing all other categories in terms of their consistency with it, implies, in practice, that whatever is taken as pivotal *is* Actor − *is* his essential nature or core being.

The topic is also extensively explored by Matza (1969).

References

BECKER, H.S. (1963). *Outsiders: Studies in the Sociology of Deviance*. Free Press.

BLUM, A. and MCHUGH, P. (1971). 'The social ascription of motives', *American Sociological Review*, vol. 36, pp. 98–109.

FROM, F. (1971). *Perception of Other People*. Columbia University Press.

GARFINKEL, H. (1967). *Studies in Ethnomethodology*. Prentice-Hall.

HALLWORTH, H.J. (1961). 'Teachers' personality ratings of high school pupils', *Journal of Educational Psychology*, vol. 52, pp. 297–302.

HALLWORTH, H.J. (1962). 'A teacher's perceptions of his pupils', *Educational Review*, vol. 14, pp. 124–33.

HARGREAVES, D.H. (1972). *Interpersonal Relations and Education*. Routledge and Kegan Paul.

HEIDER, F. (1958). *The Psychology of Interpersonal Relations*. Wiley.

HUGHES, E.C. (1945). 'Dilemmas and contradictions of status', *American Journal of Sociology*, vol. 50, pp. 353–9.

JONES, E.E. et al. (1972). *Attribution: Perceiving the Causes of Behaviour*. General Learning Press.

KELLY, G.M. (1955). *The Psychology of Personal Constructs*. (2 vols), Norton.

LOFLAND, J. (1969). *Deviance and Identity*. Prentice-Hall.

MATZA, D. (1969). *Becoming Deviant*. Prentice-Hall.

NASH, R. (1973). *Classrooms Observed*. Routledge and Kegan Paul.

RIST, R.C. (1970). 'Student social class and teacher expectations: the self-fulfilling prophecy in ghetto education', *Harvard Educational Review*, vol. 40, pp. 411–51.

ROSENTHAL, R. and JACOBSON, L.F. (1968). *Pygmalion in the Classroom*. Holt, Rinehart and Winston.

SEAVER, W.B. (1973). 'Effects of naturally induced teacher expectations', *Journal of Personality and Social Psychology*, vol. 28, no. 3, pp. 333–42.

SCHUTZ, A. (1932). *Der Sinnhafte Aufbau der Socialen Welt*. Springer.

Naturalistic Studies of Teacher Expectation Effects

J. Brophy and T. Good

[. . .] At the time that our involvement in teacher expectation research began (1969), we were (and are) convinced that expectation effects were real despite the criticisms of Rosenthal and Jacobson's (1968) study. Thus we were less interested in research using product measures to establish the reality of teacher expectation effects and more interested in research using process measures designed to reveal how teacher expectations affect teacher and student behavior. By this means we could indicate the cause-and-effect mechanisms underlying the processes by which teacher expectations become self-fulfilling. We developed the original version of the Dyadic Interaction Observation System for use in our original teacher expectation study (Brophy and Good, 1970a). This original version has been expanded and modified since, although all of the essential features that make it uniquely useful for teacher expectation research have been retained [. . .]

Observation System

Since one object of this series of studies was to see if teachers treated students differently when they held different expectations for them, an observation system was needed for classifying teacher and student behavior in situations where the teacher was dealing with individual students. Observation systems already available (Simon and Boyer, 1967) were not appropriate for this purpose, since they used the class rather than the individual student as the unit of analysis. Consequently, we constructed our own system (Brophy and Good, 1970b; Good and Brophy, 1970), guided by the following specifications:

1 The system should be geared to *dyadic* teacher-student interactions, in which the teacher is interacting with individual students

2 It should retain the *sequence* of action and reaction in each interchange, so that effects due to the behavior of the teachers can be separated from those due to the behavior of the students

3 It should be designed so that interactions can be coded by classroom observers as they occur, without requiring audio or video tapes

4 It should be sensitive to teacher behavior which might be related to the teachers' communication of their *expectations* for student performance

[. . .] The system is designed so that all dyadic contacts between a teacher and an individual student are recorded. Special emphasis is given to contacts involving school-related work, since these seem most relevant to the communication of achievement expectations. Five types of dyadic contacts are distinguished: *public response opportunities*, in which the student tries to answer a question posed by the teacher; *reading turns*, in which he reads aloud from a primer or reader; *private work-related contacts*, which concern the student's seatwork or homework, *private procedural interactions*, which concern supplies, food or drink, washroom trips, errands for the teacher, or other matters not directly related to classwork; and *behavioral evaluations*, in which the teacher singles out a student for praise or criticism of his classroom behavior. Each type of interaction is coded as it occurs, with contacts initiated by the teacher being recorded separately from those initiated by the student. Teacher praise and criticism in each type of contact are also coded whenever they occur.

The sequence of events is preserved in coding public response opportunities that occur when a student is called on to respond to a question or when a student calls out an answer and receives feedback from the teacher. Called out answers which are ignored by the teacher are not coded. Thus public response opportunities are classified into three types: *open questions*, in which the teacher poses the question, waits for students to raise their hands, and then calls on a student with his hand up; *direct questions*, in which the teacher calls on a student who has not indicated a desire to respond (the teacher names the student before asking the question or calls on a student who does not have his hand up); and *call outs*, in which a student calls out an answer before the teacher has a chance to call on someone. Direct questions are the most clearly teacher-initiated response opportunities; open questions involve initiative by both the teacher and the student; and call outs are determined almost completely by the student (although the teacher must give a feedback response rather than ignore the student).

The level of response demand built into teacher questions is also coded.

Five types of questions are identified: *process* questions, which require the student to give a detailed explanation or to explain the thinking and problem solving that underlies an answer; *product* questions, which require the student to provide a short factual answer or bit of information from memory; *choice* questions, which require the student to select from among response alternatives provided by the teacher or by a workbook; *opinion* questions, which require the student to make a prediction or give an opinion regarding some curriculum-relevant matter; and *self-reference questions*, which concern the student's personal experiences, likes and dislikes, or other personal matters. From the viewpoint of the level of demand made upon the student, process questions are usually the most difficult, followed in order by the other types of questions as listed above.

In addition to coding the type and difficulty level of response opportunities, observers also code the *quality of the student's response* (coded as correct, part correct, incorrect, or no response) and the types of *feedback reactions given by the teachers.* Teacher feedback reactions include praising, criticizing, giving the answer, giving more extensive process feedback, calling on someone else to give the answer, repeating the question, rephrasing the question or giving a clue, asking a new question, and failing to give any feedback at all.

These question-answer-feedback sequences of response opportunities are recorded in the order in which they occur, so that their sequence as well as their frequency can be determined from the coding sheets. This feature of the system makes possible the derivation of percentage scores which allows us to control for differences in frequency of different kinds of teacher-student interactions and therefore to make more direct comparisons between students than the more typically used frequency counts allow.

In addition to praise, criticism, and failure to give feedback, the process-product distinction is also used in coding teacher responses during private work-related interactions. If a teacher merely tells the student that his work is correct or incorrect, or if he merely gives the student an answer, he is coded for simple *product* feedback. However, if he takes time to explain the process by which the student can arrive at the correct answer or to explain the nature of an error that the student has made, he is coded for *process* feedback. This distinction is useful in assessing the degree to which teachers work with individual students when they are having difficulties. High rates of process feedback indicate that the teacher is working with the student, trying to help him learn the material. In contrast, low rates of process feedback imply that the teacher is simply giving the student answers rather than taking time to work with him until he clearly understands the concept or task.

Basic Methodological Procedures

With only minor variations from one study to the next, the same basic procedures for obtaining and analyzing data were used in all of the studies involving the Dyadic System. First, decisions were made about which variables should be included in a particular study. Variables pertaining to the reading group, for example, were not needed at later grades where no reading groups occur. Once the coding categories to be used in a given study were agreed upon, an appropriate coding sheet was designed, and observers practiced using the system in classrooms similar to those in which the study was to be conducted. Observer practice continued until acceptable levels of reliability (80 percent agreement) were achieved (see Brophy and Good, 1970b, for details). Then observers worked individually, each being responsible for coding one or more classrooms.

Unless hand raising is included in the study (as in Brophy and Good, 1970a), there never is more than one codable dyadic teacher-student interaction going on at any one time. Thus a single observer can code *all* dyadic interactions involving the teacher, so that only one coder is required per classroom once the coder's reliability is established.

So that data on individual students can be retrieved from the coding sheets, each student in a class is assigned a number. This number is recorded (along with other information), whenever he has a dyadic interaction with the teacher. Data are later tabulated separately for each student, and the student is assigned mean scores reflecting the *quantity* of his contacts with the teacher and percentage scores reflecting the *quality* of these contacts. The mean scores are determined by dividing the total number of contacts in a category by the number of times the student was present for observation [. . .]

Initial Study

Our initial study (Brophy and Good, 1970a) was conducted in four of the nine first-grade classrooms in a school serving a predominantly lower class population. The first grade was selected for study because Rosenthal and Jacobson had reported the strongest expectation effects at this grade level. The four classes were chosen because no student teachers were present, as they were in the other classes. Since we were mainly interested in studying typical interactions in everyday classrooms rather than in classrooms affected by special experimental treatments, we decided to use the teachers' own naturalistically formed expectations rather than try to induce expectations, as Rosenthal and Jacobson had done. Consequently, each teacher was asked to rank the children in her classroom in order of expected achievement. The instructions for ranking were kept deliberately vague to encourage the teachers to use their own complex subjective citeria in making judgments.

The teachers' rankings were then used to select children for special study. In each case three boys and three girls high on the teacher's list (highs) and three boys and three girls low on the teacher's list (lows) were selected for observation. Substitutes for each type of child (high boys, high girls, low boys, and low girls) were also identified. Whenever a sample student was absent during a scheduled observation, a substitute was observed in his place. Thus equal numbers of each type of child were observed during each observation period.

The teachers knew that the study was concerned with the classroom behavior of children of various achievement levels, but they did not realize that their own behavior as well as that of the children was being specifically observed. In addition, they thought that observations were being taken on every child in the classroom and did not know that specific subgroups had been selected for study. These cautions were necessary to insure that teachers would not possess knowledge that would allow them deliberately to affect the outcome of the study. More specific information about the research was given to the teachers later, after the observational data had been collected.

By selecting only students who were high or low on the teachers' rankings, we increased the chances of discovering differential teacher treatment related to teacher expectations. However, the school district had tracked students according to abilities, using readiness and achievement test data. Our observations were taken in the spring, after the children already had been grouped on the basis of readiness tests given in the fall and then regrouped between semesters on the basis of achievement test scores. *Therefore, at least in terms of test scores, ability differences among the children in a given room were minimal, and there was little objective support for the teachers' expectation rankings.*

Thus, although we were observing children who were placed at all extremes within the rooms, according to the teachers' subjective judgments, the tracking procedure and test data suggest that actual ability differences between children at the extremes within rooms were relatively small compared to the differences between rooms. The rooms in which we observed were ranked third, sixth, seventh, and eight among the nine first-grade classrooms.

Observations lasting an entire morning or afternoon (two of each for each class) were made on four separate days in each classroom. Data were recorded for all periods of academic activity, using one coding sheet for reading groups and another for all other situations. During nonacademic procedural activities (cleaning up, getting in line, pledging to the flag, and so on), only behavioral evaluations were coded.

In each class, one observer coded the interactions involving the six highs and the other coded the six lows. Assignments were balanced so that each observer spent half his time watching highs and the other half watching lows.

Originally, observer assignments were to be made according to convenience, with one observer watching children in the left side of the room and the other watching the children in the right side. We had expected that this plan would randomize the highs and lows across observers [. . .] However, in three of the four classrooms, dividing the children according to seating location resulted in the assignment of the six highs to one coder and the six lows to the other!

The children were seated around movable rectangular tables, with one at each end and six or eight along the sides. First-grade classrooms usually have three reading groups, and frequently there are three tables in the class. Teachers often find it convenient to assign each reading group to its own table. This facilitates giving assignments, monitoring seatwork, and other teaching activities which require different teacher behavior towards the different reading groups.

One effect of this practice, however, is to segregate the children according to achievement level. In three of the four classrooms in which we observed, the seating order, progressing from the head of one table through the middle table and back up the other table, was almost perfectly parallel to the teacher's achievement rankings! Over time this in itself would tend to polarize the classroom (increase the differences between highs and lows), because it minimizes the potential benefits that the less able students can derive from contact with the brighter students. In addition, as Rist (1970) also noted, the top group was usually seated closest to the teacher's desk, where they had easier access to her and were more likely to be noticed by her.

It is worth noting here that, although all four teachers were observed to treat children in the high and low groups differentially in ways that favored the highs, there was less favoritism by the teacher who dispersed her children randomly rather than seating them by reading groups. We suspect that teachers who seat their children randomly are more likely to treat them as individuals rather than as stereotyped group members.

Results

Raw data for each of the forty-eight children were tabulated and analyzed for group differences. The major findings will be presented in two sections (see Brophy and Good, 1970a, for details). The first section was concerned with group differences in interaction patterns which cannot be ascribed clearly to the teachers. Many of these are strictly child behavior measures, such as hand raising counts and frequencies of child-initiated private contacts. Others are teacher-child patterns which may result from behavioral differences between the groups of children, from teacher discrimination between the groups, or from a combination of these two factors. Examples

TABLE 1   Expectancy group differences in child behavior and teacher-child interaction in the Initial Study (from Brophy and Good, 1970a)

Measures	Lows	Highs
Number of times called on to answer an open question	1.71	1.96
Number of times called on to answer a direct question	1.83	2.50
Number of times called on by teacher during reading groups	4.79	3.29*
Number of times child called out answer during reading group	2.96	3.54
Procedural contacts initiated by child	3.17	5.13**
Work-related contacts initiated by child	1.79	7.38***
Procedural contacts initiated by teacher	2.58	2.04
Work-related contacts initiated by teacher	6.00	3.79
Number of behavioral criticisms from teacher	4.92	2.04***
Total teacher-initiated response opportunities	10.96	10.29
Total child-initiated response opportunities	7.92	16.04***
Total dyadic contacts with teacher	33.67	35.17
Number of times child raises hand to seek response opportunity	8.88	16.67***
Number of times called on/number of times raises hand	0.20	0.12**
Total correct answers	6.67	8.92*
Total incomplete, incorrect and "don't know" answers	4.63	2.38***
Average number of reading problems per reading turn	4.67	2.23***
Percent of total contacts involving praise from the teacher	3.88	11.00***
Precent of total contacts involving criticism from the teacher	24.33	10.75***

$* p < .10$ $** p < .05$ $*** p < .001$

here include teacher-initiated response opportunities, praise and criticism frequencies, and behavioral evaluations. These data appear in Table 1.

The data in Table 1 show large and consistent differences between the expectancy groups. The highs initiated more public response opportunities and work-related private contacts with the teacher, raised their hands more often, gave more correct and fewer incorrect answers, had fewer problems per reading turn, and received more praise and less criticism than the lows. This pattern of differences in classroom behavior was paralleled by differences favoring the highs on the Stanford Achievement Tests taken at the end of the year.

The large group differences on hand raising and on initiation of work contacts are consistent with what our model would predict for data collected late in the school year. Since no earlier data were collected, it is impossible to tell whether these differences had been present all year long or had increased as the school year progressed. In any case, it is clear that late in the school year the highs were much more active in seeking response opportunities and in going to the teacher to discuss their seatwork.

The data concerning student-initiated contacts with the teachers are particularly revealing. Lows sought out the teachers less frequently than highs even for procedural matters, suggesting that they were less teacher oriented than highs and perhaps even alienated from their teachers. Differences were even greater for work-related contacts. The lows were notably reluctant to come to the teacher to discuss their work, even though they presumably needed more help and instruction. The teacher evaluation data suggest a possible reason for this reluctance: praise and criticism are closely balanced for the highs, but the lows averaged more than six critical comments for every favorable one. Such heavy rates of criticism probably discouraged lows from seeking help from the teachers, even though they needed it more.

Differences between highs and lows were mostly in *quality* rather than *quantity* of contacts with teachers. There was little difference in the total number of contacts with teachers, but more of the contacts involving highs were response opportunities or private work-related contacts, and more were initiated by the children themselves. The differences seem clearly attributable to the behavior of the children rather than to a teacher tendency to give more response opportunities to highs or to initiate more interactions with them. In fact, measures of teacher-initiated contacts usually favored the lows, although the differences usually were not significant.

These data might mean that the teachers were attempting to compensate for the differences in child-initiated contacts by seeking out lows more frequently for individual attention. However, the evidence suggests only a slight tendency at best. Although the teachers did initiate more procedural contacts, more work-related contacts, and more total response opportunities with the lows, none of these group differences were significant. Furthermore, the difference on the measure of direct questions favored the highs, even though teachers could have compensated here for the greater tendency of the highs to call out answers and seek response opportunities through hand raising.

The only frequency measure suggesting teacher compensation which reached statistical significance was the ratio of the number of times the child was called on to answer open questions over the number of times he raised his hand. Lows were called on an average of 20 percent of the times they raised their hands, while the average for the highs was 12 percent. However, these figures were not adjusted for the group difference in hand raising frequency. When hand raising rates are adjusted the results will favor the lows, but the difference no longer approaches statistical significance. Taken together, then, the data suggest that there was a small tendency at best for teachers to compensate for the lows' lower rates of initiation of interaction by taking it upon themselves to initiate contacts with lows.

In general, the findings on quantity of contacts were somewhat at variance with those of Good (1970) and Kranz, Weber, and Fishell (1970), who reported that first-grade teachers give significantly more response opportunities to highs. Perhaps the teachers in this study were more aware of the differences in the rates of child-initiated contacts and made a clear effort to counteract these differences through their own actions. However, it seems more likely that the discrepancy was due to the tracking system used in the school. That is, it is likely that there were smaller differences in abilities and behavior between the highs and the lows in this study than in the research reported by Good (1970) and Kranz, Weber, and Fishell (1970).

Teachers' Expectations as Self-fulfilling Prophecies

Most of the differences between highs and lows reviewed in the preceding section are consistent with the notion that the teachers were treating the two groups differently because they held different expectations for them. However, these group differences do not really provide direct evidence that teachers' expectations were functioning as self-fulfilling prophecies. Since the children differed in their behavior, the group differences discussed above would appear even if the teachers were merely reacting consistently. That is, the group differences could be due solely to differences in the children and not to any direct discrimination or favoritism by the teachers. More direct evidence to support the self-fulfilling prophecy hypothesis would require data to show that the teachers were treating the groups differently in equivalent situations. The data from five such measures are presented in Table 2.

The measures in Table 2 provide direct evidence that the teachers' differential expectations for student performance were affecting their classroom behavior. The measures all involve the teachers' reactions to student attempts to answer questions or to read in the reading groups. They are all percentage measures which take into account absolute differences in the frequencies of the various behaviors involved, allowing for a direct comparison of the teachers' behavior toward the two groups in *equivalent situations.*

TABLE 2   Group differences from the Initial Study on variables related
to the communication of teacher expectations (from Brophy and Good,
1970a)

Measures	Lows	Highs
Percent of correct answers followed by praise	5.88	12.08**
Percent of wrong answers followed by criticism	18.77	6.46***
Percent of wrong answers followed by repetition or rephrasing the question or by giving a clue	11.52	27.04*
Percent of reading problems followed by repetition or rephrasing the question or by giving a clue	38.37	67.05***
Percent of answers (correct or incorrect) not followed by any feedback from the teacher	14.75	3.33***

* $p < .10$ ** $p < .05$ *** $p < .01$

The teachers consistently favored the highs in demanding and reinforcing
quality performance. Despite the fact that highs gave more correct answers
and fewer incorrect answers, they were *more* frequently praised when correct and *less* frequently criticized when incorrect or unable to respond. We
were quite surprised by these findings, in view of the stress that teacher
trainers place on the need to encourage children and to promote learning
through praise and rewards.

In view of the highs' greater success in reading and answering questions,
we were not surprised by the data in Table 1 showing that highs received
more total praise and less total criticism than lows. However, in view of the
advice given prospective teachers in educational psychology books and of
our commonsense predictions about teachers' reactions to successes and
failures by these two contrasting groups, we had expected that the percentage measures for praise of success and criticism of failure in Table 2 would
favor the lows.

Because the lows are successful less frequently, we assumed that a correct
response from one of these children would be more significant to the teacher
and more likely to elicit praise than a correct answer from one of the highs.
Similarly, we expected that teachers would be less likely to criticize the lows
for failure to respond correctly, because of their greater learning difficulty.
However, the results were precisely the opposite. The lows were only half as

likely as the highs to be praised following a correct response, and they were three times as likely to be criticized following failures. The teachers were encouraging and supportive toward the children who needed it least, but were cool and critical toward the children who most needed encouragement!

The next two measures in Table 2 show that the teachers were more persistent in eliciting responses from highs than lows. When highs responded incorrectly or were unable to respond, the teachers were more likely to provide a second response opportunity by repeating or rephrasing the question or by giving a clue. Conversely, they were more likely to give the answer or call on another child when reacting to lows in similar situations.

The final measure in Table 2 gives the percentages of instances in which the teachers gave no feedback reaction whatever following a student response. Teachers neglected to give feedback only 3.33 percent of the time when reacting to highs, while the corresponding figure for lows was 14.75 percent, a highly significant difference.

Taken together, the data in Table 2 show that the teachers took more appropriate action to elicit a good performance from the highs, and that they tended to reinforce it appropriately when it was elicited. In contrast, they tended to accept poor performance from lows, and they failed to reinforce good performance properly even when it did occur.

This differential treatment goes beyond the differences in performance between the two groups, and is the type of teacher behavior that would polarize the class over time by enhancing the motivation and performance of the highs and depressing that of the lows. In view of the data of Table 2, the contrasting patterns of student-initiated contacts with the teachers that were summarized in Table 1 are not surprising. The teachers were treating the highs in ways that would encourage these students to seek them out, while their treatment of the lows was more likely to induce alienation.

The data of Table 2 provide a glimpse of another phenomenon that appears frequently in our observations: teachers sometimes overvalue correct answers and those students who give correct answers frequently. From an objective standpoint, incorrect answers and failures are at least as useful as correct answers and successes. While the latter confirm that learning has occurred, the former are useful both as evidence of deficiencies in learning and as indicators of the nature of the difficulty. However, many teachers do not respond so objectively to right and wrong answers. Like anyone else they want to have a sense of accomplishment and success in their work. In practice this means that correct answers and successful reading are experienced as rewards by some teachers, while failures to respond or to read correctly are experienced as punishments. This is probably one of the factors involved in making teachers more willing to stick with the highs by asking them another question when they have not been able to respond to the first one. Highs are more likely to 'reward' the teacher with a correct response when given a second chance. This is less likely to occur with lows, so the teacher terminates the interaction and moves away from them.

Serious deterioration of classroom climate and effectiveness can occur if the teacher is strongly oriented toward hearing only correct answers. As the year progresses, such teachers spend more and more of their time and energy with only a select few children who receive the majority of the response opportunities and get more than their share of individual contacts with the teacher. When carried to extremes, this produces a classroom situation in which very little new learning goes on because the teacher confines questions and assignments to material she knows the children can handle. Much of the verbal interaction in such a classroom boils down to the recitation of over-learned material by high expectation students, with the teacher spending her time eliciting responses and labeling them as correct or incorrect but doing very little teaching in the normal sense of the word.

Data Limitations and Unanswered Questions

Although the results of our initial study were encouraging, certain limitations in the data and certain unanswered questions led us to initiate a series of follow-up studies. One important limitation was the small and restricted sample. Only four teachers were observed, and all were working in the same grade at the same school. How could we be sure they were typical?

In addition, the data were collected in the spring, near the end of the school year. Perhaps teachers give up on their low achieving students only after a long and determined effort to improve their performance. Perhaps at the beginning of the year there are no differences between expectancy groups. Data on this question were needed to evaluate the next step in our model. The model not only predicted that teachers would treat high and low achieving students differently, it also implied that polarization would occur as the school year progressed. That is, if teachers' classroom behavior is related to student achievement, and if teachers do in fact treat high achieving students more favorably than they treat low achieving students, the relative difference between high and low students should increase as the school year progresses.

The children should begin to respond to this differential teacher treatment with complementary behavior, reinforcing the teachers' tendency to differentiate. For example, if teachers more frequently give up on low achieving students when they make no response, and more often criticize them when they make errors, these students might learn in time that remaining silent when in doubt is the best way to 'get off the hook.' Such increasing silence might reinforce the teachers' suspicions that the students were falling hopelessly behind; it also might make the teachers more likely to call quickly on someone else to spare them further embarrassment. Systematic study of this idea required data from the beginning of the school year.

Also, the data in our original study were consistent with two earlier studies (Good, 1970; Kranz, Weber, and Fishell, 1970) in that teachers were found to be more positively responsive to high achieving students, but there was one major difference. In the earlier studies teachers were found to interact much more frequently with their highs than their lows. However, the frequency (*quantity*) of teacher interaction with high and low achieving students did not differ greatly in this study. Instead, the *quality* of interaction, *how* the teacher responded to the child, was the major indicant of differential teacher behavior.

In earlier studies classes had been grouped *heterogeneously*; however, in our study the children were grouped *homogeneously*. Perhaps when children are ability grouped so that differences between highs and lows within each classroom are smaller, the frequency of teacher contacts with different achievement groups is more similar. Additional data taken in classes which use heterogeneous grouping practices were needed to test this hypothesis [. . .]

Follow-up to the Initial Study

[. . .] To answer some of the research questions our initial study had raised, we replicated and extended it the following year (Evertson, Brophy, and Good, 1973). This follow-up study involved different kinds of students from those in the initial study, and they were grouped heterogeneously rather than homogeneously. Naturalistic classroom observations were collected over the entire fall semester to see if differential teacher expectations would lead to a gradual polarization of the class.

Data were collected in three classrooms in each of three different types of schools. In one school most of the teachers and all of the students were black, and the great majority of the students came from homes of lower socioeconomic status. The teaching staffs and student populations of the other two schools were overwhelmingly white. However, they differed in the socioeconomic status of their student population. One was similar to the black school in this regard, with the great majority of families being supported by an unskilled bread winner or by public assistance. In contrast, the students at the other white school came from middle and upper-middle class homes. Thus the three schools selected for study were different from one another in the student populations they served. This selection allowed us to see if the findings from the previous research would generalize to schools that differed from the one studied originally.

Resources were limited, so we had to choose between making a few observations in a large number of classrooms or making many observations in a few classrooms. Part of our solution to this dilemma was a decision to work only with the first grade. This was to maximize the comparability of data from all classrooms both with one another and with those in the original study. This was important because, at the time, the data from our initial study were still unique. We had developed a new observation system to do a new kind of research, and there was no body of data with which some of our findings could be compared. Replication at the first-grade level would enable us to get this kind of comparison data.

We also opted in favor of making extensive observations in a small number of classrooms. We anticipated that replications of the Rosenthal and Jacobson study and research similar to or own would begin to appear in the research literature more frequently, and that they would establish more firmly the finding that teachers' expectations sometimes act as self-fulfilling prophecies. Consequently, our interests focused on research designed to reveal more about how the process works. In particular, we wanted to test our model further, especially the hypothesis that a class will become polarized over time if the teacher consistently encourages the highs and discourages the lows.

Procedures

[. . .] The study began in late September and continued through mid-December. It was essentially a replication of our initial study, except that adjustments were made in the coding system so that a single observer could code the entire class rather than only a few children at the extremes of the teachers' rankings. The first-grade classes in each of the three schools were involved. In September teachers were given an orientation similar to the one used the previous year and were asked to rank their children according to the achievement they expected from them. At this point in the research the teachers did not know the full intent of the study.

Each of the nine classrooms was then observed sixteen times during the semester, eight mornings and eight afternoons, with observations spread across the days of the week and the weeks of the semester. A total of about forty hours of interaction data were collected from each classroom. The data were analyzed with two main questions in mind. Would the findings of the initial study be replicated? If so, would there be evidence that the differences between the low and high groups increased with time (that is, would the classes become more polarized)?

Results

Results related to the first question are reviewed in detail below. However, they can be simply summarized here. Few of the findings regarding communication of teachers' expectations were replicated across the whole sample of teachers. As a group, these nine teachers were not treating highs favorably and lows unfavorably. Three of the nine teachers did show this pattern, however.

There were considerable differences among the students ranked high, middle, and low in the teachers' rankings. Highs had a higher percentage of correct answers and fewer errors per reading turn than lows, with middles in between (middles were between highs and lows on almost all measures; exceptions to this general finding will be noted). Also, highs were more likely to make an incorrect response than to make no response at all when they did fail to respond correctly. This may be simply a knowledge or ability difference; perhaps the lows are more often stumped so completely that they cannot even offer a guess. However, it also may indicate a personality difference: perhaps highs are generally more secure and confident and lows generally more anxious and inhibited when 'put on the spot' in public response opportunity situations.

Quantitative differences in the frequency of teacher-student interactions were mixed. Highs got more public response opportunities and more reading turns than lows. Similar nonsignificant trends also were seen in the data on self-reference questions and student-initiated work and procedural contacts. However, the measures for response opportunities in reading groups and for teacher-initiated work contacts showed the opposite trend (significant in the latter case). Thus, as a group, these teachers showed evidence of attempts to compensate for the highs' tendency to be more active in seeking response opportunities and initiating contacts. Behavioral contacts were most frequent with the low group and least frequent with the middle group.

In sum, the quantitative data suggest that highs were creating extra response opportunities for themselves, but that, in general, the teachers were attempting to compensate by calling on lows more frequently and especially by frequently initiating work-related contacts with them. The only really large difference favoring the highs is on the measure of reading turns, and this may be due to what was going on in the reading groups at the time rather than to teacher favoritism. That is, early in the semester, the high groups were already reading and therefore getting reading turns, while the low groups were still on readiness work and had not yet begun to read. Thus the reading group data probably reflect appropriate teaching rather than favoritism toward highs.

The data on teacher versus student initiation of individual private contacts show a clear pattern: highs initiated more contacts with the teachers, and teachers compensated by initiating more contacts with lows. Here again is evidence that teachers were actively trying to reach the lows rather than giving up on them or allowing themselves to be continually occupied with the highs.

Data on the difficulty level of questions, on teacher praise following correct answers, and on teacher criticism following incorrect answers showed no clear trends. Highs did get more total praise from the teachers, because of a large difference in praise given during teacher-initiated private work contacts. Again, this is probably due to differences in the quality of the students' work rather than to teacher favoritism. Students in the middle groups were rarely criticized for classroom misbehavior, while the lows were most frequently criticized for this reason. A similar pattern occurred on the measure of warning over warning plus criticism, indicating that teachers were likely merely to warn the middles when they misbehaved but were more likely to criticize the lows when they misbehaved. This ties in with the finding on behavioral contacts noted earlier and reflects a more general finding seen in several of our studies: the middle group is usually less salient in the classroom than the high and low groups, and teachers are usually more detached and unemotional when dealing with them. Middles tend not to make so strong an impression on teachers as highs and lows, and they do not provoke so much emotional response from the teachers.

The findings on measures of teacher persistence in seeking responses were mixed. There were no clear trends in teacher behavior following failure to answer an initial question. Thus, the tendency of the teachers in the initial study to give up on lows but stay with highs in these situations was not replicated in this study.

When the teachers did stay with students following their failure to respond correctly, they were more likely simply to repeat the question to highs but more likely to give a clue or some kind of help to lows. Thus they were more demanding in dealing with highs in these situations. This is one finding that can be interpreted as evidence of communication of expectations, although most observers would probably see it as an appropriate teaching strategy, given the differences in the children's abilities and other evidence in the study showing that these teachers seemed to be working to involve lows and help them master the material.

Measures of the teachers' frequencies of asking a second question following a correct answer to the first question actually favored the lows, and the group effect was significant on one measure. Thus, the teachers tended to stay with the lows when they were responding successfully.

Measures of process feedback given by teachers in responding to student answers or in working with them at their desks all show that lows got more process feedback. This again indicates a tendency for the teachers to work with the lows rather than give up on them. However, one difference was significant. This was on the measure of process feedback in teacher-initiated work contacts, and it can be interpreted in tandem with the findings reported earlier that teachers gave more praise to the highs in teacher-initiated work contacts. Taken together, these findings show that the teachers were praising the students when they had done the work correctly but were stopping to give explanation and instruction when they had not. Most observers would agree that this is appropriate teaching, even though it does result in the highs getting somewhat more praise than the other students.

The findings of teacher failure to give feedback were mixed. The one significant difference showed that the teachers more frequently failed to give feedback to the highs after they had responded to questions during reading groups. This is a reversal of the findings of the initial study. However, a trend that approached significance suggested more frequent failure to give feedback to the lows following reading turns, and a third measure (failure to give feedback during general class discussions) showed no important group differences. Thus it would not be appropriate to conclude that these teachers more frequently failed to give feedback to highs than lows. It is true, however, that the finding from the initial study that teachers more frequently failed to give feedback to lows was not replicated in this study.

To summarize, few of the key findings from the initial study were replicated in the follow-up. As a group, the teachers in the follow-up study showed no evidence of favoring highs or of treating them more appropriately than lows. If anything, the opposite was true. There was considerable evidence that the teachers were consistently compensating for the tendency of highs to demand more of their attention by seeking out lows for contacts and by persistently explaining the work to lows when they needed help. Furthermore, they did this even though lows apparently created more frequent control and discipline problems by misbehaving more often than their classmates. The measures that did favor highs over lows are most likely attributable to differences in the work and behavior of the groups of students rather than to teacher favoritism.

These findings are for the teachers as a group, however, and they gloss over individual differences among them. When data for each teacher were examined individually, it was found that three teachers tended to favor the highs (behaving similarly to the teachers in the intitial study), three showed no particular pattern of group differences at all, and three showed evidence of special concern and effort directed toward the lows (in general, the opposite of the kinds of patterns seen in the initial study). The data for the three teachers who did favor highs were examined for evidence of polarization of their classes. One class did show polarization over time, while the other two showed no trend at all. Thus the findings regarding the polarization hypothesis were ambiguous.

Contrasts Between the Two Studies

The results of the two studies contrast sharply. In the first study all four teachers showed a tendency to treat the highs more appropriately than the lows in working for and reinforcing good responses (although the tendency was less noticeable in one teacher). In the second study only three of nine teachers showed that pattern, while three showed no group difference and the other three showed a contrasting pattern suggesting extra efforts to work with the lows. There were several differences between the two studies which might explain these contrasting findings.

First, the student populations were different. This apparently was not a factor, however. None of the three teachers in the lower class white school in the follow-up study, which was most similar to the school used in the initial study, showed the pattern that the teachers in the initial study had shown.

A second difference was that students in the follow-up study were grouped heterogeneously. Again, this is a possible but unlikely explanation for the difference in findings. If anything, heterogenous grouping should increase rather than decrease the likelihood that a teacher will show differences in treating the highs and lows. Since the differences between these groups are greater in heterogeneously grouped than in homogeneously grouped classes, teachers' differential expectations for achievement will be more closely fulfilled in heterogeneously grouped classrooms. Thus a teacher who found work with highs rewarding and work with lows unrewarding should be especially disposed to favor highs in a heterogeneously grouped classroom.

A counter argument can be constructed, however, based on cognitive consistency notions. It may be that teachers in homogeneously grouped classrooms expect equal performance from everyone. If so, such teachers may become especially frustrated or angered by the relatively poor performance of their lows. This, in turn, may lead them to reject the lows and favor the highs. In contrast, teachers in heterogeneously grouped classrooms may not be disturbed or frustrated by the relatively poor performance of lows because they expect it, so that they may be emotionally freer to work with lows at their individual levels without letting anger or rejection get in the way.

Carrying this argument further, it could be predicted that teachers' treatment of individual students is influenced not so much by the nature of the particular expectations they have for the students as by the discrepancy between those expectations and what the student is actually doing. Students failing to meet expectations may provoke frustration and rejection, while students exceeding expectations may provoke pleasure and good will. However, although the first part of this prediction may prove true, the second part does not square with the praise and criticism findings from the initial study, or with data from other investigators suggesting that unexpected good performance may even be negatively perceived (Leacock, 1969; Rosenthal and Jacobson, 1968). If student performance that exceeds expectation really produces pleasure and good will in teachers, it seems reasonable to hypothesize that teachers should more frequently praise lows than highs in parallel situations and should react more positively and intensely to success from lows. This does not typically occur.

Obviously, more research is needed here. It may be that some teachers are more affected by their general expectancy than by student performance, that other teachers are more affected by discrepancy between expectancy and performance, and that still other teachers are relatively unaffected by either factor.

Another difference between the studies was the time of year in which the data were taken. The observations in the first study were made late in the spring, while the follow-up was done in the first semester. There are at least two reasons to believe that expectancy group differences will be larger later in the year. The first is the polarization hypothesis already discussed. The second is a developmental progression that may exist in teachers' attempts to work with low achievers. It may be that at the beginning of the year teachers suspend judgment or take into account readiness and maturity differences while trying to bring all students up to the same criteria (he will do all right once he settles down; he has ability but he has not had any preparation, and so on). Then, when certain students consistently show relatively poor achievement, the teachers may respond with redoubled effort and determination (he is going to need a lot of extra work and individual attention). During this second phase, research would turn up no differences or perhaps even differences favoring lows on measures related to teachers' attempts to work for response.

There may come a third phase, however, if redoubled efforts still have not succeeded with certain students. The teacher may reach a point where he gives up, consciously or unconsciously, feeling that his time and efforts have not succeeded and will not succeed. Once such resignation and acceptance of failure occurs, findings like those seen in the initial study would begin to appear.

This may explain the praise and criticism findings in the initial study. If teachers had given up serious attempts to teach lows, they would have been strongly motivated in their beliefs that lows could not handle the material. As long as this belief could be retained, their failure to persist in trying to teach lows could be justified (they cannot learn), and, more generally, their self-concept as teachers could be protected and preserved (their failure is not my failure; no one could teach these students any better than I have).

Dynamics of this sort would tend to reverse 'normal' reactions. Instead of responding with satisfaction to the success of the lows, the teachers might respond with irritation. They might even fail to notice their success. Similar dynamics could reverse the 'usual' response to failure by lows. Instead of responding with patience and compassion, the teacher who had given up might well respond with criticism and rejection, not in an attempt to motivate the student, but out of a need to reassure himself that the student indeed was not making it (and, implicitly, will not make it and therefore does not merit greater teaching efforts).

In any case homogeneous versus heterogeneous grouping and first versus second semester data are likely explanations for the differences in findings between the two studies. It is also possible that the teachers' achievement rankings in the second study, collected early in the school year, reflected merely fleeting first impressions. Perhaps our teacher expectation data were obsolete and did not accurately reflect the teachers' expectations during the time that data were collected. This was not a factor, however. The teachers' expectations remained remarkably stable across the school year.

Finally, the teachers in the follow-up may have been more skillful or competent than the teachers in the initial study. In this connection it should be noted that we have frequently used the term 'failure to replicate,' and have implied in other ways that the follow-up results were unfortunate or undesirable. Actually, they provoked mixed feelings in us, depending upon whether we viewed them from the perspective of research and theory or from the perspective of the quality of education in the schools. When viewed from the first perspective, the follow-up data were distressing, since they showed that the situation was more complex than we had realized and that our theorizing about teacher expectation effects and our ability to generalize from our initial study would have to be modified. In short, we were confronted with an occupational hazard faced by all scientific investigators: 'the rape of a beautiful theory by a gang of brutal facts.'

Our distress here was mitigated, of course, by the fact that the follow-up findings were not completely negative. Three of the nine teachers did show the same pattern that had been observed in all four of the teachers studied in the initial research. Thus the follow-up did not so much completely contradict the initial findings as it complicated the interpretation of them by showing that not all teachers are affected by their expectations (the expectations we had measured, at least; unknown and unmeasured expectation effects are always a possibility).

We were pleased and impressed with the follow-up findings when we viewed them from the perspective of the quality of education in schools studied. It is encouraging that six of the nine teachers showed no evidence of giving up on the lows or otherwise treating them inappropriately, and three apparently were going out of their way to give them special help and attention. We had found the results of our initial study discouraging from this perspective, since they suggested that inappropriate teaching was typical, perhaps even universal. The follow-up data helped us to correct this overly pessimistic perspective. They showed that undesirable teacher expectation effects were not necessary or universal, and that teachers will differ in the degree to which they show these effects in their classroom behavior. This was the first naturalistic study in which undesirable expectation effects were not observed [. . .]

References

BROPHY, J., and GOOD, T. (1970a). 'Teacher's communication of differential expectations for children's classroom performance: some behavioral data,' *Journal of Educational Psychology*, 61, 365–374.

BROPHY, J., and GOOD, T. (1970b). 'Brophy-Good system (teacher-child dyadic interaction)', in A. Simon and E. Boyer (eds.), *Mirrors for Behavior: An Anthology of Observation Instruments Continued*, 1970 supplement. Volume A, Philadelphia, Research for Better Schools, Inc.

EVERTSON, C., BROPHY, J., and GOOD, T. *Communication of Teacher Expectations: Second Grade*. Report No. 92, Research and Development Center for Teacher Education, The University of Texas at Austin.

GOOD, T. (1970). 'Which pupils do teachers call on?' *Elementary School Journal*, 70, 190–198.

GOOD, T. and BROPHY, J. (1970). 'Teacher-child dyadic interactions: a new method of classroom observation', *Journal of School Psychology*, 8, 131–138.

KRANZ, P., WEBER, W., and FISHELL, K. (1970). 'The relationships between teacher perception of pupils and teacher behavior toward those pupils', paper presented at the annual meeting of the American Educational Research Association.

LEACOCK, E. (1969). *Teaching and Learning in City Schools*. New York, Basic Books.

RIST, R. (1970). 'Student social class and teacher expectations: the self-fulfilling prophecy in ghetto education', *Harvard Educational Review*, 40, 411–451.

ROSENTHAL, R. and JACOBSON, L. (1968). *Pygmalion in the Classroom: Teacher Expectation and Pupils' Intellectual Development*. New York, Holt, Rinehart and Winston.

SIMON, A., and BOYER, E. (eds.), (1967). *Mirrors for Behavior: An Anthology of Classroom Observation Instruments*. Philadelphia, Research for Better Schools, Inc.

Student Social Class and Teacher Expectations: The Self-fulfilling Prophecy in Ghetto Education[1]

R.C. Rist

[. . .] Teacher-student relationships and the dynamics of interaction between the teacher and students are far from uniform. For any child within the classroom, variations in the experience of success or failure, praise or ridicule, freedom or control, creativity or docility, comprehension or mystification may ultimately have significance far beyond the boundaries of the classroom situation (Henry, 1955, 1959, 1963).

It is the purpose of this paper to explore what is generally regarded as a crucial aspect of the classroom experience for the children involved – the process whereby expectations and social interactions give rise to the social organization of the class. There occurs within the classroom a social process whereby, out of a large group of children and an adult unknown to one another prior to the beginning of the school year, there emerge patterns of behavior, expectations of performance, and a mutually accepted stratification system delineating those doing well from those doing poorly. Of particular concern will be the relation of the teacher's expectations of potential academic performance to the social status of the student. Emphasis will be placed on the initial presuppositions of the teacher regarding the intellectual ability of certain groups of children and their consequences for the children's socialization into the school system. A major goal of this analysis is to ascertain the importance of the initial expectations of the teacher in relation to the child's chances for success or failure within the public school system. (For previous studies of the significance of student social status to variations in educational experience, cf. Becker, 1952; Hollingshead, 1949; Lynd, 1937; Warner, *et al.*, 1944).

Increasingly, with the concern over intellectual growth of children and the long and close association that children experience with a series of teachers, attention is centering on the role of the teacher within the classroom (Sigel, 1969). A long series of studies have been conducted to determine what effects on children a teacher's values, beliefs, attitudes, and, most crucial to this analysis, a teacher's expectations may have. Asbell (1963), Becker (1952), Clark (1963), Gibson (1965), Harlem Youth Opportunities Unlimited (1964), Katz (1964), Kvaraceus (1965), MacKinnon (1962), Riessman (1962, 1965), Rose (1956), Rosenthal and Jacobson (1968), and Wilson (1963) have all noted that the teacher's expectations of a pupil's academic performance may, in fact, have a strong influence on the actual performance of that pupil. These authors have sought to validate a type of educational self-fulfilling prophecy: if the teacher expects high performance, she receives it, and vice versa. A major criticism that can be directed at much of the research is that although the studies may establish that a teacher has differential expectations and that these influence performance for various pupils, they have not elucidated either the basis upon which such differential expectations are formed or how they are directly manifested within the classroom milieu. It is a goal of this paper to provide an analysis both of the factors that are critical in the teacher's development of expectations for various groups of her pupils and of the process by which such expectations influence the classroom experience for the teacher and the students.

The basic position to be presented in this paper is that the development of expectations by the kindergarten teacher as to the differential academic potential and capability of any student was significantly determined by a series of subjectively interpreted attributes and characteristics of that student. The argument may be succinctly stated in five propositions. First, the kindergarten teacher possessed a roughly constructed 'ideal type' as to what characteristics were necessary for any given student to achieve 'success' both in the public school and in the larger society. These characteristics appeared to be, in significant part, related to social class criteria. Secondly, upon first meeting her students at the beginning of the school year, subjective evaluations were made of the students as to possession or absence of the desired traits necessary for anticipated 'success.' On the basis of the evaluation, the class was divided into groups expected to succeed (termed by the teacher 'fast learners') and those anticipated to fail (termed 'slow learners'). Third, differential treatment was accorded to the two groups in the classroom, with the group designated as 'fast learners' receiving the majority of the teaching time, reward-directed behavior, and attention from the teacher. Those designated as 'slow learners' were taught infrequently, subjected to more frequent control-oriented behavior, and received little if any supportive behavior from the teacher. Fourth, the interactional patterns between the teacher and the various groups in her class became rigidified, taking on caste-like characteristics, during the course of the school year, with the gap in completion of academic material between the two groups widening as the school year progressed. Fifth, a similar process occurred in later years of schooling, but the teachers no longer relied on subjectively interpreted data as the basis for ascertaining differences in students. Rather, they were able to utilize a variety of informational sources related to past performance as the basis for classroom grouping.

Though the position to be argued in this paper is based on a longitudinal study spanning two and one-half years with a single group of black children, additional studies suggest that the grouping of children both between and within classrooms is a rather prevalent situation within American elementary classrooms. In a report released in 1961 by the National Education Association related to data collected during the 1958–1959 school year, an estimated 77.6% of urban school districts (cities with a population above 2500) indicated that they practised between-classroom ability grouping in the elementary grades. In a national survey of elementary schools, Austin and Morrison (1963) found that 'more than 80% reported that they 'always' or 'often' use readiness tests for pre-reading evaluation [in first grade].' These findings would suggest that within-classroom grouping may be an even more prevalent condition than between-classroom grouping. In evaluating data related to grouping within American elementary classrooms, Smith (1971) concludes, 'Thus group assignment on the basis of measured 'ability' or 'readiness' is an accepted and widespread practice.' [. . .]

Methodology

Data for this study were collected by means of twice weekly one and one-half hour observations of a single group of black children in an urban ghetto school who began kindergarten in September of 1967. Formal observations were conducted throughout the year while the children were in kindergarten and again in 1969 when these same children were in the first half of their second-grade year. The children were also visited informally four times in the classroom during their first-grade year.[2] The difference between the formal and informal observations consisted in the fact that during formal visits, a continuous handwritten account was taken of classroom interaction and activity as it occurred. Smith and Geoffrey (1968) have labeled this method of classroom observation 'microethnography.' The informal observations did not include the taking of notes during the classroom visit, but comments were written after the visit. Additionally, a series of interviews were conducted with both the kindergarten and the second-grade teachers. No mechanical devices were utilized to record classroom activities or interviews.

I believe it is methodologically necessary, at this point, to clarify what benefits can be derived from the detailed analysis of a single group of children. The single most apparent weakness of the vast majority of studies of urban education is that they lack any longitudinal perspective. The complexities of the interactional processes which evolve over time within classrooms cannot be discerned with a single two- or three-hour observational period. Secondly, education is a *social process* that cannot be reduced to variations in IQ scores over a period of time. At best, IQ scores merely give indications of potential, not of process. Third, I do not believe that this school and the classrooms within it are atypical from others in urban black neighborhoods (cf. both the popular literature on urban schools: Kohl, 1967; and Kozol, 1967; as well as the academic literature: Eddy, 1967; Fuchs, 1967; Leacock, 1969; and Moore, 1967). The school in which this study occurred was selected by the District Superintendent as one of five available to the research team. All five schools were visited during the course of the study and detailed observations were conducted in four of them. The principal at the school reported upon in this study commented that I was very fortunate in coming to his school since his staff (and kindergarten teacher in particular) were equal to 'any in the city.' Finally, the utilization of longitudinal study as a research method in a ghetto school will enhance the possibilities of gaining further insight into mechanisms of adaptation utilized by black youth to what appears to be a basically white, middle-class, value-oriented institution.

The School

The particular school which the children attend was built in the early part of the 1960's. It has classes from kindergarten through the eighth grade and a single special education class. The enrollment fluctuates near the 900 level while the teaching staff consists of twenty-six teachers, in addition to a librarian, two physical education instructors, the principal, and an assistant principal. There are also at the school, on a part time basis, a speech therapist, social worker, nurse, and doctor, all employed by the Board of Education. All administrators, teachers, staff, and pupils are black. (The author is caucasian.) The school is located in a blighted urban area that has 98% black population within its census district. Within the school itself, nearly 500 of the 900 pupils (55%) come from families supported by funds from Aid to Dependent Children, a form of public welfare.

The Kindergarten Class

Prior to the beginning of the school year, the teacher possessed several different kinds of information regarding the children that she would have in her class. The first was the pre-registration form completed by 13 mothers of children who would be in the kindergarten class. On this form, the teacher was supplied with the name of the child, his age, the name of his parents, his home address, his phone number, and whether he had had any pre-school experience. The second source of information for the teacher was supplied two days before the beginning of school by the school social worker who provided a tentative list of all children enrolled in the kindergarten class who lived in homes that received public welfare funds.

The third source of information on the child was gained as a result of the initial interview with the mother and child during the registration period, either in the few days prior to the beginning of school or else during the first days of school. In this interview, a major concern was the gathering of medical information about the child as well as the ascertaining of any specific parental concern related to the child. This latter information was noted on the 'Behavioral Questionnaire' where the mother was to indicate her concern, if any, on 28 different items. Such items as thumb-sucking, bed-wetting, loss of bowel control, lying, stealing, fighting, and laziness were included on this questionnaire.

The fourth source of information available to the teacher concerning the children in her class was both her own experiences with older siblings, and those of other teachers in the building related to behavior and academic performance of children in the same family. A rather strong informal norm had developed among teachers in the school such that pertinent information, especially that related to discipline matters, was to be passed on to the next teacher of the student. The teachers' lounge became the location in which they would discuss the performance of individual children as well as make comments concerning the parents and their interests in the student and the school. Frequently, during the first days of the school year, there were admonitions to a specific teacher to 'watch out' for a child believed by a teacher to be a 'trouble-maker.' Teachers would also relate techniques of controlling the behavior of a student who had been disruptive in the class. Thus a variety of information concerning students in the school was shared, whether that information regarded academic performance, behavior in class, or the relation of the home to the school.

It should be noted that not one of these four sources of information to the teacher was related directly to the academic potential of the incoming kindergarten child. Rather, they concerned various types of social information revealing such facts as the financial status of certain families, medical care of the child, presence or absence of a telephone in the home, as well as the structure of the family in which the child lived, *i.e.*, number of siblings, whether the child lived with both, one, or neither of his natural parents.

The Teacher's Stimulus

When the kindergarten teacher made the permanent seating assignments on the eighth day of school, not only had she the above four sources of information concerning the children, but she had also had time to observe them within the classroom setting. Thus the behavior, degree and type of verbalization, dress, mannerisms, physical appearance, and performance on the early tasks assigned during class were available to her as she began to form opinions concerning the capabilities and potential of the various children. That such evaluation of the children by the teacher was beginning, I believe, there is little doubt. Within a few days, only a certain group of children were continually being called on to lead the class in the Pledge of Allegiance, read the weather calendar each day, come to the front for 'show and tell' periods, take messages to the office, count the number of children present in the class, pass out materials for class projects, be in charge of equipment on the playground, and lead the class to the bathroom, library, or on a school tour. This one group of children, that continually were physically close to the teacher and had a high degree of verbal interaction with her, she placed at Table 1.

As one progressed from Table 1 to Table 2 and Table 3, there was an increasing dissimilarity between each group of children at the different tables on at least four major criteria. The first criterion appeared to be the physical appearance of the child. While the children at Table 1 were all dressed in clean clothes that were relatively new and pressed, most of the children at Table 2, and with only one exception at Table 3, were all quite poorly dressed. The clothes were old and often quite dirty. The children at Tables 2 and 3 also had a noticeably different quality and quantity of clothes to wear, especially during the winter months. Whereas the children at Table 1 would come on cold days with heavy coats and sweaters, the children at the other two tables often wore very thin spring coats and summer clothes. The single child at Table 3 who came to school quite nicely dressed came from a home in which the mother was receiving welfare funds, but was supplied with clothing for the children by the families of her brother and sister.

An additional aspect of the physical appearance of the children related to their body odor. While none of the children at Table 1 came to class with an odor of urine on them, there were two children at Table 2 and five children at Table 3 who frequently had such an odor. There was not a clear distinction among the children at the various tables as to the degree of 'blackness' of their skin, but there were more children at the third table with very dark skin (five in all) than there were at the first table (three). There was also a noticeable distinction among the various groups of children as to the condition of their hair. While the three boys at Table 1 all had short hair cuts and the six girls at the same table had their hair 'processed' and combed, the number of children with either matted or unprocessed hair increased at Table 2 (two boys and three girls) and eight of the children at Table 3 (four boys and four girls). None of the children in the kindergarten class wore their hair in the style of a 'natural.'

A second major criterion which appeared to differentiate the children at the various tables was their interactional behavior, both among themselves and with the teacher. The several children who began to develop as leaders within the class by giving directions to other members, initiating the division of the class into teams on the playground, and seeking to speak for the class to the teacher ('We want to color now'), were all placed by the teacher at Table 1. This same group of children displayed considerable ease in their interaction with her. Whereas the children at Table 2 and 3 would often linger on the periphery of groups surrounding the teacher, the children at Table 1 most often crowded close to her.

The use of language within the classroom appeared to be the third major differentiation among the children. While the children placed at the first table were quite verbal with the teacher, the children placed at the remaining two tables spoke much less frequently with her. The children placed at the first table also displayed a greater use of Standard American English within the classroom. Whereas the children placed at the last two tables most often responded to the teacher in black dialect, the children at the first table did so very infrequently. In other words, the children at the first table were much more adept at the use of 'school language' than were those at the other tables. The teacher utilized standard American English in the classroom and one group of children were able to respond in a like manner. The frequency of a 'no response' to a question from the teacher was recorded at a ratio of nearly three to one for the children at the last two tables as opposed to Table 1. When questions were asked, the children who were placed at the first table most often gave a response.

The final apparent criterion by which the children at the first table were quite noticeably different from those at the other tables consisted of a series of social factors which were known to the teacher prior to her seating the children. Though it is not known to what degree she utilized this particular criterion when she assigned seats, it does contribute to developing a clear profile of the children at the various tables. Table 1 gives a summary of the distribution of the children at the three tables on a series of variables related to social and family conditions. Such variables may be considered to give indication of the relative status of the children within the room, based on the income, education and size of the family. (For a discussion of why these three variables of income, education, and family size may be considered as significant indicators of social status, cf. Frazier, 1959; Freeman, *et al.*, 1959; Gebhard, *et al.*, 1958; Kahl, 1957; Notestein, 1953; Reissman, 1959; Rose, 1956; Simpson and Yinger, 1958.)

Believing, as I do that the teacher did not randomly assign the children to

TABLE 1   Distribution of socio-economic status factors by seating
arrangement at the three tables in the kindergarten classroom

| | Seating arrangement* | | |
Factors	Table 1	Table 2	Table 3
Income			
1 Families on welfare	0	2	4
2 Families with father employed	6	3	2
3 Families with mother employed	5	5	5
4 Families with both parents employed	5	3	2
5 Total family income below $3,000. /yr**	0	4	7
6 Total family income above $12,000. /yr**	4	0	0
Education			
1 Father ever grade school	6	3	2
2 Father ever high school	5	2	1
3 Father ever college	1	0	0
4 Mother ever grade school	9	10	8
5 Mother ever high school	7	6	5
6 Mother ever college	4	0	0
7 Children with pre-school experience	1	1	0
Family size			
1 Families with one child	3	1	0
2 Families with six or more children	2	6	7
3 Average number of siblings in family	3–4	5–6	6–7
4 Families with both parents present	6	3	2

 * There are nine children at Table 1, eleven at Table 2, and ten children at Table 3.
** Estimated from stated occupation.

the various tables, it is then necessary to indicate the basis for the seating
arrangement. I would contend that the teacher developed, utilizing some
combination of the four criteria outlined above, a series of expectations
about the potential performance of each child and then grouped the children
according to perceived similarities in expected performance. The teacher
herself informed me that the first table consisted of her 'fast learners' while
those at the last two tables 'had no idea of what was going on in the
classroom.' What becomes crucial in this discussion is to ascertain the basis
upon which the teacher developed her criteria of 'fast learner' since there had
been no formal testing of the children as to their academic potential or

capacity for cognitive development. She made evaluative judgments of the expected capacities of the children to perform academic tasks after eight days of school.

Certain criteria became indicative of expected success and others became indicative of expected failure. Those children who closely fit the teacher's 'ideal type' of the successful child were chosen for seats at Table 1. Those children that had the least 'goodness of fit' with her ideal type were placed at the third table. The criteria upon which a teacher would construct her ideal type of the successful student would rest in her perception of certain attributes in the child that she believed would make for success. To understand what the teacher considered as 'success,' one would have to examine her perception of the larger society and whom in that larger society she perceived as successful. Thus, in the terms of Merton (1957), one may ask which was the 'normative reference group' for Mrs. Caplow that she perceived as being successful.[3] I believe that the reference group utilized by Mrs. Caplow to determine what constituted success was a mixed black white, well-educated middle class. Those attributes most desired by educated members of the middle class became the basis for her evaluation of the children. Those who possessed these particular characteristics were expected to succeed while those who did not could be expected not to succeed. Highly prized middle-class status for the child in the classroom was attained by demonstrating ease of interaction among adults; high degree of verbalization in Standard American English; the ability to become a leader; a neat and clean appearance, coming from a family that is educated, employed, living together, and interested in the child; and the ability to participate well as a member of a group.

The kindergarten teacher appeared to have been raised in a home where the above values were emphasized as important. Her mother was a college graduate, as were her brother and sisters. The family lived in the same neighborhood for many years, and the father held a responsible position with a public utility company in the city. The family was devoutly religious and those of the family still in the city attend the same church. She and other members of her family were active in a number of civil rights organizations in the city. Thus, it appears that the kindergarten teacher's 'normative reference group' coincided quite closely with those groups in which she did participate and belong. There was little discrepancy between the normative values of the mixed black-white educated middleclass and the values of the groups in which she held membership. The attributes indicative of 'success' among those of the educated middle class had been attained by the teacher. She was a college graduate, held positions of respect and responsibility in the black community, lived in a comfortable middle-class section of the city in a well-furnished and spacious home, together with her husband earned over $20,000 per year, was active in a number of community organizations, and had parents, brother, and sisters similar in education, income, and occupational positions [. . .]

The organization of the kindergarten classroom according to the expectation of success or failure after the eighth day of school became the basis for the differential treatment of the children for the remainder of the school year. From the day that the class was assigned permanent seats, the activities in the classroom were perceivably different from previously. The fundamental division of the class into those expected to learn and those expected not to permeated the teacher's orientation to the class.

The teacher's rationalization for narrowing her attention to selected students was that the majority of the remainder of the class (in her words) 'just had no idea of what was going on in the classroom.' Her reliance on the few students of ascribed high social status reached such proportions that, on occasion, the teacher would use one of these students as an exemplar that the remainder of the class would do well to emulate.

> (It is Fire Prevention Week and the teacher is trying to have the children say so. The children make a number of incorrect responses, a few of which follow:) Jim, who had raised his hand, in answer to the question, 'Do you know what week it is?' says, 'October.' The teacher says 'No, that's the name of the month. Jane, do you know what special week this is?' and Jane responds, 'It cold outside.' Teacher says, 'No, that is not it either. I guess I will have to call on Pamela. Pamela, come here and stand by me and tell the rest of the boys and girls what special week this is.' Pamela leaves her chair, comes and stands by the teacher, turns and faces the rest of the class. The teacher puts her arm around Pamela, and Pamela says, 'It fire week.' The teacher responds, 'Well Pamela, that is close. Actually it is Fire Prevention Week.'

On another occasion, the Friday after Hallowe'en, the teacher informed the class that she would allow time for all the students to come to the front of the class and tell of their experiences. She, in reality, called on six students, five of whom sat at Table 1 and the sixth at Table 2. Not only on this occasion, but on others, the teacher focused her attention on the experiences of the higher status students.[4]

> (The students are involved in acting out a skit arranged by the teacher on how a family should come together to eat the evening meal.) The students acting the roles of mother, father, and daughter are all from Table 1. The boy playing the son is from Table 2. At the small dinner table set up in the center of the classroom, the four children are supposed to be sharing with each other what they had done during the day – the father at work, the mother at home, and the two children at school. The Table 2 boy makes few comments. (In real life he has no father and his mother is supported by ADC funds.) The teacher comments, 'I think that we are going to have to let Milt (Table 1) be the new son. Sam, why don't you go and sit down. Milt, you seem to be one who would know what a son is supposed to do at the dinner table. You come and take Sam's place.'

In this instance, the lower-status student was penalized, not only for failing to have verbalized middle-class table talk, but, more fundamentally, for lacking middle-class experiences. He had no actual father to whom he could speak at the dinner table, yet he was expected to speak fluently with an imaginary one.

Though the blackboard was long enough to extend parallel to all three tables, the teacher wrote such assignments as arithmetic problems and drew all illustrations on the board in front of the students at Table 1. A rather poignant example of the penalty the children at Table 3 had to pay was that they often could not see the board material.

> Lilly stands up out of her seat. Mrs. Caplow asks Lilly what she wants. Lilly makes no verbal response to the question. Mrs. Caplow then says rather firmly to Lilly, 'Sit down.' Lilly does. However, Lilly sits down sideways in the chair (so she is still facing the teacher). Mrs. Caplow instructs Lilly to put her feet under the table. This Lilly does. Now she is facing directly away from the teacher and the blackboard where the teacher is demonstrating to the students how to print the letter,'O'.

The realization of the self-fulfilling prophecy within the classroom was in its final stages by late May of the kindergarten year. Lack of communication with the teacher, lack of involvement in the class activities and infrequent instruction all characterized the situation of the children at Tables 2 and 3. During one observational period of an hour in May, not a single act of communication was directed towards any child at either Table 2 or 3 by the teacher except for twice commanding 'sit down.' The teacher devoted her attention to teaching those children at Table 1. Attempts by the children at Tables 2 and 3 to elicit the attention of the teacher were much fewer than earlier in the school year.

In June, after school had ended for the year, the teacher was asked to comment on the children in her class. Of the children at the first table, she noted:

> I guess the best way to describe it is that very few children in my class are exceptional. I guess you could notice this just from the way the children were seated this year. Those at Table 1 gave consistently the most responses throughout the year and seemed most interested and aware of what was going on in the classroom.

Of those children at the remaining two tables, the teacher commented:

> It seems to me that some of the children at Table 2 and mostly all the children at Table 3 at times seem to have no idea of what is going on in the classroom and were off in another world all by themselves. It just appears that some can do it and some cannot. I don't think that it is the teaching that affects those that cannot do it, but some are just basically low achievers.

The Students' Response

The students in the kindergarten classroom did not sit passively, internalizing the behavior the teacher directed towards them. Rather, they responded to the stimuli of the teacher, both in internal differentiations within the class itself and also in their response to the teacher. The type of response a student made was highly dependent upon whether he sat at Table 1 or at one of the two other tables. The single classroom of black students did not respond as a homogeneous unit to the teacher-inspired social organization of the room.

For the high-status students at Table 1, the response to the track system of the teacher appeared to be at least three-fold. One such response was the directing of ridicule and belittlement towards those children at Tables 2 and 3. At no point during the entire school year was a child from Table 2 or 3 ever observed directing such remarks at the children at Table 1.

> Mrs. Caplow says, 'Raise your hand if you want me to call on you. I won't call on anyone who calls out.' She then says, 'All right, now who knows that numeral? What is it, Tony?' Tony makes no verbal response but rather walks to the front of the classroom and stands by Mrs. Caplow. Gregory calls out, 'He don't know. He scared.' Then Ann calls out, 'It sixteen, stupid.' (Tony sits at Table 3, Gregory and Ann sit at Table 1.)

> Jim starts to say out loud that he is smarter than Tom. He repeats it over and over again, 'I smarter than you. I smarter than you.' (Jim sits at Table 1, Tom at Table 3.)

> Milt came over to the observer and told him to look at Lilly's shoes. I asked him why I should and he replied, 'Because they so ragged and dirty.' (Milt is at Table 1, Lilly at Table 3.)

> When I asked Lilly what it was that she was drawing, she replied, 'A parachute.' Gregory interrupted and said, 'She can't draw nothin'.'

The problems of those children who were of lower status were compounded, for not only had the teacher indicated her low esteem of them, but their peers had also turned against them. The implications for the future schooling of a child who lacks the desired status credentials in a classroom where the teacher places high value on middle-class 'success' values and mannerisms are tragic.

It must not be assumed, however, that though the children at Tables 2 and 3 did not participate in classroom activities and were systematically ignored by the teacher, they did not learn. I contend that in fact they did learn, but in a fundamentally different way from the way in which the high-status children at Table 1 learned. The children at Table 2 and 3 who were unable to interact with the teacher began to develop patterns of interaction among themselves whereby they would discuss the material that the teacher was presenting to the children at Table 1. Thus I have termed their method of grasping the material 'secondary learning' to imply that knowledge was not gained in direct interaction with the teacher, but through the mediation of peers and also through listening to the teacher though she was not speaking to them. That the children were grasping, in part, the material presented in the classroom, was indicated to me in home visits when the children who sat at Table 3 would relate material specifically taught by the teacher to the children at Table 1. *It is not as though the children at Table 2 and 3 were ignorant of what was being taught in the class, but rather that the patterns of classroom interaction established by the teacher inhibited the low-status children from verbalizing what knowledge they had accumulated.* Thus, from the teacher's terms of reference, those who could not discuss must not know. Her expectations continued to be fulfilled, for though the low-status children had accumulated knowledge, they did not have the opportunity to verbalize it and, consequently, the teacher could not know what they had learned. Children at Table 2 and 3 had learned material presented in the kindergarten class, but would continue to be defined by the teacher as children who could not or would not learn.

A second response of the higher status students to the differential behavior of the teacher towards them was to seek solidarity and closeness with the teacher and urge Table 2 and 3 children to comply with her wishes.

The teacher is out of the room. Pamela says to the class, 'We all should clean up before the teacher comes.' Shortly thereafter the teacher has still not returned and Pamela begins to supervise other children in the class. She says to one girl from Table 3, 'Girl, leave that piano alone.' The child plays only a short time longer and then leaves.

The teacher has instructed the students to go and take off their coats since they have come in from the playground. Milt says, 'Ok y'al, let's go take off our clothes.'

At this time Jim says to the teacher, 'Mrs. Caplow, they pretty flowers on your desk.' Mrs. Caplow responded, 'Yes, Jim, those flowers are roses, but we will not have roses much longer, The roses will die and rest until spring because it is getting so cold outside.'

When the teacher tells the students to come from their desks and form a semi-circle around her, Gregory scoots up very close to Mrs. Caplow and is practically sitting in her lap.

Gregory has come into the room late. He takes off his coat and goes to the coat room to hang it up. He comes back and sits down in the very front of the group and is now closest to the teacher.

The higher-status students in the class perceived the lower status and esteem the teacher ascribed to those children at Tables 2 and 3. Not only would the Table 1 students attempt to control and ridicule the Table 2 and 3 students, but they also perceived and verbalized that they, the Table 1 students, were better students and were receiving differential treatment from the teacher.

> The children are rehearsing a play, Little Red Riding Hood. Pamela tells the observer, 'The teacher gave me the best part.' The teacher overheard this comment, smiled, and made no verbal response.

> The children are preparing to go on a field trip to a local dairy. The teacher has designated Gregory as the 'sheriff' for the trip. Mrs. Caplow stated that for the field trip today Gregory would be the sheriff. Mrs. Caplow simply watched as Gregory would walk up to a student and push him back into line saying, 'Boy, stand where you suppose to.' Several times he went up to students from Table 3 and showed them the badge that the teacher had given to him and said, 'Teacher made me sheriff.'

The children seated at the first table were internalizing the attitudes and behavior of the teacher towards those at the remaining two tables. That is, as the teacher responded from her reference group orientation as to which type of children were most likely to succeed and which type most likely to fail, she behaved towards the two groups of children in a significantly different manner. The children from Table 1 were also learning through emulating the teacher how to behave towards other black children who came from low-income and poorly educated homes. The teacher, who came from a well-educated and middle-income family, and the children from Table 1 who came from a background similar to the teacher's, came to respond to the children from poor and uneducated homes in a strikingly similar manner.

The lower-status students in the classroom from Tables 2 and 3 responded in significantly different ways to the stimuli of the teacher. The two major responses of the Tables 2 and 3 students were withdrawal and verbal and physical in-group hostility.

The withdrawal of some of the lower-status students as a response to the ridicule of their peers and the isolation from the teacher occasionally took the form of physical withdrawal, but most often it was psychological.

> Betty, a very poorly dressed child, had gone outside and hidden behind the door . . . Mrs. Caplow sees Betty leave and goes outside to bring her back, says in an authoritative and irritated voice, 'Betty, come here right now.' When the child returns, Mrs. Caplow seizes her by the right arm, brings her over to the group, and pushes her down to the floor. Betty begins to cry . . . The teacher now shows the group a large posterboard with a picture of a white child going to school.

> The teacher is demonstrating how to mount leaves between two pieces of wax paper. Betty leaves the group and goes back to her seat and begins to color.

> The teacher is instructing the children in how they can make a 'spooky thing' for Hallowe'en. James turns away from the teacher and puts his head on his desk. Mrs. Caplow looks at James and says, 'James, sit up and look here.'

The children are supposed to make United Nations flags. They have been told that they do not have to make exact replicas of the teacher's flag. They have before them the materials to make the flags. Lilly and James are the only children who have not yet started to work on their flags. Presently, James has his head under his desk and Lilly simply sits and watches the other children. Now they are both staring into space . . . (5 minutes later) Lilly and James have not yet started, while several other children have already finished . . . A minute later, with the teacher telling the children to begin to clean up their scraps, Lilly is still staring into space.

The teacher has the children seated on the floor in front of her asking them questions about a story that she had read to them. The teacher says, 'June, your back is turned. I want to see your face.' (The child had turned completely around and was facing away from the group.)

The teacher told the students to come from their seats and form a semi-circle on the floor in front of her. The girls all sit very close to the piano where the teacher is seated. The boys sit a good distance back away from the girls and away from the teacher. Lilly finishes her work at her desk and comes and sits at the rear of the group of girls, but she is actually in the middle of the open space separating the boys and the girls. She speaks to no one and simply sits staring off.

The verbal and physical hostility that the children at Tables 2 and 3 began to act out among themselves in many ways mirrored what the Table 1 students and the teacher were also saying about them. There are numerous instances in the observations of the children at Tables 2 and 3 calling one another 'stupid,' 'dummy,' or 'dumb dumb.' Racial overtones were noted on two occasions when one boy called another a 'nigger,' and on another occasion when a girl called a boy an 'almond head.' Threats of beatings, 'whoppins,' and even spitting on a child were also recorded among those at Tables 2 and 3. Also at Table 2, two instances were observed in which a single child hoarded all the supplies for the whole table. Similar manifestations of hostility were not observed among those children at the first table. The single incident of strong anger or hostility by one child at Table 1 against another child at the same table occurred when one accused the other of copying from his paper. The second denied it and an argument ensued.

In the organization of hostility within the classroom, there may be at least the tentative basis for the rejection of a popular 'folk myth' of American society, which is that children are inherently cruel to one another and that this tendency towards cruelty must be socialized into socially acceptable channels. The evidence from this classroom would indicate that much of the cruelty displayed was a result of the social organization of the class. Those children at Tables 2 and 3 who displayed cruelty appeared to have learned from the teacher that it was acceptable to act in an aggressive manner towards those from low-income and poorly educated backgrounds. Their cruelty was not diffuse, but rather focused on a specific group – the other poor children.

Likewise, the incidence of such behavior increased over time. The children at Tables 2 and 3 did not begin the school year ridiculing and belittling each other. This social process began to emerge with the outline of the social organization the teacher imposed upon the class. The children from the first table were also apparently socialized into a pattern of behavior in which they perceived that they could direct hostility and aggression towards those at Tables 2 and 3, but not towards one another. The chidren in the class learned who was vulnerable to hostility and who was not through the actions of the teacher. She established the patterns of differential behavior which the class adopted.

First Grade

Though Mrs. Caplow had anticipated that only twelve of the children from the kindergarten class would attend the first grade in the same school, eighteen of the children were assigned during the summer to the first-grade classroom in the main building. The remaining children either were assigned to a new school a few blocks north, or were assigned to a branch school designed to handle the overflow from the main building, or had moved away. Mrs. Logan, the first-grade teacher, had had more than twenty years of teaching experience in the city public school system, and every school in which she had taught was more than 90 percent black. During the 1968–1969 school year, four informal visits were made to the classroom of Mrs. Logan. No visits were made to either the branch school or the new school to visit children from the kindergarten class who had left their original school. During my visits to the first-grade room, I kept only brief notes of the short conversations that I had with Mrs. Logan; I did not conduct formal observation of the activities of the children in the class.

During the first-grade school year, there were thirty-three children in the classroom. In addition to the eighteen from the kindergarten class, there were nine children repeating the first grade and also six children new to the school. Of the eighteen children who came from the kindergarten class to the first grade in the main building, seven were from the previous year's Table 1, six from Table 2, and five from Table 3.

In the first-grade classroom, Mrs. Logan also divided the children into three groups. Those children whom she placed at 'Table A' had all been Table 1 students in kindergarten. No student who had sat at Table 2 or 3 in kindergarten was placed at Table A in the first grade. Instead, all the students from Tables 2 and 3 – with one exception – were placed together at 'Table B.' At the third table which Mrs. Logan called 'Table C,' she placed the nine children repeating the grade plus Betty who had sat at Table 3 in the kindergarten class. Of the six new students, two were placed at Table A and four at ·

Table C. Thus the totals for the three tables were nine students at Table A, ten at Table B, and fourteen at Table C.

The seating arrangement that began in the kindergarten as a result of the teacher's definition of which children possessed or lacked the perceived necessary characteristics for success in the public school system emerged in the first grade as a caste phenomenon in which there was absolutely no mobility upward. That is, of those children whom Mrs. Caplow had perceived as potential 'failures' and thus seated at either Table 2 or 3 in the kindergarten, not one was assigned to the table of the 'fast learners' in the first grade.

The initial label given to the children by the kindergarten teacher had been reinforced in her interaction with those students throughout the school year. When the children were ready to pass into the first grade, their ascribed labels from the teacher as either successes or failures assumed objective dimensions. The first-grade teacher no longer had to rely on merely the presence or absence of certain behavioral and attitudinal characteristics to ascertain who would do well and who would do poorly in the class. Objective records of the 'readiness' material completed by the children during the kindergarten year were available to her. Thus, upon the basis of what material the various tables in kindergarten had completed, Mrs. Logan could form her first grade tables for reading and arithmetic.

The kindergarten teacher's disproportionate allocation of her teaching time resulted in the Table 1 students having completed more material at the end of the school year than the remainder of the class. As a result, the Table 1 group from kindergarten remained intact in the first grade, as they were the only students prepared for the first-grade reading material. Those children from Tables 2 and 3 had not yet completed all the material from kindergarten and had to spend the first weeks of the first-grade school year finishing kindergarten level lessons. The criteria established by the school system as to what constituted the completion of the necessary readiness material to begin first-grade lessons insured that the Table 2 and 3 students could not be placed at Table A. The only children who had completed the material were those from Table 1, defined by the kindergarten teacher as successful students and whom she then taught most often because the remainder of the class 'had no idea what was going on.'

It would be somewhat misleading, however, to indicate that there was absolutely no mobility for any of the students between the seating assignments in kindergarten and those in the first grade. All of the students save one who had been seated at Table 3 during the kindergarten year were moved 'up' to Table B in the first grade. The majority of Table C students were those having to repeat the grade level. As a tentative explanation of Mrs. Logan's rationale for the development of the Table C seating assignments, she may have assumed that within her class there existed one group of students who possessed so very little of the perceived behavioral patterns and attitudes necessary for success that they had to be kept separate from the remainder of the class. (Table C was placed by itself on the opposite side of the room from Tables A and B.) The Table C students were spoken of by the first-grade teacher in a manner reminiscent of the way in which Mrs. Caplow spoke of the Table 3 students the previous year.

Students who were placed at Table A appeared to be perceived by Mrs. Logan as students who not only possessed the criteria necessary for future success, both in the public school system and in the larger society, but who also had proven themselves capable in academic work. These students appeared to possess the characteristics considered most essential for 'middle-class' success by the teacher. Though students at Table B lacked many of the 'qualities' and characteristics of the Table A students, they were not perceived as lacking them to the same extent as those placed at Table C.

A basic tenet in explaining Mrs. Logan's seating arrangement is, of course, that she shared a similar reference group and set of values as to what constituted 'success' with Mrs. Caplow in the kindergarten class. Both women were well educated, were employed in a professional occupation, lived in middle-income neighborhoods, were active in a number of charitable and civil rights organizations, and expressed strong religious convictions and moral standards. Both were educated in the city teacher's college and had also attained graduate degrees. Their backgrounds as well as the manner in which they described the various groups of students in their classes would indicate that they shared a similar reference group and set of expectations as to what constituted the indices of the 'successful' student.

Second Grade

Of the original thirty students in kindergarten and eighteen in first grade, ten students were assigned to the only second-grade class in the main building. Of the eight original kindergarten students who did not come to the second grade from the first, three were repeating first grade while the remainder had moved. The teacher in the second grade also divided the class into three groups, though she did not give them number or letter designations. Rather, she called the first group the 'Tigers.' The middle group she labeled the 'Cardinals,' while the second-grade repeaters plus several new children assigned to the third table were designated by the teacher as 'Clowns.'[5]

In the second-grade seating scheme, no student from the first grade who had not sat at Table A was moved 'up' to the Tigers at the beginning of second grade. All those students who in first grade had been at Table B or Table C and returned to the second grade were placed in the Cardinal group. The Clowns consisted of six second-grade repeaters plus three students who were new to the class. Of the ten original kindergarten students who came from

TABLE 2   Distribution of socio-economic status factors by seating arrangement in the three reading groups in the second-grade classroom

Factors	Seating arrangement*		
	Tigers	Cardinals	Clowns
Income			
1 Families on welfare	2	4	7
2 Families with father employed	8	5	1
3 Families with mother employed	7	11	6
4 Families with both parents employed	7	5	1
5 Total family income below $3,000. /yr**	1	5	8
6 Total family income above $12,000. /yr**	4	0	0
Education			
1 Father ever grade school	8	6	1
2 Father ever high school	7	4	0
3 Father ever college	0	0	0
4 Mother ever grade school	12	13	9
5 Mother ever high school	9	7	4
6 Mother ever college	3	0	0
7 Children with pre-school experience	1	0	0
Family size			
1 Families with one child	2	0	1
2 Families with six or more children	3	8	5
3 Average number of siblings in family	3–4	6–7	7–8
4 Families with both parents present	8	6	1

*   There are twelve children in the Tiger group, fourteen children in the Cardinal group, and nine children in the Clown group.
** Estimated from stated occupation.

the first grade, six were Tigers and four were Cardinals. Table 2 illustrates that the distribution of social economic factors from the kindergarten year remained essentially unchanged in the second grade.

By the time the children came to the second grade, their seating arrangement appeared to be based not on the teacher's expectations of how the child might perform, but rather on the basis of past performance of the child. Available to the teacher when she formulated the seating groups were grade sheets from both kindergarten and first grade, IQ scores from kindergarten, listing of parental occupations for approximately half of the class, reading scores from a test given to all students at the end of first grade, evaluations from the speech teacher and also the informal evaluations from both the kindergarten and first-grade teachers.

The single most important data utilized by the teacher in devising seating groups were the reading scores indicating the performance of the students at the end of the first grade. The second-grade teacher indicated that she attempted to divide the groups primarily on the basis of these scores. The Tigers were designated as the highest reading group and the Cardinals the middle. The Clowns were assigned a first-grade reading level, though they were, for the most part, repeaters from the previous year in second grade. The caste character of the reading groups became clear as the year progressed, in that all three groups were reading in different books and it was school policy that no child could go on to a new book until the previous one had been completed. Thus there was no way for the child, should he have demonstrated competence at a higher reading level, to advance, since he had to continue at the pace of the rest of his reading group. The teacher never allowed individual reading in order that a child might finish a book on his own and move ahead. *No matter how well a child in the lower reading groups might have read, he was destined to remain in the same reading group. This is, in a sense, another manifestation of the self-fulfilling prophecy in that a 'slow learner' had no option but to continue to be a slow learner, regardless of performance or potential.* Initial expectations of the kindergarten teacher two years earlier as to the ability of the child resulted in placement in a reading group, whether high or low, from which there appeared to be no escape. The child's journey through the early grades of school at one reading level and in one social grouping appeared to be pre-ordained from the eighth day of kindergarten. [. . .]

The phenomenon of teacher expectation based upon a variety of social status criteria did not appear to be limited to the kindergarten teacher alone. When the second-grade teacher was asked to evaluate the children in her class by reading group, she responded in terms reminiscent of the kindergarten teacher. Though such a proposition would be tenuous at best, the high degree of similarity in the responses of both the kindergarten and second-grade teachers suggests that there may be among the teachers in the school a common set of criteria as to what constitutes the successful and promising student. If such is the case, then the particular individual who happens to occupy the role of kindergarten teacher is less crucial. For if the expectations of all staff within the school are highly similar, then with little difficulty there could be an interchange of teachers among the grades with little or no noticeable effect upon the performance of the various groups of students. If all teachers have similar expectations as to which types of students perform well and which types perform poorly, the categories established by the kindergarten teacher could be expected to reflect rather closely the manner in which other teachers would also have grouped the class.

As the indication of the high degree of similarity between the manner in which the kindergarten teacher described the three tables and the manner in which the second-grade teacher discussed the 'Tigers, Cardinals, and Clowns,' excerpts of an interview with the second-grade teacher are presented, where she stated her opinions of the three groups. Concerning the Tigers:

Q: Mrs. Benson, how would you describe the Tigers in terms of their learning ability and academic performance?
R: Well, they are my fastest group. They are very smart.
Q: Mrs. Benson, how would you describe the Tigers in terms of discipline matters?
R: Well, the Tigers are very talkative. Susan, Pamela, and Ruth, they are always running their mouths constantly, but they get their work done first. I don't have much trouble with them.
Q: Mrs. Benson, what value do you think the Tigers hold for an education?
R: They all feel an education is important and most of them have goals in life as to what they want to be. They mostly want to go to college.

The same questions were asked of the teacher concerning the Cardinals.

Q: Mrs. Benson, how would you describe the Cardinals in terms of learning ability and academic performance?
R: They are slow to finish their work . . . but they get finished. You know, a lot of them though, don't care to come to school too much. Rema, Gary, and Toby are absent quite a bit. The Tigers are never absent.
Q: Mrs. Benson, how would you describe the Cardinals in terms of discipline matters?
R: Not too bad. Since they work so slow they don't have time to talk. They are not like the Tigers who finish in a hurry and then just sit and talk with each other.
Q: Mrs. Benson, what value do you think the Cardinals hold for an education?
R: Well, I don't think they have as much interest in education as do the Tigers, but you know it is hard to say. Most will like to come to school, but the parents will keep them from coming. They either have to baby sit, or the clothes are dirty. These are the excuses the parents often give. But I guess most of the Cardinals want to go on and finish and go on to college. A lot of them have ambitions when they grow up. It's mostly the parents' fault that they are not at the school more often.

In the kindergarten class, the teacher appeared to perceive the major ability gap to lie between the students at Table 1 and those at Table 2. That is, those at Tables 2 and 3 were perceived as more similar in potential than were those at Tables 1 and 2. This was not the case in the second-grade classroom. The teacher appeared to perceive the major distinction in ability as lying between the Cardinals and the Clowns. Thus she saw the Tigers and the Cardinals as much closer in performance and potential than the Cardinals and the Clowns. The teacher's responses to the questions concerning the Clowns lends credence to this interpretation.

Q: Mrs. Benson, how would you describe the Clowns in terms of learning ability and academic performance?
R: Well, they are really slow. You know most of them are still doing first-grade work.
Q: Mrs. Benson, how would you describe the Clowns in terms of discipline matters?
R: They are very playful. They like to play a lot. They are not very neat. They like to talk a lot and play a lot. When I read to them, boy, do they have a good time. You know, the Tigers and the Cardinals will sit quietly and listen when I read to them, but the Clowns, they are always so restless. They always want to stand up. When we read, it is really something else. You know – Diane and Pat especially like to stand up. All these children, too, are very aggressive.
Q: Mrs. Benson, what value do you think the Clowns hold for an education?
R: I don't think very much. I don't think education means much to them at this stage. I know it doesn't mean anything to Randy and George. To most of the kids, I don't think it really matters at this stage.

Further Notes on the Second Grade: Reward and Punishment

Throughout the length of the study in the school, it was evident that both the kindergarten and second-grade teachers were teaching the groups within their classes in a dissimilar manner. Variations were evident, for example, in the amount of time the teachers spent teaching the different groups, in the manner in which certain groups were granted privileges which were denied to others, and in the teacher's proximity to the different groups. Two additional considerations related to the teacher's use of reward and punishment.

Though variations were evident from naturalistic observations in the kindergarten, a systematic evaluation was not attempted of the degree to which such differential behavior was a significant aspect of the classroom interactional patterns. When observations were being conducted in the second grade, it appeared that there was on the part of Mrs. Benson a differentiation of reward and punishment similar to that displayed by Mrs Caplow. In order to examine more closely the degree to which variations were present over time, three observational periods were totally devoted to the tabulation of each of the individual behavioral units directed by the teacher towards the children. Each observational period was three and one-half hours in length, lasting from 8:30 a.m. to 12:00 noon. The dates of the observations were the Fridays at the end of eight, twelve, and sixteen weeks of school – October 24, November 21, and December 19, 1969 respectively.

A mechanism for evaluating the varieties of teacher behavior was developed. Behavior on the part of the teacher was tabulated as a 'behavioral unit' when there was clearly directed towards an individual child some manner of communication, whether it be verbal, non-verbal or physical contact. When, within the interaction of the teacher and the student, there occurred more than one type of behavior, i.e., the teacher spoke to the child and touched him, a count was made of both variations. The following is a list of the nine variations in teacher behavior that were tabulated within the second-grade classroom. Several examples are also included with each of the alternatives displayed by the teacher within the class.

1 *Verbal supportive:* 'That's a very good job.' 'You are such a lovely girl.' 'My, but your work is so neat.'
2 *Verbal neutral:* 'Laura and Tom, let's open our books at page 34.' 'May, your pencil is on the floor.' 'Hal, do you have milk money today?'
3 *Verbal control:* Lou, sit on that chair and shut up.' 'Curt, get up off that floor.' 'Mary and Laura, quit your talking.'
4 *Non-verbal supportive:* Teacher nods her head at Rose. Teacher smiles at Liza. Teacher claps when Laura completes her problem at the board.
5 *Non-verbal neutral:* Teacher indicates with her arms that she wants Lilly and Shirley to move farther apart in the circle. Teacher motions to Joe and Tom that they should try to snap their fingers to stay in beat with the music.
6 *Non-verbal control:* Teacher frowns at Lena. Teacher shakes finger at Amy to quit tapping her pencil. Teacher motions with hand for Rose not to come to her desk.
7 *Physical contact supportive:* Teacher hugs Laura. Teacher places her arm around Mary as she talks to her. Teacher holds Trish's hand as she takes out a splinter.
8 *Physical contact neutral:* Teacher touches head of Nick as she walks past. Teacher leads Rema to new place on the circle.
9 *Physical contact control:* Teacher strikes Lou with stick. Teacher pushes Curt down in his chair. Teacher pushes Hal and Doug to the floor.

Table 3 which follows is presented with all forms of control, supportive, and neutral behavior grouped together within each of the three observational periods. As a methodological precaution, since the categorization of the various types of behavior was decided as the interaction occurred and there was no cross-validation checks by another observer, all behavior was placed in the appropriate neutral category which could not be clearly distinguished as belonging to one of the established supportive or control categories. This may explain the large percentage of neutral behavior tabulated in each of the three observational periods.

TABLE 3   Variations in teacher-directed behaviour for three second-grade reading groups during three observational periods within a single classroom

| Item | Variations in teacher-directed behavior | | |
	Control	Supportive	Neutral
*Observational period 1**			
Tigers	5%–(6)**	7%–(8)**	87%–(95)
Cardinals	10%–(7)	8%–(5)	82%–(58)
Clowns	27%–(27)	6%–(6)	67%–(67)
Observational period 2			
Tigers	7%–(14)	8%–(16)	85%–(170)
Cardinals	7%–(13)	8%–(16)	85%–(157)
Clowns	14%–(44)	6%–(15)	80%–(180)
Observational period 3			
Tigers	7%–(15)	6%–(13)	86%–(171)
Cardinals	14%–(20)	10%–(14)	75%–(108)
Clowns	15%–(36)	7%–(16)	78%–(188)

* Forty-eight (48) minutes of unequal teacher access (due to one group of children's being out of the room) was eliminated from the analysis.
** Value within the parentheses indicates total number of units of behavior within that category.

The picture of the second-grade teacher, Mrs. Benson, that emerges from analysis of these data is of one who distributes rewards quite sparingly and equally, but who utilizes somewhere between two and five times as much control-oriented behavior with the Clowns as with the Tigers. Alternatively, whereas with the Tigers the combination of neutral and supportive behavior never dropped below 93 percent of the total behavior directed towards them by the teacher in the three periods, the lowest figure for the Cardinals was 86 percent and for the Clowns was 73 percent. It may be assumed that neutral and supportive behavior would be conducive to learning while punishment or control-oriented behavior would not. Thus for the Tigers, the learning situation was one with only infrequent units of control, while for the Clowns, control behavior constituted one-fourth of all behavior directed towards them on at least one occasion [. . .]

Of particular interest (here) are the findings of Adams (1945), Anderson (1946), Anderson, *et al.* (1946), Preston and Heintz (1949), and Robbins (1952). Their findings may be generalized to state that children within an authoritarian classroom display a decrease in both learning retention and performance, while those within the democratic classroom do not. In extrapolating these findings to the second-grade classroom of Mrs. Benson, one cannot say that she was continually 'authoritarian' as opposed to 'democratic' with her students, but that with one group of students there occurred more control-oriented behavior than with other groups. The group which was the recipient of this control-oriented behavior was that group which she had defined as 'slow and disinterested.' On at least one occasion Mrs. Benson utilized nearly five times the amount of control-oriented behavior with the Clowns as with her perceived high-interested and high-ability group, the Tigers. For the Clowns, who were most isolated from the teacher and received the least amount of her teaching time, the results noted above would indicate that the substantial control-oriented behavior directed towards them would compound their difficulty in experiencing significant learning and cognitive growth.

Here discussion of the self-fulfilling prophecy is relevant: given the extent to which the teacher utilized control-oriented behavior with the Clowns, data from the leadership and performance studies would indicate that it would be more difficult for that group to experience a positive learning situation. The question remains unanswered, though, as to whether the behavior of uninterested students necessitated the teacher's resorting to extensive use of control-oriented behavior, or whether that, to the extent to which the teacher utilized control-oriented behavior, the students responded with uninterest. If the prior experience of the Clowns was in any way similar to that of the students in kindergarten at Table 3 and Table C in the first grade, I am inclined to opt for the latter proposition.

A very serious and, I believe, justifiable consequence of this assumption of student uninterest related to the frequency of the teacher's control-oriented behavior is that the teachers themselves contribute significantly to the creation of the 'slow learners' within their classrooms. Over time, this may help to account for the phenomenon noted in the Coleman Report (1966) that the gap between the academic performance of the disadvantaged students and the national norms increased the longer the students remained in the school system. During one of the three and one-half hour observational periods in the second grade, the percentage of control-oriented behavior oriented toward the entire class was about 8 per cent. Of the behavior directed toward the Clowns, however, 27 per cent was control-oriented behavior – more than three times the amount of control-oriented behavior directed to the class as a whole. Deutsch (1968), in a random sampling of New York City Public School classrooms of the fifth through eighth grades, noted that the teachers utilized between 50 and 80 percent of class time in discipline and organization. Unfortunately, he fails to specify the two individual percentages and thus it is unknown whether the classrooms were dominated by either discipline or organization as opposed to their combination. If it is the case, and Deutsch's findings appear to lend indirect support, that the higher the grade level, the greater the discipline and control-oriented behavior by the teacher, some of the unexplained aspects of the 'regress phenomenon' may be unlocked.

On another level of analysis, the teacher's use of control-oriented behavior is directly related to the expectations of the ability and willingness of 'slow learners' to learn the material she teaches. That is, if the student is uninterested in what goes on in the classroom, he is more apt to engage in activities that the teacher perceives as disruptive. Activities such as talking out loud, coloring when the teacher has not said it to be permissible, attempting to leave the room, calling other students' attention to activities occurring on the street, making comments to the teacher not pertinent to the lesson, dropping books, falling out of the chair, and commenting on how the student cannot wait for recess, all prompt the teacher to employ control-oriented behavior toward that student. The interactional pattern between the uninterested student and the teacher literally becomes a 'vicious circle' in which control-oriented behavior is followed by further manifestations of uninterest, followed by further control behavior and so on. The stronger the reciprocity of this pattern of interaction, the greater one may anticipate the strengthening of the teacher's expectation of the 'slow learner' as being either unable or unwilling to learn [. . .]

Poor Kids and Public Schools

It has been a major goal of this paper to demonstrate the impact of teacher expectations, based upon a series of subjectively interpreted social criteria, on both the anticipated academic potential and subsequent differential treatment accorded to those students perceived as having dissimilar social status. For the kindergarten teacher, expectations as to what type of child may be anticipated as a 'fast learner' appear to be grounded in her reference group of a mixed white-black educated middle class. That is, students within her classroom who displayed those attributes which a number of studies have indicated are highly desired in children by middle-class educated adults as being necessary for future success were selected by her as possessing the potential to be a 'fast learner.' On the other hand, those children who did not possess the desired qualities were defined by the teacher as 'slow learners.' None of the criteria upon which the teacher appeared to base her evaluation of the children were directly related to measurable aspects of academic potential. Given that the I.Q. test was administered to the children in the last week of their kindergarten year, the results could not have been of any benefit to the teacher as she established patterns of organization within the class.[6] The I.Q. scores may have been significant factors for the first- and second-grade teachers, but I assume that consideration of past performance was the major determinant for the seating arrangements which they established.[7]

For the first-grade teacher, Mrs. Logan, and the second-grade teacher, Mrs. Benson, the process of dividing the class into various reading groups, apparently on the basis of past performance, maintained the original patterns of differential treatment and expectations established in the kindergarten class. Those initially defined as 'fast learners' by the kindergarten teacher in subsequent years continued to have that position in the first group, regardless of the label or name given to it.

It was evident throughout the length of the study that the teachers made clear the distinctions they perceived between the children who were defined as fast learners and those defined as slow learners. It would not appear incorrect to state that within the classroom there was established by the various teachers a clear system of segregation between the two established groups of children. In the one group were all the children who appeared clean and interested, sought interactions with adults, displayed leadership within the class, and came from homes which displayed various status criteria valued in the middle class. In the other were children who were dirty, smelled of urine, did not actively participate in class, spoke a linguistic dialect other than that spoken by the teacher and students at Table 1, did not display leadership behavior, and came from poor homes often supported by public welfare. I would contend that within the system of segregation established by the teachers, the group perceived as slow learners were ascribed a caste position that sought to keep them apart from the other students.

The placement of the children within the various classrooms into different reading groups was ostensibly done on the promise of future performance in the kindergarten and on differentials of past performance in later grades. However, the placement may rather have been done from purely irrational reasons that had nothing to do with academic performance. The utilization of academic criteria may have served as the rationalization for a more fundamental process occurring with the class whereby the teacher served as the agent of the larger society to ensure that proper 'social distance' was maintained between the various strata of the society as represented by the children.

Within the context of this analysis there appear to be at least two interactional processes that may be identified as having occurred simultaneously within the kindergarten classroom. The first was the relation of the teacher to the students placed at Table 1. The process appeared to occur in at least four stages. The initial stage involved the kindergarten teacher's developing expectations regarding certain students as possessing a series of characteristics that she considered essential for future academic 'success.' Second, the teacher reinforced through her mechanisms of 'positive' differential behavior those characteristics of the children that she considered important and desirable.

Third, the children responded with more of the behavior that initially gained them the attention and support of the teacher. Perceiving that verbalization, for example, was a quality that the teacher appeared to admire, the Table 1 children increased their level of verbalization throughout the school year. Fourth, the cycle was complete as the teacher focused even more specifically on the children at Table 1 who continued to manifest the behavior she desired. A positive interactional scheme arose whereby initial behavioral patterns of the student were reinforced into apparent permanent behavioral patterns, once he had received support and differential treatment from the teacher.

Within this framework, the actual academic potential of the students was not objectively measured prior to the kindergarten teacher's evaluation of expected performance. The students may be assumed to have had mixed potential. However, the common positive treatment accorded to all within the group by the teacher may have served as the necessary catalyst for the self-fulfilling prophecy whereby those expected to do well did so.

A concurrent behavioral process appeared to occur between the teacher and those students placed at Tables 2 and 3. The student came into the class possessing a series of behavioral and attitudinal characteristics that within the frame of reference of the teacher were perceived as indicative of 'failure.' Second, through mechanisms of reinforcement of her initial expectations as to the future performance of the student, it was made evident that he was not perceived as similar or equal to those at the table of fast learners. In the third stage, the student responded to both the definition and actual treatment given to him by the teacher which emphasized his characteristics of being an educational 'failure.' Given the high degree of control-oriented behavior directed toward the 'slower' learner, the lack of verbal interaction and encouragement, the disproportionally small amount of teaching time given to him, and the ridicule and hostility, the child withdrew from class participation. The fourth stage was the cyclical repetition of behavioral and attitudinal characteristics that led to the initial labeling as an educational failure.

As with those perceived as having high probability of future success, the academic potential of the failure group was not objectively determined prior to evaluation by the kindergarten teacher. This group also may be assumed to have come into the class with mixed potential. Some within the group may have had the capacity to perform academic tasks quite well, while others perhaps did not. Yet the reinforcement by the teacher of the characteristics in the children that she had perceived as leading to academic failure may, in fact, have created the very conditions of student failure. With the 'negative' treatment accorded to the perceived failure group, the teacher's definition of the situation may have ensured its emergence. What the teacher perceived in the children may have served as the catalyst for a series of interactions, with the result that the child came to act out within the class the very expectations defined for him by the teacher.

As an alternative explanation, however, the teacher may have developed the system of caste segregation within the classroom, not because the groups of children were so dissimilar they had to be handled in an entirely different manner, but because they were, in fact, so very close to one another. The teacher may have believed quite strongly that the ghetto community inhibited the development of middle-class success models. Thus, it was her duty to 'save' at least one group of children from the 'streets.' Those children had to be kept separate who could have had a 'bad' influence on the children who appeared to have a chance to 'make it' in the middle class of the larger society. Within this framework, the teacher's actions may be understood not only as an attempt to keep the slow learners away from those fast learners, but to ensure that the fast learners would not so be influenced that they themselves become enticed with the 'streets' and lose their apparent opportunity for future middle-class status.

In addition to the formal separation of the groups within the classroom, there was also the persistence of mechanisms utilized by the teacher to socialize the children in the high reading group with feelings of aversion, revulsion, and rejection towards those of the lower reading groups. Through ridicule, belittlement, physical punishment, and merely ignoring them, the teacher was continually giving clues to those in the high reading group as to how one with high status and a high probability of future success treats those of low status and low probability of future success. To maintain within the larger society the caste aspects of the position of the poor *vis a vis* the remainder of the society, there has to occur the transmission from one generation to another the attitudes and values necessary to legitimate and continue such a form of social organization.

Given the extreme intercomplexity of the organizational structure of this society, the institutions that both create and sustain social organization can neither be held singularly responsible for perpetuating the inequalities nor for eradicating them (cf. Leacock, 1969). The public school system, I believe, is justifiably responsible for contributing to the present structure of the society, but the responsibility is not its alone. The picture that emerges from this study is that the school strongly shares in the complicity of maintaining the organizational perpetuation of poverty and unequal opportunity. This, of course, is in contrast to the formal doctrine of education in this country to ameliorate rather than aggravate the conditions of the poor.

The teachers' reliance on a mixed black-white educated middle class for their normative reference group appeared to contain assumptions of superiority over those of lower-class and status positions. For they and those members of their reference group, comfortable affluence, education, community participation, and possession of professional status may have afforded a rather stable view of the social order. The treatment of those from lower socio-economic backgrounds within the classrooms by the teachers may have indicated that the values highly esteemed by them were not open to members of the lower groups. Thus the lower groups were in numerous ways informed of their lower status and were socialized for a role of lower self expectations and also for respect and deference towards those of higher status. The social distance between the groups within the classrooms was manifested in its extreme form by the maintenance of patterns of caste segregation whereby those of lower positions were not allowed to become a part of the peer group at the highest level. The value system of the teachers appeared to necessitate that a certain group be ostracized due to 'unworthiness' or inherent inferiority. The very beliefs which legitimated exclusion were maintained among those of the higher social group which then contributed to the continuation of the pattern of social organization itself [. . .]

Notes

1 This paper is based on research aided by a grant from the United States Office of Education, Grant No. 6–2771. Original Principal Investigator, Jules Henry (deceased) Professor of Anthropology, Washington University. Current Principal Investigators, Helen P. Gouldner, Professor of Sociology, Washington University, and John W. Bennett, Professor of Anthropology, Washington University. The author is grateful for substantive criticism and comments from John Bennett, Marshal Durbin and Helen Gouldner on an earlier draft of this paper.

2 The author, due to a teaching appointment out of the city, was unable to conduct formal observations of the children during their first-grade year.

3 The names of all staff and students are pseudonyms. Names are provided to indicate that the discussion relates to living persons, and not to fictional characters developed by the author.

4 Through the remainder of the paper, reference to 'high' or 'low' status students refers to status ascribed to the student by the teacher. Her ascription appeared to be based on perceptions of valued behavioral and cultural characteristics present or absent in any individual student.

5 The names were not given to the groups until the third week of school, though the seating arrangement was established on the third day.

6 The results of the I.Q. Test for the kindergarten class indicated that, though there were no statistically significant differences among the children at the three tables, the scores were skewed slightly higher for the children at Table 1. There were, however, children at Tables 2 and 3 who did score higher than several students at Table 1. The highest score came from a student at Table 1 (124) while the lowest came from a student at Table 3 (78). There appear to be at least three alternative explanations for the slightly higher scores by students at Table 1. First, the scores may represent the result of differential treatment in the classroom by Mrs. Caplow, thus contributing to the validation of the self-fulfilling prophecy. That is, the teacher by the predominance of teaching time spent with the Table 1 students, better prepared the students to do well on the examination than was the case for those students who received less teaching time. Secondly, the tests themselves may have reflected strong biases towards the knowledge and experience of middle-class children. Thus, students from higher-status families at Table 1 could be expected to perform better than did the low-status students from Table 3. The test resulted not in a 'value free' measure of cognitive capacity, but in an index of family background. Third, of course, would be the fact that the children at the first table did

possess a higher degree of academic potential than those at the other tables, and the teacher was intuitively able to discern these differences. This third alternative, however, is least susceptible to empirical verification.

7 When the second-grade teacher was questioned as to what significance she placed in the results of I.Q. tests, she replied that 'They merely confirm what I already know about the student.'

References

ADAMS, R.G. 'The Behavior of Pupils in Democratic and Autocratic Social Climates.' Abstracts of Dissertations, Stanford University, 1945.

ANDERSON, H. *Studies in Teachers' Classroom Personalities.* Stanford: Stanford University Press, 1946.

ANDERSON, H., BREWER, J. and REED, M. 'Studies of Teacher's Classroom Personalities, III. Follow-up Studies of the Effects of Dominative and Integrative Contacts on Children's Behavior.' *Applied Psychology Monograph.* Stanford: Stanford University Press, 1946.

ASBELL, B. 'Not Like Other Children.' *Redbook,* 65 (October, 1963), pp. 114–118.

AUSTIN, MARY C. and MORRISON, COLEMAN. *The First R: The Harvard Report on Reading in Elementary Schools,* New York: Macmillan, 1963.

BECKER, H.S. 'Social Class Variation in the Teacher-Pupil Relationship.' *Journal of Educational Sociology,* 1952, 25, 451–465.

CLARK, K.B. 'Educational Stimulation of Racially Disadvantaged Children.' *Education in Depressed Areas.* Edited by A.H. Passow. New York: Columbia University Press, 1963.

COLEMAN, J.S., *et al. Equality of Educational Opportunity.* Washington, D.C.: United States Government Printing Office, 1966.

DEUTSCH, M. 'Minority Groups and Class Status as Related to Social and Personality Factors in Scholastic Achievement.' *The Disadvantaged Child.* Edited by M. Deutsch, *et al.* New York: Basic Books, 1967.

EDDY, E. *Walk the White Line.* Garden City, N.Y.: Doubleday, 1967.

FRAZIER, E.F. *Black Bourgeoisie.* New York: The Free Press, 1957.

FREEMAN, R., WHELPTON, P. and CAMPBELL, A. *Family Planning, Sterility and Population Growth.* New York: McGraw-Hill, 1959.

FUCHS, E. *Teachers Talk.* Garden City, N.Y.: Doubleday, 1967.

GEBHARD, P., POMEROY, W., MARTIN, C. and CHRISTENSON, C. *Pregnancy, Birth and Abortion,* New York: Harper and Row, 1958.

GIBSON, G. 'Aptitude Tests.' *Science,* 1965, 149, 583.

HARLEM YOUTH OPPORTUNITIES UNLIMITED *Youth in the Ghetto.* New York: HARYOU, 1964.

HENRY, J. 'Docility, or Giving the Teacher What She Wants.' *Journal of Social Issues,* 1955, II, 2.

HENRY, J. 'The Problem of Spontaneity, Initiative and Creativity in Suburban Classrooms.' *American Journal of Orthopsychiatry,* 1959, 29, 1.

HENRY, J. 'Golden Rule Days: American Schoolrooms.' in *Culture Against Man.* New York: Random House, 1963.

HOLLINGSHEAD, A. *Elmtown's Youth.* New York: John Wiley and Sons, 1949.

KAHL, J.A. *The American Class Structure.* New York: Holt, Rinehart and Winston, 1957.

KATZ, I. 'Review of Evidence Relating to Effects of Desegregation on Intellectual Performance of Negroes.' *American Psychologist*, 1964, 19, 381–399.

KOHL, H. *36 Children*. New York: New American Library, 1967.

KOZOL, J. *Death at an Early Age*. Boston: Houghton Mifflin, 1967.

KVARACEUS, W.C. 'Disadvantaged Children and Youth: Programs of Promise or Pretense?' Burlingame: California Teachers Association, 1965. (Mimeographed.)

LEACOCK, E. *Teaching and Learning in City Schools*. New York: Basic Books, 1969.

LYND, H. and LYND, R. *Middletown in Transition*. New York: Harcourt, Brace and World, 1937.

MACKINNON, D.W. 'The Nature and Nurture of Creative Talent.' *American Psychologist*, 1962, 17, 484–495.

MERTON, R.K. *Social Theory and Social Structure*. Revised and Enlarged. New York: The Free Press, 1957.

MOORE, A. *Realities of the Urban Classroom*. Garden City, N.Y.: Doubleday, 1967.

NOTESTEIN, F. 'Class Differences in Fertility.' *Class, Status and Power*. Edited by R. Bendix and S. Lipset. New York: The Free Press, 1953.

PRESTON, M. and HEINTZ, R. 'Effects of Participatory Versus Supervisory Leadership on Group Judgment.' *Journal of Abnormal Social Psychology*, 1949, 44, 345–355.

REISSMAN, L. *Class in American Society*. New York: The Free Press, 1959.

RIESSMAN, F. *The Culturally Deprived Child*. New York: Harper and Row, 1962.

RIESSMAN, F. 'Teachers of the Poor: A Five Point Program.' Burlingame: California Teachers Association, 1965. (Mimeographed.)

ROBBINS, F. 'The Impact of Social Climate upon a College Class.' *School Review*, 1952, 60, 275–284.

ROSE, A. *The Negro in America*. Boston: Beacon Press, 1956.

ROSENTHAL, R. and JACOBSON, LENORE. *Pygmalion in the Classroom*. New York: Holt, Rinehart and Winston, 1968.

SIGEL, I. 'The Piagetian System and the World of Education.' *Studies in Cognitive Development*. Edited by D. Elkind and J. Flavell. New York: Oxford University Press, 1969.

SIMPSON, G. and YINGER, J.M. *Racial and Cultural Minorities*. New York: Harper and Row, 1958.

SMITH, L. and GEOFFREY, W. *The Complexities of an Urban Classroom*. New York: Holt, Rinehart and Winston, 1968.

SMITH, M. 'Equality of Educational Opportunity: The Basic Findings Reconsidered.' *On Equality of Educational Opportunity*. Edited by F. Mosteller and D.P. Moynihan. New York: Random House, 1971.

WARNER, W.L., HAVIGHURST, R. and LOEB, M. *Who Shall Be Educated?* New York: Harper and Row, 1944.

WILSON, A.B. 'Social Stratification and Academic Achievement.' *Education in Depressed Areas*. Edited by A.H. Passow. New York: Teachers College Press, Columbia University, 1963.

Index